D1030643

4.19.79

'A fully-equipped duke costs as much to keep up as two dreadnoughts. They are just as great a terror and they last longer.' So said Lloyd George, that fiery duke-baiter, in 1909. *Amazing Grace* surveys the dukes of Great Britain in their prime, chiefly during the eighteenth and nineteenth centuries. Dukes were expected to bring something extra to the grand manner, writes Mr Turner, 'something which unmistakably conveyed that here was a man who owned Belgravia, or Eastbourne, or Ben Lomond.' He offers an anecdote-packed study of 'godhead, eccentricity, *noblesse oblige*, self-indulgence and grand-landlordism'; but his eye for the outrageous does not prevent him from paying tribute to those dukes to whom humanity has been much indebted.

In these pages will be found a Duke of Somerset who cut £20,000 from a daughter's inheritance because she sat down while he slept; a Duke of Montague who dressed up as the Emperor of China to woo a madwoman and separate her from her wealth; a Duke of Bolton who toured Europe with his mistress and a clergyman to marry them as soon as the Duchess died; a Duke of Bridgewater who was jilted and then made a vast fortune cutting canals; a Duke of Sutherland who 'improved' a county by emptying it of people; a Duke of Portland who cut carriage tunnels underneath his park and buried a ballroom; and a Duke of Northumberland who defiantly assured a Coal Commission that he owned all minerals in his lands right down to the centre of the earth and was very happy with this arrangement.

All noble life is here, in these eye-opening pages.

Amazing Grace

Amazing Grace

THE GREAT DAYS OF DUKES

E. S. Turner

LONDON
MICHAEL JOSEPH

First published in Great Britain by Michael Joseph Ltd
52 Bedford Square, London, W.C.1
1975

© 1975 by E. S. Turner

ISBN 0 7181 1362 4

Set and printed in Great Britain by
Northumberland Press Ltd Gateshead,
in Baskerville type, eleven point leaded, and bound
by James Burn at Esher, Surrey

CONTENTS

ILLUSTRATIONS

Richard Grenville, first Duke of Buckingham and Chandos: a Grand Tour by yacht to save money

George Granville Leveson-Gower, first Duke of Sutherland: the landlord who emptied the glens

Worksop Manor, seat of the Dukes of Norfolk in the Dukeries

Alnwick Castle, seat of the Dukes of Northumberland: 'Look around! I myself have measured out all these things.'

The mausoleum built by the fifth Duke of Rutland to his Duchess: her four dead children welcome her to Heaven

Charles Spencer Churchill, ninth Duke of Marlborough: two rich American wives

'You people of great families and hereditary trusts and fortunes are not like such as I am, who, whatever we may be by the rapidity of our growth and even by the fruit we bear, flatter ourselves that, while we creep on the ground, we belly into melons that are exquisite for size and flavour, yet still we are but annual plants that perish with our season, and leave no sort of trace behind us. You, if you are what you ought to be, are in my eye the great oaks that shade a country, and perpetuate your benefits from generation to generation.'

Edmund Burke to the third Duke of Richmond, 1772

'Is it not monstrous that a small number of men, several of whom take the title of duke and earl from towns in this very neighbourhood, towns which they never saw, which never heard of them, which they did not form, or build, or establish, I say is it not monstrous that individuals so circumstanced should be invested with the highest of conceivable privileges —the privilege of making laws? Dukes and earls indeed! I say there is nothing in a masquerade so ridiculous.'

Mr Millbank, in Disraeli's Coningsby

'A fully-equipped duke costs as much to keep up as two dreadnoughts. They are just as great a terror and they last longer.'

David Lloyd George at Newcastle-on-Tyne, 1909

AUTHOR'S NOTE

This book surveys the dukes of Great Britain in their settled prime, which was chiefly in the eighteenth and nineteenth centuries.

It starts with the upsurge of duke-making after the Civil War, a process which continued apace under William III, Anne and George I. By the end of George I's reign there were two score dukes in Britain, as against today's twenty-six. Thereafter the creation of dukes fell away to a slow trickle. The book ends with the 1930s when the power and the glory of the upper aristocracy had been severely diminished.

This survey is not concerned with royal dukes, apart from the half-dozen bastards of Charles II. The Dukes of York, Lancaster, Gloucester, Clarence, Cornwall, Cumberland, Kent, Edinburgh, Connaught, Sussex, Rothesay, Albany and Windsor do not figure in these pages.

The dull dukes—and there have been many—have been ruthlessly discarded; and for space reasons a number of others, both worthy and notorious, are omitted. For the reader's comfort the tortuosities of genealogy and inheritance have been heavily pruned. The military campaigns of Marlborough and Wellington are touched on only lightly.

Although the chapters preserve a rough chronology, the book does not aspire to be a history of Britain in terms of dukes.

ACKNOWLEDGEMENTS

The author and publisher are grateful to the following for permission to reproduce illustrations: the National Portrait Gallery for portraits of the Duke of Lauderdale, the Duke of Monmouth, the Duke of Newcastle (Thomas Pelham-Holles), the first Duke of Marlborough, the third Duke of Richmond, the fourth Duke of Queensberry, the first Duke of Sutherland, and the ninth Duke of Marlborough; the British Library for two lithographs of the Duke of Newcastle (William Cavendish), portraits of the first Duke of Northumberland (Hugh Smithson), the first Duke of Buckingham and Chandos, the Duke of Wharton, the third Duke of Bridgewater, and pictures of Blenheim Palace, Worksop Manor, Alnwick Castle, and the Duchess of Rutland's mausoleum; Dulwich College Picture Gallery for the portrait of the first Duke of Bedford; Radio Times Hulton Picture Library for the picture of Chatsworth; the Illustrated London News and Sketch Limited for three lithographs of the first Duke of Wellington; and *Punch* for the cartoon of the ninth Duke of Bedford.

The author would like to express his especial indebtedness to the *Complete Peerage* and the *Dictionary of National Biography*, both of which furnished indispensable background.

ACKNOWLEDGEMENTS

INTRODUCTION

Why a book about dukes? Do not marquesses and earls furnish an equally satisfying study of godhead, eccentricity, *noblesse oblige*, self-indulgence and grand landlordism? Of course they do. But a dukedom is the highest rank of nobility and those who held it in the great days of subordination enjoyed an especial adulation and awe. They were expected to bring something extra to the grand manner, something which unmistakably conveyed that here was a man who owned Belgravia, or Eastbourne, or Ben Lomond. Lesser men addressed them as 'Your Grace'—and grace has pleasing connotations not only of elegance but of divinity. At the mere mention of a duke's name in a public address listeners uncovered their heads. In their coronets dukes were content with eight strawberry leaves, not a vulgar mixture of strawberry leaves and fat pearls. When dukes achieved paternity the whole countryside was expected to rejoice; when their sons came of age the whole countryside became blind drunk; and when they died the whole countryside came to a halt. Dukes, more than other noblemen, supported their rank by keeping people standing, not only artists and tradesmen but their fathers-in-law. At the domestic hearth they addressed their first-born sons, not as Charles or George, but by the names of towns, like Titchfield or Tavistock, or even—as the Duke of Wellington did—by the name of a Portuguese

river, Douro. (Trollope's Duke of Omnium says: 'The use
of Christian names is, I think, pleasant and hardly common
enough among us. I almost forget my boy's name because the
practice has grown up of calling him by a title.')

Dukes were not necessarily the brightest ornaments of their
line. Often their forebears—mere knights, barons and earls—
were men of far greater achievement. It might take centuries
of service, solicitation and aggrandisement before a family
reached the point at which it could sustain a duke, and there
was no assurance that the candidate would be worthy of the
honour when it came. However, it was a rare duke who could
afford the luxury of feeling humble, or dare to plead lack of
capacity, or retreat into a life of piety. There he was, a most
puissant and most excellent prince, and it was necessary to
make the best of it. He had inherited a string of boroughs and
was responsible for the votes of those who lived in them. He
was expected to be Lord Lieutenant of his county, or of
some other county, which made him responsible for raising
and drilling volunteers. He had church livings to fill—more
than forty of them, if he was born into Chatsworth. If there
was a forest going a-begging, he would surely wish to be
made ranger of it, with a free house, and the privilege of
presenting a buck now and then to his friends, and no
questions asked if he helped himself to the timber from
time to time. If his leanings were political he would expect
to be offered a government post sooner or later. And since
he was a duke, he was liberally qualified to govern Ireland
as Viceroy or to represent his country in Paris. As Lord
Eustace Percy, a duke's son, has modestly explained, 'Large
private responsibilities do tend to form in their possessors a
certain talent for public affairs.'*

Unlike their French counterparts, the dukes of Britain
had enough sense, as a rule, to spend much of the year on
their estates and look after 'their' people. They were not
expected to live in cupboards at Court. Their hospitality
was often prodigious and by no means limited to their own
set; it is sad that literary men so often bit the hands that fed

* Lord Eustace Percy: *Some Memories*

them. Occasionally the mob broke the windows of even the best-loved 'dooks', regarding them as symbols of privilege. Sheer eminence has always attracted criticism, as a mountain peak attracts the worst of the weather. The demagogue Lloyd George knew what he was doing when, in his Limehouse speech of 1909, he selected dukes as the enemies of the nation. Winston Churchill pretended to come to their rescue, while mocking them still further.

It is an old radical belief that men have been given titles for deeds which merited flogging at the cart's tail. The reasons for making men dukes were many and not always creditable. They include:

for winning great victories in the field

for public and political services

for fascinating a male Sovereign

for fascinating a female Sovereign

for betraying a Sovereign (i.e. for services to Protestantism)

for being a bastard of the Sovereign

for having ancestors who served the State well

for having an ancestor who was unfairly executed

for defeating, subduing or otherwise taming the Scots or Irish

for supporting, or not opposing, parliamentary reform

for marrying a duchess

for amassing, or inheriting, or marrying into, enormous landed wealth

Sometimes dukes were created for a combination of these reasons. At times it is almost impossible to tell why a man was raised to the top rank. The first Duke of Ancaster seems to have been honoured because he had a clever brother. The dukes of this creation rate no entries in the *Dictionary of National Biography*, though the fourth Duke receives an honourable mention in the *Complete Peerage* for leaving a legacy to a dwarfish drinking companion whom he used to hurl at his fellow roustabouts, as other men would throw a bottle. In general, a dukedom went only to those with large estates; a fortune in the funds was not regarded as an adequate stake in the country. A successful military commander like

Marlborough or Wellington had to be rewarded with lands
as well as titles.

If this book shows anything, it shows how often the highest
rank was won by those families with the greatest talent for
bedding heiresses. In the eighteenth century there were two
ways in which a man might win a fortune in a day. One was
by intercepting the homeward Acapulco galleon on the high
seas; the other was by marrying a rich woman. In the nineteenth century there were no more treasure galleons, but
there were proud, full-sailed heiresses in plenty; and because
they were such valuable prizes they were heavily guarded
and escorted. There is hardly a ducal family which has not
benefited at some stage by the rich spoils of marriage. Writing
in 1884, Lord Ronald Gower said of the Dukes of Sutherland:
'I wish I could think that their promotion was owing to deeds
performed by land or sea; but if the truth must be told, the
family have been more distinguished by their luck and their
alliances than in the senate or in the field. For generations
they appear to have wedded heiresses or co-heirs of peers;
and in the marriage of my grandfather, the first Duke of
Sutherland, to the greatest heiress in three kingdoms their
achievements in that respect may be said to have culminated.'*
The fifth Duke of Sutherland has echoed these sentiments. It
is no secret that the vast wealth of the Westminsters stemmed
from the marriage of a Cheshire baronet, whose family had
already been enriched by an heiress, to scatter-brained Mary
Davies, who owned the gold-bearing lands of Westminster
and Mayfair.

Even when the long-sought dukedom had been secured,
more heiresses were often necessary to defray the cost of
ducal living. The first Duke of Montagu, anxious to extend
the glories of his Boughton seat, dressed up as the Emperor
of China in order to woo the widowed, rich but mad Duchess
of Albemarle, this being the only way of separating her
from her money. In more recent times the Dukes of Marlborough were among those who went to America for their
heiresses. The eighth Duke lost little time in spending his

* Lord Ronald Gower: *My Reminiscences*

bride's money on central heating for Blenheim Palace. He
did not have to dress up in imperial garb to win her. It was
enough to be an English duke.

It would have been sensible and seemly if no more dukes
had been created after the Duke of Wellington. The later
nineteenth-century creations had little to justify them except
that those elevated were great landlords; they may have lived
dignified and philanthropic lives, but that was no reason for
making them dukes. In 1955 a dukedom was offered by
Queen Elizabeth II to that former scourge of dukes, Sir
Winston Churchill, who declined it. So far no dukes have
renounced their hereditary titles, though in 1954 the
Marquess of Graham, resident in Rhodesia, showed great
lack of interest in the news that he had become seventh Duke
of Montrose. It is customary for hereditary dukedoms to be
accepted, with a smile or a shrug, along with all accompanying lands, no matter by what remote and devious links they
have reached the recipient. The notion of voluntarily
restoring an inherited estate to the people, or to the Crown
which originally bestowed it, would be regarded as a betrayal
not only of one's forebears but of one's descendants, as the
third Duke of Richmond made very clear to his fellow peers
in 1780. The Dukes of Northumberland never questioned
their rights to all the minerals buried under their lands,
right down to the centre of the earth. Why should they under-
mine the principle of property? If a duke, of all people, once
doubted his right to possession, all possession would be at an
end. One of the more poignant moments in these pages is
when the eighth Duke of Northumberland is called before
the Coal Commission in 1919:

Sir Leo Chiozza Money: As a coal owner, what service
do you perform to the community?
Duke of Northumberland: As the owner of the coal I
do not think I perform any service to mankind, not as the
owner of the coal.

The Duke's royalties from minerals at this time were

£84,000 gross. Some of the miners on the Commission were unable to see why he should receive such sums. But when asked, 'Do you not think it is a bad thing to own as much as you do?' he replied, 'No, I think it is an excellent thing in every way.'

There spoke a true English duke.

PREAMBLE

There were no dukes in Britain until 1337. In that year Edward III created his son, the Black Prince, Duke of Cornwall. With the title went a duchy.

Earlier English kings had called themselves Dukes of Normandy or Aquitaine; but Edward, having claimed the throne of France, felt himself free to create dukes in his own lands. His successors also bestowed dukedoms on their sons.

In 1483 the rank of duke was conferred on a commoner, John Howard, who became Duke of Norfolk. The title was extinguished, along with its owner, in the last battle of the Wars of the Roses.

Under the Tudors the handful of dukes lived dangerously. In 1521 the third Duke of Buckingham was beheaded by Henry VIII for supposedly coveting the Crown; he was too strong a magnate and had built the last private castle to be raised in England. One who wept to see his fate, and then begged his lands, was Thomas Howard, second Duke of Norfolk, who had won back the dukedom by defeating the Scots at Flodden. The rapacious Howards had to perform fearful duties for their monarch. The third Duke of Norfolk steered two queens—Anne Boleyn and Catherine Howard—to the block; both were his nieces. The King then executed the Duke's son, the Earl of Surrey, on charges of treason and would have executed the Duke for the same offence had not death claimed the Throne.

Henry VIII's handsome bully, Charles Brandon, Duke of Suffolk, who married a sister of the King when he already had a wife, was fortunate enough to die with his head on. In 1551 his sons Henry and Charles were both carried away on the same day by the sweating sickness. The younger son enjoyed the rank of duke for only half an hour.

Henry VIII's policy had been to break the power of the great nobles. Ironically, by giving away the Church spoils to his henchmen, he founded the immense fortunes of a later generation of nobles who were able to overturn one royal house and dominate another.

After Henry's death the history of dukes continues to be the history of the block. In 1552 the Duke of Somerset, Protector of the infant Edward VI, founder of Somerset House and Syon House, was beheaded on trumped-up charges brought by the Duke of Northumberland. In the following year the Duke of Northumberland was beheaded by Mary for trying to put his daughter-in-law, Lady Jane Grey, on the throne. Lady Jane's father, a new Duke of Suffolk, also went to the block.

Elizabeth, whose chief vexations were caused by earls, killed off the last remaining duke in 1572 and disinherited his heirs. He was Thomas Howard, fourth Duke of Norfolk, who cherished the perilous notion of marrying Mary Queen of Scots and becoming her consort. 'Alas!' said Mary, 'what has the House of Howard suffered for my sake!' But the House of Howard brought most of its troubles on itself. Elizabeth, at all events, was grateful to a Howard for commanding the fleet which, with some aid from the Almighty, routed the Armada.

For a whole generation there were no dukes in Britain. Then James I revived, and dishonoured, the rank by conferring it on the young George Villiers, with whom he was besotted. This fortunate young gentleman, recruited to the post of cupbearer, rose from esquire to earl in just over two years, as against seven for the previous favourite. He had to wait six more years to become Duke of Buckingham, in order to avoid outraging the old nobility. Between them king and favourite sold for cash all ranks from earl downwards. The Duke continued in favour under Charles I, but came to a violent end.

The Civil War broke out in 1642. After the Battle of Worcester the future Charles II fled the country, as did the second Duke of Buckingham, son of the murdered favourite. Some of their time was spent in France, where fascinating dukes and marquesses were thick on the ground. In 1660 the Stuart dynasty was restored.

REPLENISHING THE RANKS

1

A wise king awards few titles of honour. This advice was given to Charles II by his boyhood governor, who became Duke of Newcastle. However, something had to be done at the Restoration to placate and strengthen an aristocracy that had become wasted, especially in its upper ranges. Almost the only duke surviving was that corrupter of royal innocence, the second Duke of Buckingham, who had deserted Charles in exile but was there to greet him at Dover, ready to advance an interrupted career as rake, mischief-maker, 'chymist, fiddler, statesman and buffoon'. To replenish the store of dukes, the King hit upon a plan of singular cynicism: for almost every duke he created from existing stock, he bred another from a current mistress. Of the six ducal lines sired by the Fount of Honour, four are still with us.

Within a year of acceding Charles raised five subjects to dukedoms. They included a madman, who became Duke of Norfolk; a young man who was created Duke of Hamilton only because he had married the right woman at the right time (Anne, Duchess of Hamilton, who had inherited the dukedom after the second Duke fell at Worcester); and the architect of the Protestant Ascendancy in Ireland, who became Duke of Ormonde.

Why make a madman a duke? The Howards, deprived of the highest rank since Elizabeth beheaded the fourth Duke of

Norfolk, were choking with frustrated ambition. They had
lands, lineage and a tradition of State service. In their ducal
palace at Norwich they drank from gold goblets and handled
the coal with silver tongs. Like potentates, they were greeted
by cathedral bells and cannon. During New Year festivities
their three carriages, one of them a specially-built fourteen-
seater, went about the town picking up lady guests.* Unhappily, the family's candidate for a dukedom, Thomas
Howard, lived in exile in Padua where a severe illness had
left him deranged. He was not in the class of the 'cannibalistic idiot' who, on a later occasion, was disqualified from
becoming a Duke of Queensberry, but he was in no state to
wear a coronet in public. However, in the family's view, an
insane duke was better than no duke at all, and more than
ninety nobles were induced to petition for a restoration of
this ancient dukedom. Late in 1660 Thomas Howard was
created fifth Duke of Norfolk. In 1677 he died, still at Padua,
and his brother Henry succeeded him. This sixth Duke
figures dubiously in the memoirs of that doughty cavalier,
Sir John Reresby, who says the Howards suspected him of
fatally gelding a young blackamoor servant and, assuming
he would be convicted of felony, began to solicit the King
for his estates. Lawyers and a surgeon inspected the putrefied
corpse but could find no sign of malpractice. It was, says
Sir John, 'a black and most ridiculous piece of malice'. The
sixth Duke later sought to appease Reresby, who found it hard
to forgive the conduct of a noble family on the make.

Among those who knelt to the new King at Dover was the
professional soldier who had survived the interregnum as
General-in-Chief of All Land Forces in the Three Kingdoms
and Joint Commander of the Navy. General George Monk
had fought for Charles I and spent three years in the Tower;
then, when the Civil War ended, he had consented to serve
Cromwell against the country's enemies, meaning the Dutch,
the Irish and the Scots. The Protector esteemed him as an
'honest and simple-hearted fellow' and gave him his own
regiment of Foot Guards, which became the Coldstream. In

* *Journal* of E. Browne, quoted by Macaulay

1660, with Parliament half-foundering in disgrace, Monk marched on London and, after much secret negotiation, was deputed to greet the new Stuart. In a sense he was the midwife of the Restoration; or, as Horace Walpole says, he 'furnished a hand to the heart of a nation'. Charles heaped honours and lands on him and created him Duke of Albemarle. Clarendon classed the Duke as a sensible man 'with no fumes of religion to turn his head'; Bishop Burnet thought he had 'steered dexterously on a strong tide'. and felt it a pity he lived long enough to make his stupidity evident;* the Earl of Ailesbury, conceding that the Duke was 'naturally of heavy parts and illiterate', praised his good judgment and caution.† During the Great Plague the Duke stayed in London (which was more than the King did), visiting pest-houses and drawing up preventive measures. Immediately afterwards he was at sea again fighting the Dutch; and when his ship grounded he petrified the gentlemen volunteers by threatening to fire his pistol into the magazine if she were faced with capture. From these desperate scenes he was called back to establish order in London after the Great Fire. If he was a blockhead, it is a pity there were not more like him. His Duchess was the one-time seamstress Nan Clarges, a rabid royalist, whom he got with child while in the Tower. Pepys was among the many who vilified her; after accepting Albemarle's hospitality he reported: 'The Duke has sorry company, dirty dishes, bad meat and a nasty wife at table.' Materially, the Duke fared well under the new regime. He moved into Cromwell's old estate of New Hall in Essex, with its four rows of great elms a mile long. In Walpole's *Royal and Noble Authors* he is credited with a book of military precepts, one of which is a warning that if swords are issued to common soldiers half the weapons 'will on the first march be broken with cutting boughs'.

The King was slower to pay his debt to his boyhood governor, William Cavendish, Marquess of Newcastle. This romantic equestrian was a grandson of Sir William Caven-

* Bishop Burnet: *History of My Own Time*
† Earl of Ailesbury: *Memoirs*

dish and the formidable 'Bess of Hardwick', who used the
wealth of four husbands to build five great mansions (Chatsworth, Oldcotes, Bolsover, Worksop and Hardwick Hall)
and founded two ducal lines of Cavendishes: the Devonshires
and the Newcastles. The Marquess, a self-indulgent general,
had raised the North for Charles I but walked out on the
God of Battles after seeing his forces squandered by Prince
Rupert at Marston Moor. While he was self-exiled in Europe
seven out of his eight parks were ravaged, only Welbeck
being spared; and his castle at Bolsover was half-demolished.
At Antwerp, living off his friends, he set up a riding school
and published an uncommonly lavish book on equitation.
For his second wife he had married the busy-brained Margaret
Lucas, that incurable philosopher and fantasist who became
known as Mad Madge. She had been unhappy in her post at
the court of Queen Henrietta Maria, wife of Charles I, where
she was thought 'a natural fool', but under the Cavalier's
protection she expanded; her fancies, instead of lying 'like
a swarm of bees in a round heap', flew abroad 'to gather
honey from the sweet flowery rhetoric of my Lord's discourse'.
It was a pity that, on the Restoration, the Marquess had to
leave her in Flanders as security for his debts; nor did he
find it easy to raise the cash to redeem her. His dukedom,
which came in 1665, had to be solicited. In the patent creating
him Duke of Newcastle-on-Tyne the King said: 'We shall
always retain a sense of those good principles he instilled into
us.' Among them were: a man cannot be too civil to women;
and a too devout man may be a bad king.

The Duke now concentrated on restoring his estates and
exercising his horses. Near Welbeck he built a five-mile
racecourse and drew up his own rules for riding—no slashing at
competitors, or pulling their bridles. But the skills of dressage
were his obsession. In his book *A General System of Horsemanship* he says that anyone who asks, 'What is a horse good
for that can do nothing but dance and play tricks?' might
as well subsist on nothing but acorns and water. He scoffs at
'the absurd fault of some horsemen who by seeing imitate,
and imagine they ride as I do', and regrets that there are riders

who think buttocks are for sitting on, instead of perching 'upright on the twist'. He will have no cruel measures in training. Mares should not be 'covered' when in a place of confinement, 'for every natural action of this kind ought to be performed with freedom and love and not by violence or constraint'. He condemns 'the ridiculous practice of tying the left testicle to generate a male and the right a female', but advocates a usage no more sensible: 'Place a cloth before the mare's face, of which colour you please, that she may conceive a colt of the same.'

While the Duke educated his horses, engaged in swordplay and generally acted the Elizabethan, his Duchess sat in Welbeck Abbey weaving her conceits and allegories, refining her cogitations, dreaming of fame everlasting and wondering whether her lord was overheating himself. He would have done better to wonder whether his lady was not overheating herself. Did he ever hear her calling her footman-amanuensis, 'John! John! I conceive!'? Literary creation, as she admitted, was gruelling work:

> When I did write this book I took great pains,
> For I did walk and think and break my brains.

Both of them wrote plays. The Duke and Dryden between them turned a Molière play into *Sir Martin Mar-All*, which Pepys saw eight times, rating it the best comedy ever written; but he thought the Duke's comedy *The Humorous Lovers* was the silliest play ever staged. The Duchess's plays are a producer's despair. Where other dramatists bring on spear-carriers, she calls for a chorus of moral philosophers and natural philosophers, who hold dissertations of enormous tedium. In her copious prefaces she admits she has no hopes of seeing her plays acted, but at least they are not cribbed from the masters:

> I could not steal their wits, nor plots out take,
> All my plays' plots my own poor brain did make.

However, she received some assistance from her husband, who wrote many of the bolder lines, like 'In plain English, I would have your maidenhead!' and, in less plain English, 'Let us meet in the next close, there under some sweet hedge to taste Love's aromatic banquet at your table.' Such passages, from *The Lady Contemplation*, are carefully credited to the Duke in the text. According to the Duchess, he had been a great lover in his day and perhaps it seemed sensible to draw on his experience; though, for a woman who claimed to have been 'bred to elevated thoughts', she could turn out indelicacies with the best.

In the field of philosophy the Duchess ploughed her own furrow, refusing 'to be led by the nose by Authority and Old Authors'. Total ignorance could not prevent her from explaining wind, tides, noise or atoms. No writer showed off more indefatigably. Out it all teemed: dialogues between earth and darkness, 'a moral discourse on corn', explanations of colics, speeches suitable for a dying virgin, a quarter-drunk gentleman and a half-drunk gentleman. In her fantasy *The Blazing World* the soul of the Duchess flies in a secretarial capacity to a golden utopia, the empress of which chops logic with castrated savants. Descending to Welbeck in an invisible car, the souls of the two ladies espy the Duke of Newcastle overheating himself as he sits upright on the twist and, uninvited, enter his body; 'and had there been some such souls more the Duke would have been like the Grand Signior in his Seraglio, only it would have been the Platonic Seraglio'. Alas, even in this Platonic Seraglio there is jealousy.

The Duke, carrying gallantry to its last extremity, publicly praised his wife's wit and invention, assuring her that when Shakespeare and Spenser lay under oblivion her works would survive; and she never ceased to esteem his talents and dignity, and to mourn the depredations of war which had cost him £1,000,000. She wrote his life and listed his opinions; among them, a belief that too many young men were going up to the universities, and that news-sheets overheated the people's brains. Occasionally the Duchess descended on London,

theatrically dressed, in a black-and-silver cavalcade which
set all the boys and girls running. Pepys thought her comely,
but with 'many black patches, because of pimples about her
mouth'. Evelyn met her when she invited herself to the Royal
Society and was shown how to turn roast mutton into pure
blood; he called her 'a mighty pretender to learning, poetry
and philosophy'. As such she sent copies of her works to the
universities and was fulsomely thanked for her services to
Learning's Commonwealth. She was in danger of being made
a cult figure like Amanda Ros of a later day. Virginia Woolf
thinks the Duchess had 'a vein of authentic fire', something
'noble and Quixotic and high-spirited, as well as crack-
brained and bird-witted'.* Her splendid epitaph in Westminster Abbey says she came of 'a noble familie', in which
'all the brothers were valiant, and all the sisters virtuous'.

The man who had to work hardest for his dukedom
under Charles II was that vizier with the 'Saracen fiery face',
John Maitland, who was created Duke of Lauderdale in 1672.
Charles abhorred the anarchic squalor of Scotland and
handed the country over to Lauderdale to keep in some sort
of subjection, even if it meant loosing hundreds of wild
Highlanders on the Lowlands. No one could have ruled
Scotland for two decades without high administrative talent
and skill in the exercise of patronage; these assets the Duke
possessed, along with ruthlessness, craft and treachery, all
useful qualities when dealing with the Scots nobility.

At the English Court men who spoke 'high Scotch' were
natural butts. Like James I the Duke had a tongue too big
for his mouth, which made him 'bedew' those he addressed,
and his red hair was in every sense a shock. Ailesbury said he
was for ever 'uttering bold jests for wit, and repeating good
ones of others and ever spoiled them in relating them, which
delighted the good King much'. He picked his ears in the
Presence Chamber and performed other private acts publicly.
To keep Lauderdale's fingers out of the royal snuff-box, the
King wore a special shaker tied to his wrist by a string.

* *Collected Essays*

Ailesbury tells how the courtiers, anxious to deter the Duke from inviting himself to the King's private suppers, filled two syllabub glasses, handing one to the King and the other, which contained horse urine, to the Duke. When the King pronounced his syllabub to be very good, the Duke drained his glass and loyally commented that no one had such a taste as His Majesty. 'In some little time it worked as was natural, and the King perceiving it cried out, "My Lord Lauderdale is sick," and they carried him away, and the King was never troubled more with him on such diverting occasions.'*

The Duke's friendships were formed for what they might yield. He had 'a selfishness that never slept' and was 'completely free of a belief in generosity of character and of the embarrassments of gratitude ... a bold and unabashed liar, he was as eloquent against what he called "damned insipid lies" as Hotspur was against women's oaths'. Yet he was prepared to stoop to the truth if it suited him. Strangely, the red boor was well versed in Latin, Greek and Hebrew, but he abominated music—'he had rather hear a cat mew than the best music in the world; and the better the music the more sick it made him'. As a debauchee he was rated in the high Roman class. He has been called an addict of 'bestial revels, the pleasures of which it is a shame even to speak', and 'that most terrible of all things—a dirty old man'.†

In 1672 this decaying satyr married the Countess of Dysart, a rapacious widow whose family owned Ham House, beside the Thames. She and the Duke embellished it until, as Evelyn says, it was 'like a great Prince's'. As joint rangers of Richmond Park they did their best to keep the common people out, while exploiting its resources. In Scotland the Duke also lived in the grand manner. One day as the table was being prepared for an important dinner in his castle of Thirlstane, near Lauder, he discovered that there was a shortage of plate, a situation which could be remedied only by sending a running footman across the Lammermuir Hills to his other castle at

* Earl of Ailesbury: *Memoirs*
† Osmund Airy in *Charles II* and *Quarterly Review*, April 1844

Lethington, fifteen miles away. The footman returned with
the necessary items in time for dinner.* It sounds improbable,
but running footmen prided themselves on their power to
outstay horses.

In 1684 Charles conferred a dukedom on a magnate who
lived in old-fashioned baronial splendour at Badminton,
Gloucestershire. He was Henry Somerset, Marquess of Worcester, who now became Duke of Beaufort. The reasons given
for advancing him were that he was descended from Edward
III by John de Beaufort and had served the King well. His
Civil war record had been undistinguished and he had
drawn a liberal dole from Cromwell, though at the end he
had been active to restore the monarchy. Convinced of his
loyalty, Charles had made him Lord President of Wales and
as such, on his progresses, he had been treated like royalty.
Roger North, who visited Badminton in 1680, said the Marquess 'had about two hundred persons in his family, all
provided for'. Every day nine tables were laid, each for a
carefully defined group of servants, and all in a large hall
where 'the whole lay in front of him that was chief'. The
method of governing this great family was 'admirable and
easy'. No liveried servants attended the top table, but 'those
called gentlemen only'; and there was 'no sitting at table
with tobacco and healths, as the common use is'. All the
household were busy, the ladies embroidering for the State
beds, the servants brewing beer and making soap and
candles (the malt for the beer lay drying on the leads of
the house). All horses were bred on the estate, used until
unfit and then pensioned off.

Badminton set an example of old-world order in a corrupt
age. 'The children of the family', says North, 'were bred
with a philosophical care. No inferior servants were permitted to entertain them, lest some mean sentiments or
foolish notions and fables should steal into them; and nothing was so strongly impressed upon them as a sense of
honour.' Lord Arthur Somerset, aged about five, rebuked
a visiting judge for hanging criminals. 'The judge told him

* Chambers's *Book of Days*

that if they were not hanged they would kill and steal. "No," said the little boy, "you should make them promise upon *their honour* they will not do so and then they will not." '*

The best-known duke of the Restoration, George Villiers, second Duke of Buckingham, had won back his forfeited estates by a desperate, but dazzling, stratagem while Cromwell was still alive. The lands had gone to Lord Fairfax, the former Parliamentary general. It seemed to the Duke, in exile, that the best way to get them back was to slip into England and win the hand of Fairfax's daughter Mary. She was on the point of marrying an earl but succumbed instantly to the Villiers charm, as did her father. The Duke later made his peace with Parliament. Within twenty-four hours of Charles's landing at Dover he had also made his peace with the king he deserted. He then took over Wallingford House, Westminster, where he was born, and set about establishing himself as the wittiest, most popular and most personable of the King's subjects. In so doing, Ailesbury estimates, he got through £20,000 a year for twenty years and incurred debts of £40,000 as well.

As a statesman the Duke was incapable of adjusting the nocturnal routine of a profligate to the needs of the nation. He lost the favour of the King as often as he gained it. He was sent to the Tower for pulling one marquess's nose and again for knocking off another marquess's wig; and yet again for casting the King's horoscope, a treasonable exercise calling for the imagining of that unimaginable thing, the King's death. Charles weathered some angry scenes in Buckingham's company, notably when the Duke was suspected of having been behind the waylaying, in St James's, of that proud Irish Cavalier, the Duke of Ormonde by the grudge-ridden knave Colonel Blood. The Colonel had every intention of carrying off Ormonde to Tyburn and hanging him there like a common criminal; but, like the master crooks of fiction, he was so anxious to stage a diabolical revenge that the victim escaped. The Earl of Ossory, Ormonde's son was certain enough of Buckingham's guilt to denounce him before the King; if

* Roger North: *Life of Francis North*

Ormonde died violently, his son warned, 'I shall pistol you, though you stood behind the King's chair, and I tell it you in His Majesty's presence that you may be sure I will keep my word.' Buckingham's complicity in the affair is doubtful. Later Blood accused him of unnatural offences against women and was ordered to pay the Duke £30,000.*

The Duke's contempt for narrow standards was best shown by his taking the Countess of Shrewsbury for mistress after mortally wounding her husband in a duel—a three-a-side encounter with swords, possibly watched by the Countess. When the Duchess of Buckingham (Mary Fairfax) objected to the Duke's proposal to bring his mistress under the family roof, the Duke said he had anticipated her scruples and had ordered a coach to take her to her father's house. Like the King, the Duke felt that wives and mistresses ought to be able to get along together. It was all too much for Pepys, who wrote: 'This will make the world think that the King hath good councillors when the Duke of Buckingham, the greatest man about him, is a fellow of no more sobriety than to fight about a whore.' The King failed to persuade the Duke not to live openly with another man's wife. In the House of Lords trustees of the young Earl of Shrewsbury complained that a child of the adulterers had been buried in Westminster Abbey, a tolerant fane which was still accepting ducal bastards a hundred years later. Eventually Parliament forced a break-up of the liaison by threatening fines of £10,000 on each partner if it continued; a penalty which would have been an impressive one even under Puritan rule.

In his turn the Duke offered domestic advice to the King. He suggested that the barren Queen be spirited away to a far plantation, or shut in a nunnery, so that Charles could marry again; but, says Bishop Burnet, the King rejected this counsel with horror. It was the Duke who introduced the actresses Nell Gwynn and Mary Davis to the King's notice. He was eager to see his cousin, the Countess of Castlemaine, replaced by a French mistress, but forgot to send a yacht to fetch Louise de Kéroualle, who was left fuming

* Hester Chapman: *Great Villiers*

on the dunes at Dieppe for a couple of weeks. This was typical of his disdain for practical administration.

The Duke never doubted that he could lead an army, command a warship, run an embassy, control the Exchequer or write a play (his comedy *The Rehearsal* deflated the overblown verse drama of the day). As a 'chymist' he thought he had got nearer to finding the Philosopher's Stone than anyone else. Of more practical use was his attempt to break the Venetian mirror monopoly by setting up a glass factory at Vauxhall. If he had a good quality, it was his belief in religious tolerance.

It was not unusual to say of a deceased enemy that he had worn himself out by whoring. Bishop Burnet detected 'the madness of vice' in the Duke's person; at the end his conversation was 'as much avoided as ever it had been courted'. He did not die, as Pope says, in 'the worst inn's worst room'. Thrown while hunting, he sat on wet grass while overheated and died in the house of a respectable tenant near Helmsley, on his Yorkshire estates. The display at his funeral in Westminster Abbey eclipsed that accorded to Charles II.

SIX ABOVE THE BLANKET

2

Samuel Pepys was not alone in thinking that Charles II was 'mighty kind ... to his bastard children'. Of these he had more than a dozen, a not excessive total by royal standards; Augustus the Strong, King of Saxony, who died in 1733, has been credited with 364. Charles made dukes out of six of his bastards, with revenues payable by the taxpayer to their descendants in perpetuity. Three of them, by three different mothers, were christened Charles; and three of them, all by one mother, were styled Fitzroy, a traditional and even coveted name for royal children born on the wrong side of the blanket (Henry VIII's son by Elizabeth Blount, a lady in waiting, had been named Henry Fitzroy and created Duke of Richmond). Charles would have rejected the notion that raising his natural sons to dukedoms was being 'mighty kind' to them, or mighty unfair to the taxpayers, or that there was anything wrong in breeding his own nobility from a string of mistresses.

When he came to the throne in 1660 Charles already had one acknowledged bastard, born in 1649 to Lucy Walters (a 'beautiful strumpet', according to John Evelyn) at Rotterdam. This was the future Duke of Monmouth and Buccleuch. The King spent his first night in England with the Countess of Castlemaine, the former Barbara Villiers, who had married her Earl the year before, at the age of eighteen. This promiscuous delinquent remained in favour for about ten years, during which she bore the King six children. The boys became the Dukes of Cleveland, Grafton and Northumberland. In 1670, by Nell Gwynn, the King fathered a boy who became Duke of St Albans. Finally in 1672 his French mistress Louise de Kéroualle gave birth to a boy who was created Duke of Richmond. Four of these ducal lines— Buccleuch, Grafton, St Albans and Richmond—still prosper.

The bastard dukes were variously supported by the Privy Purse, the Excise, the Post Office, the Law, the Army and even the Church. Into their laps were tossed Garters, Privy Councillorships and sinecures; they became admirals, colonels of regiments, governors of castles and islands, lords lieutenant of counties, constables, butlers, rangers of forests. Monmouth, who lacked education, was an obvious choice as Chancellor of Cambridge University. As if to show that the duties of Master of the Horse could be carried out by any ten-year-old, the ten-year-old Duke of Richmond was given that appointment (in fact, he employed three commissioners). Some of these posts were more ornamental than lucrative. The urgent need was to find heiresses for these needy young men, who in the main were spirited and good-looking. Charles was especially pleased at securing the Earl of Arlington's daughter for Grafton.

The sons of a profligate father and three profligate mothers seem to have grown up in amity together, taking embarrassments in their stride. Pepys saw Lucy Walters's son Monmouth riding in a coach with the King, the Queen and the Countess of Castlemaine, which was Charles's idea of a family outing. Evelyn describes an occasion when Northumberland, St Albans and Richmond, 'base sons' of three 'prostitute creatures', attended communion in Whitehall together, joining the King between the rails, in the presence of three bishops. Were the three 'prostitute creatures' also present, linked in a common glow of pride and piety? Probably not, for Richmond's French mother disliked the other two mistresses. Were the bishops moved by distaste, compassion, duty or self-importance? We can only guess. In

1685 Charles, on his deathbed, sent for his illegitimate sons and blessed them, showing a peculiar tenderness towards Richmond, the youngest. His best-loved but most exasperating son, Monmouth, was not present and was soon to lose his handsome head to Jack Ketch.

The Duke of Monmouth's career invites the taunt: 'Why was he born so beautiful? Why was he born at all?' Dryden, noting that the Duke was the King's favourite son, speculates

> Whether, inspired by some diviner lust,
> His father got him with a greater gust ...*

Ambitious, conceited, dashing, the Duke caused his father many anxieties. His Life Guards officers engaged in nose-slitting; and the Duke, in company with the second Duke of Albemarle, slew a harmless beadle on a Sunday morning while 'beating the watch'. The costs of wild living were only partly defrayed by a levy on the export of new drapery, worth £8,000 a year. As Master of the Horse he drew £5,000, but new sources of revenue had constantly to be found. Appointed Captain-General, he defeated the Covenanters at Bothwell Brig and showed leniency to the enemy. His downfall began with the Popish Plot when the country, distrustful of the King's Roman Catholic brother James, clamoured for a Protestant heir. The Duke pretended to be that heir, which drew from his angry father a statement that he had married nobody but the Queen. In 1685, with James newly on the throne, Monmouth attempted to raise the West Country and had himself crowned king in the market place at Taunton. The Whigs were not anxious to risk another civil war to throw out the Stuarts and Monmouth was not their idea of a legitimate replacement. As Macaulay says: 'All honest and sensible persons were unwilling to see a fraud which, if practised to obtain an estate, would have been punished with the scourge and the pillory.'† The Duke paid for his folly and so did all too many of his West Country supporters at

* *Absalom and Achitophel*
† *History of England*

the Bloody Assize. Had the Duke waited three more years, and thrown in his lot with William Cavendish and John Churchill, he might have lived long in the land. With his execution the Monmouth dukedom died out. He had been Duke of Monmouth and Buccleuch, having married Anne Scott, Countess of Buccleuch in her own right. His widow remained Duchess of Buccleuch and kept her lands. Unseared by the events of 1685, she lived to be a cheerful, if arrogant, septuagenarian. In Dalkeith Palace she maintained a near-royal estate, keeping everyone standing and receiving guests under a canopy. No letter could be submitted to her except through a gentlewoman in waiting. On her death her grandson became second Duke of Buccleuch. As the generations passed the family became enormously prosperous through marriage and inheritance and it may well be the richest ducal family today. Macaulay asserts that even in his time West Countrymen looked to the Buccleuchs for support when Bills affecting them were before Parliament, on the grounds that their forebears had bled copiously for the first Duke. There is a story that the fifth Duke found among his papers a certificate showing that Charles II had legally espoused Lucy Walters. Loyally he presented it to Queen Victoria, who thanked him and put it on the fire.

Possibly Charles was not the father of all the brood laid at his door by the Countess of Castlemaine; but faced with a mother who threatened to dash out the babe's brains on the floor if he denied paternity, he gave in. Her sons were not 'duked' until after she had been created Duchess of Cleveland, to mark her 'noble descent' and 'her own personal virtues'. Charles Fitzroy, who became Duke of Southampton and, on his mother's death, Duke of Cleveland, lived a life void of interest. Possibly he had hoped to live in his mother's great Tudor castle at Nonsuch, a gift from Charles, but the Duchess sold it for scrap. This ducal line became extinct in 1774. Henry Fitzroy, whom the King was slow to recognise, was created Duke of Grafton. He was handsome, rough and reckless. He fought two duels to punish aspersions, probably well founded, on his mother and on each occasion slew the

brother of an earl. In 1648 an actor known as 'Scum' Good-
man was fined £1,000 for conspiring to poison Grafton and
his brother Northumberland, with whose mother he had
been having an affair; evidently the sons had resented his
admission to the all-welcoming bed. The fine seems a modest
one for trying to extinguish two royal dukes, but there was
clearly more to the case than met the eye. In 1685 the Duke
of Grafton led troops against his half-brother, Monmouth;
and three years later he showed an equal lack of compunction
in deserting his uncle, James II. At Beachy Head in 1690
he commanded the seventy-gun *Grafton* with distinction
and died the same year, aged twenty-seven, besieging Cork.
His fortunes had been sustained by a £7,000 tax on imported wines, a pension of £4,700 on the Post Office and
nearly £3,000 as a sealer in the Law Courts. His wife, whom
he bedded when she was fourteen, was a daughter of the
Earl of Arlington, and from her the second Duke inherited
the splendid estate of Euston Park, in Suffolk. The third of
the Fitzroys, George, was created Duke of Northumberland.
Evelyn thought him handsome, well-shaped and 'of all His
Majesty's children the most accomplished and worth the
owning'. He is remembered for the way in which he tried to
shed his dull wife Catherine, the widow of an Army officer.
The Duke of Grafton, taking pity on him, suggested convey-
ing the lady to a convent in Europe and there shutting her
away as a punishment for lack of charm. Northumberland
leaped at this idea, which recalls the Duke of Buckingham's
proposals for getting rid of Charles II's Queen. He told his
wife that they were going with his brother on a sea cruise,
and would be able to fall in love afresh. The Duchess was
delivered in a high state of indignation at a convent in
Ghent, where the Mother Superior, under some pressure,
signed her in as a voluntary entrant. However, she found her
way back to Britain and exacted redress from her husband.
He died without issue in 1716 and the dukedom became
extinct.

It is supposed that Nell Gwynn had to use crude pressure
on the King to secure her boy's ennoblement. One story is

that, in a gesture worthy of the Countess of Castlemaine, she held the nameless babe out of the window until the King cried, 'Save the Earl of Burford!' In another story Nell says to the child, 'Come here, you little bastard, and speak to your father.' When the King protests, 'Nay, Nelly, do not give the child such a name,' the mother retorts, 'Your Majesty has given me no other name by which I may call him.' Thanks to some such stratagem, the little bastard was named Charles Beauclerk and created a baron and an earl to be going on with; the dukedom of St Albans came when he was fourteen. In 1688 he fought with the Imperial Army against the Turks, which spared him any agony of conscience over betraying James II. Later he served the new King in the field, and was given by him a set of coach horses 'spotted like leopards'. He drew a £2,000 pension, some of which came from ecclesiastical first fruits, and £1,200 a year as Hereditary Grand Falconer. His line has left little trace in the history books.

The King's son by his French mistress was named Charles Lennox and created Duke of Richmond; the first of seven dukes of that line to be called Charles. He was conceived during a break from a Newmarket race meeting, when the King visited Louise de Kéroualle, that tool of Louis XIV, at nearby Euston Hall, kindly lent by Lady Arlington. The French Ambassador was there in a pimping capacity and the stocking was thrown as if the King were bedding a bride. The Duke of Richmond brought no distinction to his appointments and was never sure of his politics or religion. His rewards included the castle of Richmond in Yorkshire and the Lennox lands in Scotland, and a grant of one shilling on every chaldron of coals shipped to London from Newcastle, which produced £12,000 a year, steadily rising. Early in the nineteenth century the grant was extinguished by a payment of nearly £500,000. The public has rarely had to pay such a bill for a night's gallantry.

The Duke bought an estate at Goodwood, in Sussex, which later became a great horse-racing centre, appropriately enough since the Duke was the by-product of a race meeting. Debt and dissipation began to engulf him. In 1719 he forced his eighteen-year-old son, the Earl of March, to marry the young daughter of the Earl of Cardigan in order to raise money to settle a debt. As a reward, the Earl was sent off on a three years' Grand Tour. Returning to London, he visited the theatre, was dazzled by a beauty in the audience, asked who she was and was told 'your wife'. He then fell in love with her and, as duke and duchess, they lived happily ever after.

A DELUGE OF DUKES

3

A golden age of duke-making followed the 'Glorious Revo-lution' of 1688, in which the Protestant William of Orange dislodged his Roman Catholic uncle, James II, from the Throne. The new King was anxious that the Whigs, who seized the credit for the Revolution, should not presume to rule through him; but 1688 in effect saw the beginning of half a century of domination by the great Whig families. Prominent among them were the ducal Devonshires, Bed-fords, Newcastles and Rutlands.

The way in which the coup was achieved was 'in almost every part discreditable to England', says Macaulay. It was effected without bloodshed, 'principally owing to an act of ungrateful perfidy, such as no other soldier ever committed'.*
This refers to the defection from James's army of John Churchill, later the great Duke of Marlborough. Sir Winston Churchill has demanded to know why his ancestor should be branded as infamous when those who earned their duke-doms by intriguing against James in their private homes have been hailed as the architects of a new Britain.

In 1688 the stakes were high and the penalty for failure was still the block. Only three years earlier the Duke of Monmouth's head had rolled and the West Country had been strewn with human carrion. Two years before that,

* *History of England*

44

Lord William Russell had been executed for complicity in the Rye House Plot.

The cause was that of Protestantism, which was under active attack by James, encouraged by the Roman Catholic tyrannies of France and Spain. For those noblemen living in great prosperity and comfort on former monastery lands the possibility of a restoration of the old faith, with the aid of their Catholic Majesties, was too poignant to be borne. So was the idea of Ireland as a French or Spanish satellite.

James had shown little finesse in trying to convert his country to Rome. He intimidated and purged the Bench. He introduced Roman Catholic officers into an army much expanded since Monmouth's rising; but the middle and lower ranks jeered at the Mass. By 1687 James had dismissed seventeen lords lieutenant for resisting his policies. Of these, fourteen were earls and one was a duke, the sixth Duke of Somerset, who was master of Alnwick Castle, Syon and Petworth. As First Lord of the Treasury the 'proud duke', as he is known to history, was asked to introduce the Papal nuncio at St James's. When he refused, saying he would be subject to a heavy penalty in law, James said, 'I would have you fear me, as well as the law.' To this the Duke astutely replied, 'I cannot fear your Majesty as long as I commit no offence. I am secure in your Majesty's justice.' Another notable exchange occurred when James required the seventh Duke of Norfolk to carry the Sword of State into his Popish chapel. The Duke stopped at the door, where the King said, 'My Lord, your father would have gone farther.' The reply was, 'Your Majesty's father was the better man and he would not have gone so far.'

It was a Cavendish from Chatsworth, a great-great-grandson of Bess of Hardwick, who was the leading plotter against James: William Cavendish, fourth Earl of Devonshire and later first Duke. His early life was a record of brawls and duels. In 1685, after a clash with a Colonel Culpeper in the Presence Chamber, he was fined £30,000 by the King's Bench, with a direction that he be detained until it was paid. It is probably history's highest fine for hooliganism. Escaping from custody he fled to Chatsworth and, as bold as any mediaeval baron, imprisoned the force which came to take him. The new King, James, did not want this quarrelsome nobleman at Court, but still less did he relish the notion of his plotting with fellow Protestants in the country. An order to attend Court was declined with excuses, one of which was that the Duke was busy rebuilding Chatsworth, as indeed he was; but he was also (according to a sympathetic historian) brooding over the fate which threatened the Constitution and the peril to the national religion. To guide his principles he read the great Roman authors, notably Tacitus, on power and liberty. 'Satisfied that a Prince's governing by law deserved his allegiance, yet could he never digest the notion of passive obedience to tyrants, that is to such as would bend a legal constitution to their own arbitrary will and pleasure.'* By 1687 he was deep in the plot to bring over William of Orange, presiding at secret meetings in Derbyshire and Yorkshire. He was one of the seven who signed the formal invitation to William. Among the others were his fellow Whig, the Earl of Shrewsbury, and the Tory schemer, the Earl of Danby, both of whom later received dukedoms.

When William landed at Torbay, Devonshire and Danby raised the banner of Protestantism in the Midlands and the North respectively. Devonshire was joined at Nottingham by Princess Anne, who had deserted her father, the King. Churchill's defection from his high command at Salisbury was the death-blow to James's hopes. With Churchill went the young Duke of Grafton, who had persuaded himself that the cause of Protestantism and the Constitution outweighed the ties of blood. Grafton's fellow bastard, the Duke of Northumberland, was Lord of the Bedchamber on the night that James seized the Great Seal and fled. As such he slept inside the bedchamber. James charged him not to open the doors to suitors until the usual time and he obeyed. He then mustered his troop of Life Guards and declared for William. As it happened, James had his own bastard duke in the

* Joseph Grove: *Lives of Earls and Dukes of Devonshire* (1763)

field—James Fitzjames, his soldier son by Churchill's sister Arabella, created Duke of Berwick in 1687. Unable to hold Portsmouth, of which he was governor, Berwick fled to join his father in France (where, as a Marshal of France, he later fought against his uncle, John Churchill, by then Duke of Marlborough). Two dukes remained loyal to James, though their performance was spiritless—as was that of their master. One was Henry Cavendish, second Duke of Newcastle, son of the great equestrian, who was expected to raise the North as his father had done. Humiliated by his troops, he withdrew to Welbeck and refused to take an oath to William. The other was the Duke of Beaufort, that grandee of Badminton, who tried vainly to hold Bristol for James. He later made his peace with William and in 1690 entertained him at Badminton, where he had already entertained the two previous monarchs. He was a good survivor.

William was hardly on the Throne before he faced supplications for dukedoms, Garters, regiments and much else from his helpers. He showed an initial wariness, but ended by dealing out dukedoms with a free hand to the deserving and undeserving alike. Among the first to be honoured was that devious Whig, Charles Paulet, sixth Marquess of Winchester, who in 1689 was created Duke of Bolton. The Paulets owed their influence and prosperity to Henry VIII. Their most valiant performer was the fifth Marquess, the 'great loyalist' who held Basing House for more than two years against Cromwell. His son, now Duke of Bolton, had assisted William's cause, masking his activities by a display of eccentricity scarcely distinguishable from madness, the idea being that his mental state could be blamed if it turned out that he had backed the wrong side. Since he was a very rich man, he spared no expense in his follies, which took the form of travelling about the country with four coaches and one hundred horsemen, holding nocturnal revels. Bishop Burnet describes his conduct:

He was a man of a strange mixture; he had the spleen to

a high degree and affected an extravagant behaviour; for many weeks he would take a conceit not to speak one word; and at other times he would not open his mouth till such an hour of the day, when he thought the air was pure; he changed the day into night and often hunted by torchlight and took all sorts of liberties to himself, many of which were very disagreeable to those about him. In the end of King James's reign he affected an appearance of folly which afterwards he compared to Junius Brutus's behaviour under the Tarquins. With all this he was a very knowing, and a very crafty politic man; and he was an artful flatterer, when that was necessary to compass his end, in which generally he was successful; he was a man of profuse expense and of a most ravenous avarice to support that; and though he was much hated, yet he carried matters before him with such authority and success, that he was in all respects the great riddle of the age.*

Sir John Reresby is not certain whether the Duke's 'madness' was feigned or real. Abraham de la Pryme, who refers in his *Diary* to the Duke's nocturnal hunting in Swaledale, says that 'when King William was come in he was then a man of quite another nature'. The Duke's successors were an undistinguished crew and the dukedom died out in 1794. Those leading plotters, Devonshire, Danby and Shrewsbury, had to wait until 1694 for their dukedoms. The preamble to Devonshire's patent pays tribute to:

one who, in a corrupted age ... had consistently retained the manners of the ancients and would never suffer himself to be moved either by the insinuations or the threats of a deceitful Court, but equally despising both, like a true asserter of liberties, stood always for the laws, and when he saw them violated beyond all redress, he appealed to us; and we advising him how to shake off that tyranny, he, with many other peers, drawn over to us by his example and advice, gave us the greatest assistance towards a most

* Bishop Burnet: *History of My Own Time*

Absolute Victory without blood, and so restoring the ancient rights and religion.

So far the Duke of Devonshire has appeared only as brawler, builder and plotter, but his personality, when unthwarted, was far from rude. Sir Samuel Garth, the poet, praised his 'easy grandeur'. A posthumous tribute by 'A Lady' describes him as one

> Whose awful sweetness challenged our esteem,
> Our sex's wonder and our sex's theme;
> Whose soft commanding looks our breasts assailed;
> He came and saw and at first sight prevailed.

Among those on whom he at first sight prevailed were the mothers of his several natural children. Charles II is said to have warned him off Nell Gwynn; but in his sixties he rivalled that King in taking a young actress into his keeping. She was Anne Campion, who died aged nineteen. He gave her a fine tomb with an inscription in Latin enumerating her virtues and bearing his initials 'G.D.D.' (*Gulielmus Dux Devoniae*).

The Duke's other pleasures were building, litigation, racing and cock-fighting. He found practical politics a dingy game, despising the traffic in 'dirty little boroughs sold like bullocks at Smithfield Market'. Equally he despised the traffic in places. As Lord High Steward he forcefully spurned a large sum for the liberty to fill vacancies in his gift. The intermediary proposed to bring a list of three names for each place and the Duke was to choose from them.

For his own tomb the Duke wrote this inscription: 'A Faithful Subject of Good Princes, a Hater of Tyrants and Hated by Them.' His death was celebrated with an 'Ode for Vocal and Instrumental Music After the Italian Manner', performed by leading singers hired to 'weep Devonio's fate'. It was the dreariest of verse, but ducal grandeur made such tributes inescapable.

Devonio had gambled and won, and his dukedom still sur-

vives. His fellow plotter, Charles Talbot, Earl of Shrewsbury,
who had taken a large sum to Holland to finance William's
invasion, was created Duke of Shrewsbury. He was a son of
the 'wicked Countess' who cohabited with the Duke of Buckingham. Though he held many State offices he had no relish
for living high and dangerously. He said he would rather
see his son a cobbler than a courtier, a hangman than a
statesman. As he had no son, the dukedom died out, never
to be revived. Thomas Osborne, Earl of Danby, wanted to be
created Duke of Pontefract, but the honour fell on Leeds.
He has some claim to be called the founding father of the
Tory Party. Under Charles II he had been a mighty, but
unlucky, intriguer and corrupter of Parliament. Caught up
in the scandal of the King's traffickings with Louis XIV he
had spent five years in protective custody in the Tower.
William created him Marquess of Carmarthen in 1689. The
Whigs were jealous of the favour shown to the man known
as 'King Thomas', 'Tom the Tyrant', or, from his sick
aspect, the 'White Marquess'. This dukedom survived until
1964, when the twelfth Duke died heirless.

In 1694 another dukedom went to a son-in-law of the
second Duke of Newcastle. John Holles, Earl of Clare, had
lent a modest hand with the Revolution, but his chief claim
to advancement was based on his inheritance by marriage
of most of the Cavendish estates, later augmented by those
of Baron Holles of Ifield. With an income of £40,000 a
year he found it intolerable that he should not be a duke,
and took offence when William declined his solicitations.
Relenting, William talked of making him Duke of Clarence,
but was informed that this title was reserved for the Blood
Royal; so the dukedom of Newcastle-on-Tyne was created
afresh for one who had done little but marry wealth and
inherit it. Unlike the first Duke of Newcastle he was disagreeable to his wife, mocked her literary style and signed
his letters to her 'Yours faithfully'.*

No controversy attended the elevation of William Russell,
fifth Earl of Bedford, to a dukedom, also in 1694. The Rus-

* A. S. Turberville: *A History of Welbeck Abbey*

sells, who had prospered mightily under the early Tudors, owned monastery lands in many countries, notably Cambridgeshire, Bedfordshire and Devon. By their zeal and enterprise in draining the Fens they had virtually added an agricultural county to the kingdom. The fifth Earl financed whaling ventures and built the first wet dock in Britain at Rotherhithe. He was responsible for a fine piazza laid out to Inigo Jones's design in Covent Garden, which was also ducal property. The biggest sorrow of his troubled life came when his son, Lord William Russell, who had secured the lands of Bloomsbury by marriage, was sentenced to death in 1683 for complicity in the Rye House Plot. The Earl petitioned Charles II in moving terms and then tried to secure a pardon by an offer of up to £100,000 tendered by way of the Duchess of Portsmouth, his *maîtresse-en-titre*. Even this failed. In 1688 the Earl lent only moral support to the plotters. After William landed, James appealed to the head of the House of Russell for help, saying, 'You are a good man and could render me today essential service.' To this the Earl replied, 'For myself, Sire, I am old and weak, but I once had a son who could indeed have served your Majesty.' James seemed fated to give his dukes openings for crushing retorts. Under William the attainder of Lord William Russell was wiped out. The patent to the dukedom conferred on the father made it clear that it was a recognition of Lord William's 'martyrdom' in the cause of freedom; the dead man was described with an excess of generosity as 'the ornament of his age, whose merit it is not enough to transmit by history to posterity'. In the *Complete Peerage* the martyr is a 'canonised ruffian'; his least lovable performance had been an attempt to ensure that the condemned Earl of Stafford should not escape the penalty of being disembowelled alive. It would have been more honest to award the Russells a dukedom on the same grounds that John Holles obtained his—namely, because they had great possessions, or better still, to mark the family's achievement in draining the Fens. But the Whigs badly wanted a martyr in the guise of a freedom fighter and they got one. The elderly

Duke accepted his honour quietly. According to the Earl of Ailesbury the Russells at Woburn 'kept a good house for eating among themselves, but no hospitality'.

The Russells' success put ideas into the head of that inextinguishable scoundrel, the Earl of Montagu; a man who, in a corrupt and venomous age, wore his dishonour with an easy grace and betrayed with audacity and panache. He too began to solicit a dukedom. It was he who had stood up in Parliament to incriminate Danby in the negotiations with Louis XIV, his motive in this perilous game being to win a huge pension from France. As ambassador in Paris he had wooed and won the young Countess of Northumberland, on whom Charles was thought to have cast his eyes, either for himself or his brother James. She was worth £6,000 a year. He also amused himself in Paris with a daughter of the Countess of Castlemaine, removing her from her convent to his embassy; for which the mother angrily denounced him to Charles. His greatest romance was still to come. In 1692, his unhappy wife having died, he set siege to another heiress, worth £7,000. She was the deranged widow of the second Duke of Albemarle, who had inherited a fortune from her father, the second Duke of Newcastle. Imperious and childish she let it be known, after the death of her husband, whom she drove to drink, that she would marry none but a sovereign prince. Several unfastidious suitors tried to woo her, but in vain. Montagu, rising to the challenge, bribed her attendants, dressed himself as the Emperor of China, and reinforcing his serpent's charm with oriental flatteries, won her hand; an arrangement which seems to have satisfied the Court of Chancery.

Having secured the widow, Montagu confined her on £3,000 a year in Montagu House, London, where she was served on bended knee until her death at an advanced age. Feeling himself now prosperous enough to support a dukedom—he had been an earl since 1689—he wrote to the King an impudent letter of solicitation. After recalling the antiquity of his family, and the losses it had sustained in the Wars of the Roses, he complained, 'I am now below the two younger branches, my lords Manchester and Sandwich.' He went on:

> I have to add to my pretensions the having married the
> Duke of Newcastle's eldest daughter, and it has been the
> practice of all your predecessors, whenever they were so
> gracious as to keep up the honour of a family by the
> female line, to bestow it upon those who married the
> eldest, without there were some personal prejudices to
> the person who had that claim. I may add another pre-
> tension which is the same for which you have given a duke-
> dom to the Bedford family, the having been one of the
> first and held out to the last in that cause which for the
> happiness of England brought you to the Crown. I hope
> it will not be thought a less merit to be alive and ready
> in all occasions to venture all again for your service, than
> if I had lost my head when Lord Russell did ...

The suppliant ended by hoping that these services would
compensate for 'other wants of merit'.* However, William,
whose estimation of the English aristocracy by now must
have been very low, declined the solicitation. His successor,
Queen Anne, gave Montagu the dukedom in 1705, to oblige
Sarah, Duchess of Marlborough, whose youngest daughter
had married Montagu's son. Montagu had triumphed
mightily, by perfidy, avarice, insolence, nerve and charm,
but in the end it had needed the whisper of a termagant to
crown the edifice.

William had his own Dutch supporters to reward. His
leading soldier was Marshal Frederick Schomberg, a
German-born, French-naturalised warrior with more than
half a century's service under many rulers. His spoils of war
included a palace in Berlin. The Marshal's adherence to
William resulted in the immediate angry confiscation of his
estates in France and the loss of his French nationality.
Though he had fought under many flags, the Marshal had
his own ideas on the niceties of military honour, and he
described John Churchill as 'the first lieutenant-general I

* *Calendar of State Papers (Domestic)* 1694-5

ever remember to have deserted his Colours'. In 1689
Schomberg was naturalised British and given a dukedom.
'The Duke of Schomberg' sounded oddly in English ears;
Schomberg was, in fact, a Rhine castle. Parliament was asked
to compensate him for his lost French lands and awarded
him £100,000. He visited the Commons to express his thanks,
setting a precedent for the Duke of Wellington after his
Spanish victories. William appointed the new Duke to command the under-strength forces in Ireland, where he faced
a difficult winter. In order to pay the troops he had recourse
to his £100,000, a suitable rate of interest on the grant being
agreed. With his royal master, and against his professional
judgment, he fought the Battle of the Boyne, and was sabred
and shot while rallying his French troops. He was buried in
St Patrick's Cathedral, Dublin, where more than thirty years
later the Dean and Chapter installed a stone with a scathing
inscription by Swift—later modified—deploring the failure
of his heirs to honour so great a general. The Duke's sons,
Charles and Meinhard, became second and third Dukes
and lived on the interest of their father's grant. The
dukedom died out in 1719.

Fierce indignation was aroused by the liberality with which
William sought to reward his most trusted lieutenant and
counsellor, William Bentinck, who occupies the unhappy
classification of 'favourite'. The *Complete Peerage* says: 'His
personal beauty ... was great and not improbably was the
cause of his early favour with the King, whose appreciation
of its existence in the male sex resembled that of his ancestor
James I.' However, Macaulay is sure that their friendship
was 'as warm and pure as any that ancient or modern history
records'.* It is probable that the King as a young man owed
his life to Bentinck, who nursed him with all but suicidal
devotion through smallpox, contracting the disease himself.
Soon after the Revolution Bentinck was appointed to the
intimate office of Groom of the Stole, then worth £5,000 a
year, and created Earl of Portland. The King plied him with
estates, but over-reached himself in 1696 when he proposed

* *History of England*

to give his countryman a large portion of Denbighshire, worth
£100,000, for an annual rent of 6s 8d. Parliament objected
strongly, as did the Welsh; and the King angrily dropped the
plan. It is the way of favourites to accept all that is going;
Bentinck, an aloof, wary figure, seems not to have doubted
that his services deserved to be rewarded with huge portions
of an alien kingdom. Gradually he became much put out
over the King's attachment to a less dour Dutch favourite,
Arnold van Keppel. If William had any intention of creating
Bentinck a duke he stayed his hand; however, in 1716
George I bestowed on Bentinck's son Henry the Dukedom
of Portland in token of his father's services. This son lost
much of the family wealth in the South Sea Bubble. His
son William, the second Duke, acquired Welbeck by
marrying a Cavendish, thus uniting the Chatsworth and
Welbeck lines founded by Bess of Hardwick, and thereafter
the Dukes of Portland had the surname of Cavendish-
Bentinck.

KING JOHN

4

With John Churchill, Duke of Marlborough, we come to a dukedom earned by merit, an uncommon phenomenon in ducal records. But the man who, in Parliament's words, 'signally retrieved the honour of the nation', was severely punished for trying to uphold what he had retrieved. The inscription on his monument at Blenheim tells how he 'Broke the Power of France ... Rescued the Empire from Desolation; Asserted and Confirmed the Liberties of Europe'. These were grave offences and the Duke paid the penalty for them.

The Great Captain's campaigns must be left to the military histories. It is necessary, however, to summarise what he did. Sir Winston Churchill has set it out simply: he commanded the armies of Europe against France in ten campaigns, never fought a battle he did not win, never besieged a fortress he did not take, 'never rode off any field except as a victor'.* By that forced march of redcoats to the Danube, culminating in the Battle of Blenheim, he changed the balance of Europe; no one dared tell the Sun King that his invincible army was scattered, save Madame de Maintenon. As the Duke wrote to his Duchess, 'Within the memory of man there has been no victory so great as this.' Blenheim was followed by Ramillies, Oudenarde, Malplaquet and the reduction of

* Sir Winston Churchill: *Marlborough*

almost every fortified town in Flanders. There was a time when, but for the opposition of his ally, Prince Eugene, he could have marched on Paris and put the Court of Versailles to flight, which would have been a bracing spectacle indeed. Sir Winston praises equally the Duke's diplomacy which held together the Grand Alliance—'upon his person centred the union of nearly twenty confederate states'. Not only was he a Titan, says his descendant, but he was a virtuous and benevolent being, capable of drawing harmony and design from chaos. The Blenheim monument asserts that he achieved these ends by 'Wisdom, Justice, Candour and Address'.

The War of the Spanish Succession is not everybody's favourite war. Southey's poem 'After Blenheim' expresses a common sentiment:

> 'It was the English', Kaspar cried,
> 'Who put the French to rout;
> 'But what they fought each other for
> 'I could not well make out.
> 'But everybody said,' quoth he,
> 'That 'twas a famous victory.'

What they fought each other for was the hegemony of Europe; and, on Britain's part, the right to throw out a Catholic king without being invaded by Catholic Majesties sworn to restore him, or his successors, by force of arms. The Protestant King, William III, was hardly on the Throne before the country was plunged into wasting wars in Ireland and Europe. Badly needed, in those bitterly factious times, was an old-fashioned victory, giving an excuse for bonfires, feasting, bell-ringing, illuminations, parades, anthems, odes and panegyrical sermons; a victory so concussive and absolute as to make it evident that Britain had leaders capable of humbling her enemies as well as trafficking with them. Such a victory was Blenheim, which men found no difficulty in classing with Crecy and Agincourt. In a victory poem, 'The Campaign', commissioned by the Whigs, Addison likened our 'god-like leader' to an angel who,

> ... pleased the Almighty's orders to perform,
> Rides in the whirlwind and directs the storm.

In no quarter was a burst of glory more necessary than in the guilt-ridden Army, which had been so superbly pulled together again by the man who had done so much to demoralise it.

When Marlborough ushered those three French generals into his coach at Blenheim he was fifty-four years of age. His record up to then had been a bespattered one. His first post was as page to the future James II, who took his sister for mistress; and his first financial reward was £5,000 given him by Charles II's mistress, the Countess of Castlemaine, for services rendered. Men were praised for their beauty in those days and none more than young Churchill; with beauty went exquisite, perhaps too exquisite, manners. After marrying Sarah Jennings he sobered down and took up the soldier's life. His light-voiced courtesy survived the rough life of camps; according to the Earl of Ailesbury, 'he could not chide a servant, and was the worst served possible, and in command he could not give a harsh word, no not to the meanest sergeant, corporal or soldier.' The Earl of Chesterfield, who knew the Duke well, said he possessed 'the Graces' in the highest degree; 'his manner was irresistible, by either man or woman'; 'he could refuse more gracefully than other people could grant'. On the debit side, the Duke was 'eminently illiterate; wrote bad English and spelled it still worse ... he had no brightness, nothing shining in his genius ... he had, most undoubtedly, an excellent plain understanding, with sound judgment'—and the Graces did the rest.* Chesterfield does not allude to the notorious parsimony, which supposedly led the Duke to snuff out the candles in his tent until only one was left.

There was one field from which Churchill did not ride with honour, and that was Salisbury in 1688. Defecting from James II at a critical moment, along with the young Duke

* John Bradshaw (ed.): *Letters and Characters of the Earl of Chesterfield*

of Grafton, he left the King a letter explaining politely that he was motivated by conscience and religion. He had been appointed Lieutenant-General *after* William's landing and had sworn to defend James to the last drop of blood, failing to make clear that he meant the royal person only. Marshal Schomberg, William's leading soldier, was disgusted. By family standards, it was an odd proceeding: Churchill, an ex-lover of the Countess of Castlemaine, riding off with that lady's bastard, who much admired him, in betrayal of the bastard's uncle who had debauched Churchill's sister. William rewarded the defector with the earldom of Marlborough and confirmed his appointment as Lieutenant-General, but did not trust him far; and in 1692 sent him to the Tower for communicating with James at St Germain. It was a period when loyalties were badly blurred. Not every Whig was sure that the Revolution was a safe thing, or that it had been a good thing; it seemed sensible to have a toe in the other camp. The Tories, the party of the Crown and the Church of England, were even less certain that the Revolution had been a good thing; and the stauncher Whigs denounced them as secret Jacobites. Many resented that the country was being ruled (in the phrase of John Sheffield, Duke of Buckingham) by 'a parcel of Dutch footmen', as compared with 'a parcel of Popish priests' in the previous reign and 'a parcel of French whores' in the reign before that. Marlborough had no firm political alignment, though he was to owe his later military fame to Whig support. All his life he maintained what Sir Winston Churchill has called 'undefined, mysterious and to a large extent meaningless relations with St Germain'. Aware of the frailty of his English nobles, William leaned on his Dutch advisers; but by 1698 Marlborough was back in William's trust. Meanwhile his wife, Sarah, had reduced Princess (later Queen) Anne to a state of emotional dependence on her; they called each other 'Mrs Freeman' and 'Mrs Morley'.

When the War of the Spanish Succession began in 1701, Marlborough was Commander-in-Chief in Holland and plenipotentiary. William died in 1702 and on Anne's succession 'Mr Freeman' became Captain-General of the Forces. After his successful opening campaign in Flanders that year the delighted Queen created him Duke of Marlborough. Sarah was against the idea, saying she had no great taste for grandeur and did not care whether she was first through a door or five hundredth. She also believed, as did her husband, that they had no adequate estate to sustain a dukedom. However, Marlborough thought the rank would enable him to deal more easily with the rulers of Europe. Parliament, while praising the Duke's services, voiced 'inexpressible grief' that they could not accede to the Queen's request that a grant of £5,000 a year from Post Office revenues should be entailed on the Duke's heirs; they reminded Anne of the excessive grants to favourites under William. Much annoyed, the Queen offered the Marlboroughs a private pension of £2,000 a year from the Privy Purse, which they declined. After the victory of Blenheim in 1704 she persuaded Parliament to bestow on Marlborough the royal manor of Woodstock, with 15,000 acres, plus £100,000 of public money to raise a ducal palace which should be half-home, half-monument. After Ramillies, Parliament found it possible after all to entail the Post Office pension on the Duke's heirs.

Meanwhile the Emperor in Vienna, anxious to show gratitude, offered to make Marlborough a Prince of the Holy Roman Empire, a title the Duke thought would give him still higher status in the Grand Alliance. However, the Emperor seemed reluctant to find a principality to go with the title. Marlborough insisted that he wanted no empty honour and expected a vote in the Imperial Diet, so eventually the Emperor's successor gave him the small principality of Mindelheim, in Bavaria. Sarah thought the idea of their becoming highnesses quite ridiculous.

It was a bizarre war, with the Duke pitted time and again against his sister's bastard, the Duke of Berwick, Marshal of France. The courtesies which he extended to his allies were equally extended to his nephew; the two often sent trumpets to each other to arrange for facilities to travellers, or to exchange prisoners. 'You may be sure,' the Duke wrote to Berwick in 1708, 'the difference of parties will not hinder me from having that friendship for you that becomes me towards my relations.' Once the Duke wrote to Berwick and Marshal Boufflers apologising for failing to attack when the rules of war seemed to require it. But there were less innocent contacts than this, as when, after the siege of Lille, Marlborough and Berwick met secretly to discuss peace terms, and the French minister Torcy arrived to offer enormous bribes to halt the war.

The power wielded by Marlborough, as generalissimo, plenipotentiary and prince, was almost without parallel. What worried his enemies at home was the power that he, his Duchess and their dependants exerted at Court. To his troops, whom he looked after so conscientiously, he might be Corporal John, but in London he was mocked as King John. The costliness of some of his victories, notably Malplaquet in 1709, was causing unrest. Incautiously, the Duke followed that battle with a request to be made Captain-General for life. Swift's view was that by this time the Duke had no intention of 'settling the Crown in his family', his heir being dead, but that he wanted to keep the war going for the sake of the pay. The Tories took up this sorry cry. They came to power in 1710 determined to stop the war, if necessary by vilifying the man conducting it. As it happened the Duke's position at Court was collapsing as a result of Sarah's quarrel with the Queen, who had a new female favourite manipulated by the Tories. To hasten his fall, the second Duke of Argyll,* who had soldiered under Marlborough, began jeering at the competence of 'our mighty Prince of Blenheim'. When the Queen called Argyll to a private consultation he became so carried away with jealousy and patriotism that (in Swift's words) he 'suddenly answered that Her Majesty need not be in pain; for he would undertake whenever she commanded to seize the Duke at the head of his troops and bring him

---

* This dukedom was created by William III in 1701. The first Duke was one of three men who shared the blame for the Glencoe massacre

away either dead or alive.'* Marlborough, who had secured
Argyll his promotions and his Garter, said: 'I cannot have
a worse opinion of anybody than the Duke of Argyll.'

In 1711 Marlborough arrived home to find himself accused
of corruption. The Tories charged him with levying illegal
percentages on the Army's bread contract and on the pay of
his foreign troops. These moneys, Marlborough showed,
were used for secret service and intelligence purposes (none
denied that his intelligence was of a high order). He cited
the authority of a royal warrant for such usages and his
European allies certified that the deductions had been
authorised and correctly used. None the less, Parliament
voted him guilty of appropriating about £200,000; but aware
of the weakness of their case they chose not to prosecute. The
Queen, now virulently against the Marlboroughs, dismissed
the Duke from all his offices. Sarah was called on to give up
the gold key she held as Mistress of the Robes. When she
refused the Duke returned it himself, which earned him a
place in Swift's precious symposium 'Of Those Who Have
Made a Mean Contemptible Figure in Some Action or
Circumstance of Their Life.' Sarah then qualified herself
for admission to the same list by storming out of the royal
lodgings and taking the locks and mantelpiece with her. In
Parliament Earl Poulett accused the Duke of trying to kill
off as many officers as possible and thus fill his pockets by the
sale of commissions. When the Duke sent a challenge, the Earl
lost his nerve and was arrested for his own protection.

The Duke was not left entirely friendless. Indignation at
his treatment was voiced by the future Duke of Chandos,
to whose fingers had stuck large sums in his capacity of
Paymaster-General of the Forces Abroad and who used his
wealth to build a splendid mansion at Canons (Chapter
Six). It was a protestation of loyalty which would have been
better unvoiced.

Marlborough was replaced at the head of the Army by
the second Duke of Ormonde, who proceeded to draw the
same percentages on pay and contracts, and in accordance

* Swift: *Memoirs Relating to the Change in the Queen's Ministry*

with the notorious 'restraining orders' the war was ended. Furious at the betrayal of British arms the Duke's old soldiers tore out their hair and ripped up their uniforms. Under the Treaty of Utrecht the Duke lost his principality but he and his successors retained the title of Prince of the Holy Roman Empire. Ormonde later went over to the Jacobites and died in exile.

It cannot be denied that the Duke earned vast sums on the battlefield. Estimates vary, but his *annual* emoluments worked out roughly as follows:

As Plenipotentiary	£7,000
As General of the English Forces	£10,000
As Master of the Ordnance	£3,000
As Colonel of the Guards	£2,000
From the States-General	£10,000
Pension from the Post Office	£5,000
Travelling allowance	£1,825
Table allowance	£1,000
Percentage from contractors for secret service purposes	£15,000

The Duchess's annual receipts included:

As Groom of the Stole	£3,000
As Ranger of Windsor Park	£1,500
As Mistress of the Robes	£1,500
As Keeper of the Privy Purse	£1,500

The total comes to £62,325 (multiply by ten or twelve for modern equivalent). Yet this was not all. After the quarrel with Anne, Sarah claimed the £2,000 pension offered nine years earlier from the Privy Purse and exacted it with full arrears. There were also valuable gifts of pictures and jewellery to the Duke from the dignitaries of Europe. An unexpected bonus was a sum of £100,000 which the fortunate pair made in the South Sea Bubble. The foregoing takes no account of the gift of Woodstock manor and its mighty palace.

Harried by libellers, the Duke drew £50,000 of his earnings and set off into 'exile' in Europe. Oddly, his departure was accelerated by the outcry over the death in Hyde Park of another duke who is thought to have dreamed of wearing a crown, by virtue of his royal descent: the fourth Duke of Hamilton. He had just been named ambassador to France and was preparing to take up his appointment when he was insulted by Lord Mohun, during a lawsuit. In a bloodthirsty duel the two seconds also fought; and General Macartney, who was accused of thrusting at the Duke as he lay prostrate, fled the country. The Tories pretended it was a vile plot by bullies from Marlborough's armies to slay the Queen's envoys.

In 1714 Queen Anne died. The succession had been in the balance, but in a melodramatic move the Queen's deathbed was invaded by the Dukes of Shrewsbury, Somerset and Argyll, who induced her to hand the Lord Treasurer's white staff to Shrewsbury, thus confounding any plans the Tory Bolingbroke might have had of frustrating the Hanoverian succession. Marlborough arrived back in England on the day the Queen expired. The people welcomed him as a hero, remembering that this, after all, was the man who had humbled six marshals of France and shaken the Sun King's throne; and the Duke by no means discouraged their adulation. George I restored him to his military offices. The rest of his life was spent trying to still family quarrels and to expedite the building of Blenheim, of which only one wing was finished in his time. Most of the days he lived in such pomp as he could muster at Holywell House, near St Albans. His physical decline was accelerated by strokes. In 1716, during an invasion scare, the Court sent to ask his advice. 'They found him with all the appearance of a driveller in an armed chair,' says the Earl of Shelburne. 'All that they could get him to say was, "Keep the Army together; don't divide it".'* However, he was still the Duke of Marlborough and his servants made what money they could out of exhibiting him. When he died, nine dukes followed his coffin.

* Lord Fitzmaurice: *Life of Earl of Shelburne*

The Army introduced a new mourning drill, the orders being 'Reverse your arms' and 'Rest on your arms reversed'. In performing it the troops were required to assume a 'melancholy posture', but the men who had followed Corporal John did not have to force their grief. Swift lost no time in defiling the Duke's grave:

> His Grace! impossible! what, dead!
> Of old age too, and in his bed! ...
> Threescore, I think, is pretty high;
> 'Twas time in conscience he should die ...

The funeral, said Swift, elicited no widows' sighs, no orphans' tears:

> Let pride be taught by this rebuke
> How very mean a thing's a Duke;
> From all his ill got honours flung,
> Turned to that dirt from which he sprung.*

The tempestuous Sarah was now the richest woman in Britain. Clearing up the Duke's effects, she opened a drawer and found there the tresses she had hacked from her head in a tantrum, a display which he had affected not to notice. She had always loved her lord as he had always loved her, and she decided to honour him by forcing the builders to finish Blenheim; a course which had the further attraction that it would infuriate his foes.

Sarah's stormy reputation did not prevent her receiving proposals of marriage. One of them came from the sixth Duke of Somerset, the 'proud duke' famous because he stopped £20,000 from the inheritance of a daughter who sat down in his presence when she was supposed to be on duty guarding his sleep. He lived in great state at Petworth, where a major-domo would appear with a device resembling a crozier and announce three times—first *forte*, then *piano*, then *pianissimo* —'My Lord Duke of Somerset', following it with 'Your Grace's dinner is on the table'.† Lower servants were for-

---

* *A Satirical Elegy on the Death of a Late Famous General*
† Philip Thicknesse: *Memoirs and Anecdotes*

bidden to speak to him; all communication was by signs. When he drove abroad outriders scoured the nearby roads to prevent common people staring at him, though one un-tutored peasant held up a pig to look at him over the hedge. Sarah rejected the idea of an alliance between Petworth and Blenheim. She did so supposedly in these terms, which have a touched-up air: 'If I were young and handsome as I was, instead of old and faded as I am, and you could lay the empire of the world at my feet, you should never share the heart and hand that once belonged to John, Duke of Marlborough.'* To soften the blow, the proud duchess helped the proud duke to find another bride. Between them they could surely have disciplined Sarah's troublesome daughters and grand-daughters. The Duchess's way with one of her grand-daughters, Lady Anne Egerton, was to black out her portrait and inscribe it, 'She is blacker within'.

Sarah lived out her life quarrelling, making wills and buying up land, which she thought 'will be the last thing taken from us'. Though she had done well out of the South Sea Bubble, she distrusted stocks. The dukedom passed through her daughter Henrietta to her grandson, Charles Spencer, who did not even bear the name of Churchill.† He was a spendthrift and boasted he never dirtied his hands with silver, which meant he never had to wait for a sedan chair. Sarah, suing for part of her husband's personal pro-perty, demanded possession of his diamond-hilted sword. She told the court: 'That sword my Lord would have carried to the gates of Paris. Am I to live to see the diamonds picked off one by one and lodged at the pawnbroker's?'‡

---

* Sir Winston Churchill: *Marlborough*
† The fifth Duke of Marlborough was given permission to reassume the name
‡ Lord Wharncliffe (ed.): *Letters of Lady Mary Wortley Montagu*

THE SCORN AND WONDER

5

In the annals of precocity there is no more outrageous performer than the first and last Duke of Wharton. The zeal and determination with which he set out to disgrace his dukedom command a certain awe. In his day double-dealing was regarded as a form of political prudence, but the Duke of Wharton gave treachery a bad name.

Philip Wharton was born in 1698, his baptism being attended by his King and future Queen. He was the eldest son of 'Honest Tom', first Marquess of Wharton, the great rake of Protestantism and Whig 'party boss', and author of the jingle 'Lilliburlero' which, as he boasted, 'sang a king out of three kingdoms', Swift rated 'Honest Tom' as 'the most universal villain I ever knew'. At the age of thirteen young Wharton knew long passages of Virgil and Horace by heart and was dabbling in metaphysics. His father taught him how to make Parliamentary speeches, with appropriate gestures and inflections. At sixteen, without his parents' consent, he was married by a Fleet parson to a general's fifteen-year-old daughter who, on his father's insistence, was returned to her parents after a week's use. He already had a lust for low life. The death of his disgusted father left him a marquess at sixteen, master of Wharton Hall in Westmorland and the converted bishop's palace of Wooburn in Buckinghamshire (no connection with the Bedfords'

The first and last Duke of Wharton: 'flagitious, yet not great'

Woburn), and owner of estates in Ireland. One of the Parliamentary seats he controlled was Malmesbury, for which Addison was Member. Under his father's will Wharton was required to go to Geneva to steep himself in Protestantism; it was there that 'Honest Tom' had endured what Macaulay calls an atmosphere of 'Geneva bands, heads of lank hair, upturned eyes, nasal psalmody and sermons three hours long'. Wharton was more attracted to the small courts of Europe, which had need of graceful, wealthy young noblemen. His bear-leader was a severe Huguenot, whom eventually he abandoned in Switzerland, leaving him as a punning present a half-tamed Pyrenean bear, 'the most suitable companion in the world that could be picked out for you'. In his mood of liberation he was irresistibly drawn to the court of the Pretender (James Edward, son of James II) at Avignon, to whom he made an introductory gift of a fine charger. The Pretender received him cordially and offered him the dukedom of Northumberland, which Wharton at first hesitated to accept. Many lost souls frequented the Pretender's court, including the titular Duke of Perth, who as James II's right-hand man in Scotland had introduced the thumbscrews to supplement the boot (his dukedom was as valueless as the one offered to Wharton). At St Germain the wanderer relieved James II's widow of £2,000 to help the Jacobite cause but reputedly spent the money on gambling. Then, in Paris, he went out on a spree with the aides-de-camp of the British Ambassador and scandalously drank the Pretender's health. These seditious follies were not held against the wanderer on his return to Britain in 1716. He is said to have spread the tale that he had to be a Jacobite until he had paid off the Pretender's bankers, to whom he was in pawn.

It was unthinkable that the brilliant son of such a great Whig and Protestant could really go astray. The Whigs wooed him. Soon, though under age, he talked himself into a seat in the Irish House of Peers, where he supported Government measures. Under Whig pressure George I was induced in 1718 to create Wharton a duke. Three years earlier the same Whigs had persuaded the King to confer the dukedom

of Newcastle on the young Thomas Pelham-Holles (Chapter
Eight) and he was fast becoming a pillar of the party. Why
should not the bribe work again? Why not 'nobble them
young'? The patent to Wharton's dukedom said: 'As it is
to the honour of subjects who are descended from an illustrious family to imitate the great example of their ancestors
we esteem it no less our glory as a King, after the example
of our predecessors, to dignify eminent virtues by similar
rewards.' Wharton was not yet twenty-one. Within a month
of his elevation the King's 'right trusty and entirely beloved
cousin' voted against the Government. He could deliver a
forceful oration when he took the trouble, but his finest
forensic efforts tended to be directed against his own party.
In 1720, speaking for the Opposition, he attacked the South
Sea Bill. The artificial rise in stock, he said, was 'a dangerous
bait which might decoy unwary people to their ruin'; and
furthermore the Company might become as wealthy and
powerful as to endanger the nation's liberties. Ignoring his
own warning, Wharton invested £120,000 and lost it. During
a debate on this Bill the Duke grievously insulted Earl
Stanhope with a classical allusion. Stanhope countered with
a reference to the elder Brutus who whipped his profligate
son to death for a betrayal of liberties and said: 'The Romans
did not allow young nobles to speak until they understood
good manners and propriety of language.' So incensed was
Stanhope that he had an attack and died next day. This
weighed on the Duke to the extent that in 1724 he published
a panegyric on Stanhope in *The True Briton*, praising his
'glorious disinterestedness' and 'uncorrupt views'.

Besides dissipating his fortune in stocks, the Duke spent
hugely on the routine debaucheries expected of a president
of the Hell-Fire Club. He had enormous resilience, both
physical and spiritual, and would make powerful speeches
denouncing vice in between visits to brothels. When the
King ordered the closing of the Hell-Fire Club the Duke
read extracts from the Bible to support the royal decree.
The parasitic cleric Edward Young contrived to wheedle
£1,000 from him towards a new building at All Souls, where

an inscription commemorated his munificence to the Muses. Young also obtained from the Duke the preposterous sum of £2,000 for a poem, *The Universal Passion*; stung by criticism, the Duke said it was worth £4,000. The Duke's own verse is indifferent stuff. His journal *The True Briton*, which ran from 1723 to 1724, greatly vexed the Government, but the most readable parts of it today are the advertisements for treatises on venereal disease and for superior washballs. The last issue ends with the promise: 'I shall continue to the end of my life in a steady resolution of inviolably pursuing the True Interest of my King and Country.'

Lady Mary Wortley Montagu had her eye on Wharton. In 1724 she noted that 'twenty very pretty fellows', headed by the Duke and calling themselves the Schemers, were meeting three times a week in Viscount Hillsborough's house 'for the advancement of that branch of happiness which the vulgar call whoring'. The procedure was for each member to come masked, with a masked lady, on the strict understanding that no female identity was to be divulged, and that no lady should speak. There was music and plenty of refreshment; the ladies pointed to what they wished to eat and it was then carried to an apartment, to a table behind a screen, or to a garret. That same year Lady Mary noted that the Duke of Wharton had been reconciled to his Duchess, had brought her to town and was distractedly fond of her. 'There is nothing pleasanter,' she wrote, 'than the remarks of some pious ladies on the conversion of so great a sinner.'*

By 1725 the Duke's debts were such that he began selling off his estates, those in Buckinghamshire being bought by the Duchess of Marlborough. The Court of Chancery allowed him £1,200 a year. It was impossible to live on this in England, so he set off abroad to renew acquaintance with his country's enemies. In Vienna the Pretender gave him a Garter and sent him as envoy to Madrid, with orders to help the second Duke of Ormonde with plans for the next invasion of Britain. The attainted Ormonde, who had succeeded Marlborough

---

* Robert Halsband (ed.): *Letters of Lady Mary Wortley Montagu*

as Captain-General in Flanders, had already seen one Armada dispersed by storm and was not eager to be associated with another.* While in this nest of Jacobites the Duke of Wharton received an order to return to Britain, which he tossed from his carriage window. To a friend he wrote: 'I had rather carry a musket in an Old Muscovite Regiment than wallow in riches by favour of the Usurper.' By now he was calling himself Duke of Wharton and Northumberland and the Pretender's Prime Minister. Frequently drunk, and obnoxious when sober, he boasted how he proposed to humble the British Government. To the British Ambassador, Sir Benjamin Keene, he said:

> You may look on me as Sir Philip Wharton, Knight of the Garter, running a race with Sir Robert Walpole, Knight of the Bath—running a course, and he shall be hard pressed, I assure you. He bought my family pictures, but they shall not remain long in his possession; that account is still open; neither he nor King George shall be six months at ease as long as I have the honour to serve in the employment I am now in.

The Ambassador treated this drunken bluster cavalierly and was challenged to meet with sword and pistol; but overnight the appointment was cancelled. 'What a pleasure it must have been to have killed a Prime Minister!' commented Keene.†

In 1726 the Duke of Newcastle got hold of a cypher, in French, outlining the 'Project of the Duke of Wharton to Re-Establish the Pretender'. Under this scheme the Pretender was to form an alliance with the Emperor and the King of Spain, with an undertaking, on his mounting the

---

* This Duke died in exile at Avignon. Asking to be assisted to an armchair, he said to a German baron: 'Excuse me, sir, if I make some grimaces in your presence, but my physician tells me I am at the point of death.' The Baron, whose courtesy matched that of the Duke, said, 'Ah, my Lord Duke, I beg you will not put yourself under any constraint on my account.'

† William Seward: *Anecdotes*

British Throne, to sell Minorca and Gibraltar to Spain and allow the Emperor large trading advantages, notably through Ostend. There was to be the usual Spanish invasion linked with a Scottish rising. This document created no great panic in London.

The Duke's wife died in 1726 and a few weeks later he sought permission to marry one of the Spanish Queen's maids of honour, Maria Theresa O'Byrne, daughter of an Irish colonel in the Spanish service. When the Queen refused consent on the grounds that he was a resourceless exile, he took to his 'deathbed' until she relented. Recovering quickly, he applied himself to becoming a Roman Catholic.

Shortly before George I's death in 1727 Wharton expressed a desire to spend the 'evening of his days' (he was not yet thirty) under the King's protection, but the Usurper 'did not see fit' to receive any application from him. He therefore decided to spend the evening of his days attacking his fellow countrymen in Gibraltar, then under protracted siege. The Pretender, fatigued by his Prime Minister's follies, advised against this course. Infiltrating the Spanish forces as a volunteer, the Duke contrived to get lightly wounded in the leg while drunk; but at least once, indulging his talent for gaining attention, he boldly harangued the defenders of the Rock who, discovering his identity, were unwilling or unable to terminate his performance. For his spirit he was appointed a 'colonel aggregate' of an Irish regiment fighting for Spain. The Gibraltar exploit put an end to any remaining hopes of returning to Britain, where he was now declared an outlaw and all his funds were cut off.

Friendless, he wandered about Europe, as debauched and needy an English milord as the oldest innkeepers could recall. The Pretender's remittances grew fewer and he was forced to hold daily levees of creditors. At times he lacked the price of a shirt. In 1729 the third Duke of Bedford had two 'conferences' with him in a room above the English Coffee House in Paris and reported that 'no theatre-discarded poet was ever so shabby and that none of Shakespeare's strolling Knights of the Garter had ever so dirty a

Star and Ribbon'.* Yet he was still capable of inviting himself to a convent and parading his knowledge of religion; after which he would again slide into dissipation.

Towards the end he published an open letter explaining why he supported 'James III'. The Whigs, he said, had betrayed their country and Magna Carta; they had become the corrupt tools of the Court; they had destroyed the liberty of the Press; the nation's honour and treasure were being sacrificed to enlarge the domains of Hanover. He now asserted that he had been the Pretender's man since that first meeting at Avignon. 'I was struck with a becoming awe when I beheld Hereditary Right shining in every feature of his countenance and the politeness of education illustrating the majesty of his person. How charmed was I when I heard the purity of the English tongue warmly expressing the sentiments of a True Briton ...' The Pretender was 'rather like a patriot weeping over the ruins of his country than an injured, exiled Monarch lamenting his private wrongs'. Since that time, the Duke said, he had felt it necessary to 'temporise' with the British Government, while preparing to serve the Pretender's cause. Eventually it had been too much for him—'I scorned to keep my seat in Parliament where bribery had more weight than truth.' He served at Gibraltar because he was 'unwilling to lose an opportunity of learning something of the art of war', but the British Government had made a grievance of it. All this ill usage came from 'a set of men whom my father dragged from obscurity'.†

Finally the sick profligate was reduced to living on a regimental dole in Spain, scorned by his superiors. In 1731, on his way to take the waters in Catalonia, he was picked up unconscious by monks, who took him to a convent to die. The nuns buried him, a diseased relic of Britain's highest order of chivalry, in common ground. His dukedom was extinguished with him. His widow, after some years of privation, was able to live in England in a manner suitable to her rank.

* Earl of March: *A Duke and His Friends*
† *Select Pieces Written by the Late Duke of Wharton* (1731)

Wharton's life reads at times as if it was designed to be a 'cautionary tale' by Hilaire Belloc. It was superbly summed up by Pope, in his *Moral Essays*:

> Wharton, the scorn and wonder of our days,
> Whose ruling passion was the lust of praise:
> Born with whate'er could win it from the wise,
> Women and fools must like him, or he dies;
> Though wond'ring senates hung on all he spoke,
> The club must hail him master of a joke.
> Shall parts so various aim at nothing new?
> He'll shine a Tully and a Wilmot too:
> Then turn repentant, and his God adores
> With the same spirit that he drinks and whores;
> Enough, if all around him, but admire,
> And now the punk applaud, and now the friar ...
> A fool, with more of wit than half mankind,
> Too rash for thought, for action too refined;
> A tyrant to the wife his heart approves,
> A rebel to the very King he loves;
> He dies, sad outcast, of each Church and State,
> And harder still! flagitious, yet not great.
> Ask you why Wharton broke through ev'ry rule?
> 'Twas all for fear the knaves should call him fool.

Horace Walpole saw in Wharton one of 'those vigorous exuberancies of genius' born to full manhood and 'expanding all their powers of understanding at the first appearance'. He was 'the model which Charles James Fox set himself to copy, thinking that excess of vice and libertinism would give a relief to his excellent parts, by proving how brightly they could emerge from the most dissolute indulgences, and how little they wanted application and industry.'*

It takes a rare talent to be flagitious *and* great.

---

* Horace Walpole: *Memoirs (George III)*

A PRIDE OF SEATS (1)

6

If the Palace of Blenheim was not so much a home as a monument, the same applied to other ducal seats; but instead of honouring military fame they commemorated and glorified family power, social impregnability and political influence. They were a declaration of dynastic intent; an affirmation of faith in the law of subordination; and a celebration of the mystique of aristocracy.

A rough specification for a ducal seat was a mansion, castle or palace supporting at least a hundred servants, reached by a drive a mile long through a walled park with a thousand head of deer. The dwelling would be on a slight eminence, reflected in water, with its outlook unimpaired by ugly villages. Such an effect was not achieved overnight; it might be necessary to have the builders in for ten, twenty or even thirty years. The third Duke of Argyll, anxious to erect a clan capitol in the Highlands, began to build a neo-Gothic castle at Inveraray in 1744, but because of obstruction, rebellion, dishonesty, fire, transport difficulties and, not least, the need to remove and rebuild the town of Inveraray, the castle was not completed until 1773.

In the hundred years following the Civil War the creation and remodelling of noblemen's seats was a considerable industry; a selfish industry which did nothing to help the nation's balance of payments but yielded splendour, elegance

and beauty unabashed, with only occasional lapses into
ugliness and ostentation. It involved not only quarrying and
felling, but the 'serpentining' or strangling of rivers, the
creation of lakes, the removal or redistribution of hills, the
planting of parklands, the displacement of communities,
the opening up of vistas and, not least, the erection of enclosing walls (the proud Duke of Somerset had a thirteen
mile rampart round his Petworth estate, using enough bricks
to build a string of model villages).

This quest for grace, amplitude and privacy was produced
only at nightmare cost. If the noble owner hoped to entertain
his sovereign—and which duke did not?—he had to provide
gilded State rooms adorned, not with miscellaneous bargains
from the Grand Tour, but with old masters. In the work of
embellishment wealth was scattered across the whole range of
arts, sciences and trades. It went to the Laguerres and Verrios,
the brothers Adam, the Talmans and Kents, the weavers of
tapestries, the designers of vast wrought-iron gates, the
casters of statues, the moulders of urns. A seat was useless
without stabling for up to sixty horses, and with stables went
riding schools and gallops. To be self-supporting the house
needed its dairy, laundry, bakery, brew-houses, hot-houses,
ice-houses and fruit walls. The livelihood of thousands
depended on the satisfaction of noble whim. Easily forgotten
are the installers of artificial echoes, the fountain designers
and mechanics, the builders of grand cascades, waterfalls,
artificial weeping willows and other manifestations of 'the
puerile fancy by which waterworks were contrived to wet
the unwary, not to refresh the spectators'.* A less frivolous
whim was that for classical death-houses, private pantheons
which would not only segregate and glorify the family dead
but grace the landscape, while promoting sober thoughts of
mortality. Another expensive taste was that for wild animals.
The second Duke of Richmond maintained a popular
menagerie at Goodwood. The animals included wolves,
tigers, lions, 'lepers' (presumably leopards), bears and a
'woman tyger' which was restricted to a bread diet. The

* Rev. Irvin Eller: *History of Belvoir Castle*

Duke's correspondence contains items like: 'Your Grace has heard, without doubt, and wept, the misfortune of the poor elephant that was burnt with the vessel he came in.'[*]

If it was possible to resist installing waterworks and menageries, it was less easy to ignore the major changes of taste in landscape gardening; for by his gardens as much as by his mansion was a nobleman judged. At the end of the seventeenth century the geometrical school of the Dutch and French still held sway. The grounds at Chatsworth were like those of Versailles or Fontainebleau. Evelyn has described how Ham House, as extended by the Duke of Lauderdale, sat amid 'parterres, flower gardens, orangeries, groves, avenues, courts, statues, perspectives, fountains, aviaries and all this at the banks of the sweetest river in the world.' The Duke of Beaufort's seat at Badminton was the centre of 'an asterisk of glades'. They were 'cut through the wood of all the country round, four or five in a quarter ... Divers of the gentry cut their trees and hedges to humour his vistas; and some planted their hills in his lines, for compliment, at their own charge.'[†] (The eccentric Earl-Bishop of Derry liked his vistas improved with spires and caused several churches to be fitted with them at others' expense.)

In the Augustan age the geometrical lay-out was replaced by a more natural landscape, lightly sprinkled with classical allusions in the form of statues, temples and obelisks. With Lancelot ('Capability') Brown the fashion again changed. Most of the embellishments were removed and an unnatural naturalness supervened, its essentials consisting of a gently rolling landscape with tree-capped mounds, the whole enclosed in forest greenery; and if there was a 'capability' of a lake, then a lake appeared. Today we see the finished landscape, with its noble trees; but the aristocrats of the day often had to live through ceaseless grubbing and soil-shifting, suffering mightily in the cause of fashion. Brown, of course, overdid it. Not everybody hated those geometrical parterres, or wanted the wild to reach the walls of the house. A wit

---

[*] Earl of March: *A Duke and His Friends*
[†] Roger North: *Life of Francis North*

said he hoped to pre-decease Brown, as he had no wish to find the Elysian Fields landscaped by him. In his reign of forty-odd years this popular autocrat, once a gardener at Stowe, remoulded nearly one hundred and fifty estates. Among the dukes who employed him were those of Marlborough, Devonshire, Northumberland and Grafton. When the second Duke of Montrose bore his Manners bride to Buchanan Castle in Dumbartonshire, she burst into tears at the treeless scene; he saved his marriage by calling in Brown.* James Fitzgerald, first Duke of Leinster, offered Brown £1,000 on landing in Ireland, but the landscapist pleaded that 'he had not yet finished England'.† It was left to Humphrey Repton late in the eighteenth century to restore the formal flower garden between house and landscape.

The great palace of Blenheim was conceived in years of glory and executed in a storm of derision and malice. It had been begun, on Queen Anne's personal orders, in 1705. The venerable Sir Christopher Wren was then Surveyor-General, but Marlborough asked for John Vanbrugh, his underling, to be given the commission. This playwright-architect had shown his capacity at Castle Howard and was ready to fill England with works of weight and majesty. It is hard to escape the feeling that Blenheim was to be as much a monument to himself as to the Duke. By 1710, when the Tories came to power, the palace was not half finished and had cost about twice as much as the original estimate of £100,000. It was to become the Augustan equivalent of the Concorde project. On Marlborough's fall the Queen ordered building to stop. A sum of £60,000 was outstanding to the contractors, workmen and architect and they were invited to invoice the man in whose honour the building was being erected. Vanbrugh, by now a knight, was incensed at the thought of his half-built colossus ending up as a moss-grown folly. Building was resumed under a Whig government, the bill being chargeable against the late Queen's estate, but the

* (Sixth) Duke of Montrose: *My Ditty Box*
† Dorothy Stroud: *Capability Brown*

next ten years were consumed in litigation and vituperation. In his will the Duke left £50,000 to be spent over five years on completing the palace. Sarah, by bullying and parsimony, was able to get the work finished in half the time. She erected a column with a toga-clad John on the top and had his bones buried in a Rysbrack mausoleum, with the dragon Envy snarling beneath. She even installed a statue of Anne, the first begetter of these splendours.

The feud with Vanbrugh, went on. In 1722, just after Marlborough's death, the architect wrote to his friend Jacob Tonson, the bookseller, exclaiming at the reports of the Duke's vast wealth, which included a million 'moving about' in loans, exclusive of rents, mortgages, £5,000 a year from the Post Office, South Sea stock and annuities, 'besides what God Almighty knows of in foreign banks'. Such was the man who would pay neither his workmen nor his architect. 'But he has given his widow (may a Scotch ensign get her!) £10,000 a year to spoil Blenheim in her own way; £12,000 a year to keep herself clean and go to law.'

In 1725 he had another sad tale to tell Tonson. He had called at Blenheim with his wife, the Earl of Carlisle and others, hoping to see the palace at leisure, only to find that the Duchess had left express orders that neither he nor his wife was to be allowed into the park. As a result they had to kick their heels all day at the inn. He described Sarah as 'that b—— b—— b—— old b—— the Duchess of Marlborough'.* A year later he died. At least the Blenheim feud had not lessened the demand for his services as a builder of heavyweight seats for dukes; for he had rebuilt his own house at Claremont, in Surrey, for the future Duke of Newcastle, remodelled Kimbolton Castle for the Earls (later Dukes) of Manchester, extended Grimsthorpe Castle for the Dukes of Ancaster and built Floors Castle for the Dukes of Roxburghe.

Defoe, who saw Blenheim still unfinished, said it was 'too big for any British subject to fill, if he lives at his own expense', a view with which later dukes must heartily have

* *Gentleman's Magazine*, March and May 1837

concurred. He found 'out-houses fit for the lodgings of a regiment of guards rather than of livery servants' and a one-arch rialto, which had cost £20,000, without a river.* Under the fourth Duke of Marlborough the rialto was to be redeemed from ridicule by Capability Brown, who dammed the River Glyme and created two lakes to give the bridge a purpose. Brown remarked that the Thames would never forgive him for what he had done at Blenheim. For many years Blenheim boasted 'a very remarkable polysyllabical articulate echo', capable of repeating seventeen syllables on a calm day and twenty by night; but by the nineteenth century the echo was reported much diminished.†

A notable hazard for visitors to Blenheim was the rapacity and insolence of the servants. Arthur Young, the agriculturist, and the Hon. John Byng, both of them great appraisers of noblemen's seats, protested vigorously. 'The vile custom of not being able to visit a house without paying for the sight, as if it was exhibited by a *showman*, is detestable', Young wrote, 'but when it extends to double and quadruple the common fees and impudence, the exorbitancy calls aloud for that public notice to be taken out of it, which its meanness so well deserves.' He thought noblemen were probably unaware how the magnificence of their seats was tarnished 'by the scoundrel insolence of the lowest of their servants'.‡ No obstacle other than the greed of domestics appears to have been put in the way of travellers of social standing who wished to look over great houses in the owners' absence; by the century's end certain mansions were open to the general public on set days.

Another controversial monument to Marlborough's wars was Canons, raised at Edgware by James Brydges, first Duke of Chandos. Much of the £200,000 it absorbed came from the profits of the post of Paymaster-General of the Forces Abroad, which Brydges held from 1705 to 1713. It was assumed that

---

* Daniel Defoe: *A Tour Through England and Wales*
† *A New Description of Blenheim* (1814)
‡ Arthur Young: *A Six Weeks' Tour Through the Southern Counties* (1768)

the holder of such an office would make fat profits out of it, investing public money for his own benefit. Brydges had inherited substantial wealth, some of it from a mercantile grandfather, and he was eager to cut a splendid figure. He survived the inevitable investigation into his accounts and any suspicion seems to have dissolved in amused admiration of a self-made prince who had his own Swiss Guard to attend him to his own chapel and his own choir to break into music on his approach. Perhaps it was his liberality, as contrasted with Marlborough's stinginess, that disarmed his potential enemies. On George I's Coronation he was created Earl of Caernarvon and in 1719, for no apparent reason, he was raised to a dukedom. Swift called him 'a very worthy gentleman, but a great complyer with every Court'.

According to Defoe, Canons was erected in only three years; bearing in mind the two-score years taken to complete Blenheim, it was a striking advertisement for private enterprise as against state planning. In Italy, as Defoe says, it was enough for one generation of a family to draw the design, leaving it to the next to build; but at Edgware the Duke had adopted the French King's method—'He saw and it was made.' Defoe apologises for his poor attempt at describing this Palladian 'prodigy'. We simply learn that the columns and pilasters were lofty and beautiful, the windows very high, with all possible ornaments, and that rows of statues stood along the roof. The effect was of 'brightness of fancy, goodness of judgment'. Since the mansion was set in highwayman-haunted country the Duke took precautions against marauders. In the huge gardens and outhouses he kept a constant night guard, who called out an 'all's well' at set times and places. Under the roof of Canons dwelled 120 persons, 'and yet a face of plenty appears in every part of it; nothing needful is withheld, nothing pleasant is restrained; every servant in the house is made easy and his life comfortable; and they have the felicity that it is their lord's desire and delight that it should be so.'*

Canons was a blend of welfare state and trading principal-

* Daniel Defoe: *A Tour Through England and Wales*

ity. Other dukes lived off their estates, but Chandos lived off the world, calling for ostriches, storks or mocking birds, avocadoes or anchovies, as fancy might dictate. He was also a dilettante industrialist, dabbling in mines, glass-works, soap-works and clay-pits. Off Anglesey he encouraged oyster fishing. At Canons he had a laboratory where he extracted metals from ores. There was much of the modern tycoon about him: not only was he a director of several companies, including the Turkey Company, but he owned a yacht.

It was as patron of the arts that the 'princely Chandos' most enjoyed himself. Handel spent two years at Canons, composing anthems for the ducal chapel, and produced his first English oratorio, *Esther*, for the Duke. Handel did not, however, compose music for dining, drawing the line at creating flourishes for the replacement of one opulent dish by another. Among literary visitors was Pope, who left a mocking account of the establishment in his *Epistle to Lord Burlington*. It was all too proud, too Brobdingnagian, too wastefully lavish, too symmetrical. Here is the dining-room:

> Is this a dinner? this a genial room?
> No, 'tis a temple, and a hecatomb,
> A solemn sacrifice, performed in state,
> You drink by measure, and to minutes eat.

Music was the signal, not only for plate-changing, but for worship:

> And now the chapel's silver bell you hear,
> That summons you to all the pride of prayer;
> Light quirks of music, broken and uneven,
> Make the soul dance upon a jig to Heaven ...

The lake at Canons had no function except to sharpen the keenness of the northern wind. The summer-house gave no shade. Wherever one looked, there was an encompassing wall.

> No pleasing intricacies intervene,
> No artful wildness to perplex the scene;
> Grove nods at grove; each alley has a brother,
> And half the platform just reflects the other.

Pope had suitable words for his host, the genius of the place:

> Who but must laugh, the master when he sees,
> A puny insect, shivering at a breeze.

Or again:

> My lord advances with majestic mien,
> Smit with the mighty pleasure to be seen.

The sneering guest, having dined and prayed, says:

>   I take my leave
> Sick of his civil pride from morn to eve;
> I curse such lavish cost, and little skill,
> And swear no day has ever passed so ill.

Pope admits that 'hence the poor are clothed, the hungry fed', but challenges the motive:

> What his heart denies
> His charitable vanity supplies.

The poet's consolation is that it cannot last:

> Another age shall see the golden ear
> Imbrown the slopes and nod on the parterre,
> Deep harvest bury all his pride has planned,
> And laughing Ceres reassume the land.

In the poem the Duke's house was disguised as 'Timon's villa', but nobody was deceived. The attack misfired and almost certainly was regretted. Pope sent the Duke a self-exculpatory letter, which was received with civil scepticism. The Duke was also a target for Swift in 'The Dean and the Duke' which began:

> James Brydges and the Dean had long been friends,
> James is be-duked; of course, the friendship ends ...

It went on to celebrate the financial misfortunes which later befell the Duke:

> Oh! Wert thou not a Duke, my good Duke Humphry,
> From bailiffs' claws thou scarce could keep thy bum free!

For all his commercial flair, the Duke lost £300,000 in the South Sea Bubble; or, as Swift put it, 'all he got by fraud is lost by stocks'. He had enough left to start building a town house which was to fill one whole side of Cavendish Square, but he changed his mind and bought a house in St James's Square. His third wife brought him a timely £40,000. After his death attempts to sell Canons intact were unsuccessful and it was pulled down for the materials.

Pride was not a failing of the second Duke of Chandos. The tale goes that when dining at the Pelican in Newbury he heard a commotion in the inn yard. They told him that a drunken ostler had led out his wife, a chambermaid, with a halter round her neck and was proposing to sell her. 'We will go and see the sale,' said the Duke. He was so impressed by the woman's beauty and her patience in a difficult situation that he bought her and made her his own wife.* In the third Duke, however, pride was to blame for a domestic tragedy. In 1778 his infant daughter was due to be christened, with George III and his Queen as sponsors. For the occasion the Duke spent £3,000 on rich canopies, furnishings and brilliant illuminations at his London home. The christening clothes cost £700. Under the unaccustomed glare the babe took fright and was seized with convulsions. The ceremony was stopped, the royal and noble guests left and the victim

* *Notes and Queries*, IV, 6

Chatsworth in the time of the first Duke of Devonshire: a geometrical mirage in the wilderness

of magnificence died next day.*

In the Augustan age the grandest of the ducal seats was probably Chatsworth, despite the piecemeal way in which it was developed. It will be recalled that the first Duke of Devonshire began to rebuild Bess of Hardwick's mansion as a pretext for absenting himself from the Court of James II. The dwelling lay in 'a waste and houling wilderness' beside the stormy torrent of the Derwent. A traveller approaching from Sheffield needed the services of a guide across the moors. At last, reaching the edge of a precipice, he would look down on a prodigy of a palace in the valley, like a mirage of Versailles. In those times awe of wild scenery was profound. Bishop Kennet thought the situation 'somewhat horrid', but summed up: 'The truth is that the glorious house seems to be Art insulting Nature and the imminent mountain seems to be Nature despising Art and triumphing over the attempts of it.'†

The Duke began by rebuilding the south front, but the building itch inherited from his great-great-grandmother drove him to transform the east as well. These operations, under William Talman, consumed ten years. The Duke then laid out immense geometrical gardens on a scale to dazzle the Sun King himself. After three years the urge to resume rebuilding proved insuperable and the Duke set about the west front and then the north. The twenty years task was completed in the year of his death, 1707. By then the back of the building had become the front, which called for a total rearrangement of the grounds. This task was later tackled with energy and imagination by the fourth Duke, who straightened a bend in the Derwent, abolished a whole chain of reservoirs, redistributed bridges and stables and moved part of the encroaching village of Edensor. Even during the twenty years of upheaval in the main building life was lived in great grandeur. Marshal Tallard, who was taken at Blenheim, said that when accounting to his royal master

* *Annual Register*, 1778; and Sir W. Besant: *London in the Nineteenth Century*
† Joseph Grove: *Earls and Dukes of Devonshire*

for his years of captivity in England he would leave out the days he had spent at the most beautiful palace in the world. Celia Fiennes, that hardy traveller, was impressed by Chatsworth's endless gardens, walks, groves, aviaries and waterworks (including the metal 'weeping' willow). Indoors, she was fascinated by the ducal bathroom, with hot and cold water cocks and windows of 'private' glass, which apparently was shown to visitors. The bath was cut from an entire block of white marble lightly veined with blue; 'it was as deep as one's middle on the outside and you went down steps into the bath big enough for two people.'

Much less satisfactory was the hostelry maintained by the Dukes of Devonshire at the nearby spa of Buxton. In what sounds, from Celia Fiennes's account, like 'the worst inn's worst room', were four beds shared by complete strangers, who were required, when necessary, to lie three in a bed; and all the time there was the commotion of people going to the bath and returning. As a result nobody stayed more than two or three nights. The beer provided by the Duke was 'so bad that very little can be drank'.*

Another imitation of Versailles was Boughton, in Northamptonshire, built by the first Duke of Montagu with his mad Duchess's money. As Ambassador to Louis XIV he had been delighted with the sight of fountains playing in his honour and thereafter hankered for a *grand palais* of his own, preferably with superior waterworks. The French King lent him an architect and a gardener, and Boughton emerged as a *château* with twin courtyards. He also built a semi-regal palace in London, Montagu House, where the British Museum now stands. These dwellings raised by a scoundrel passed to a practical joker. The second Duke, according to his mother-in-law, Sarah Churchill, still retained at fifty-two the tastes of a boy of fifteen, liking nothing better than to get people into his gardens and wet them with squirts, or to put things in their beds and make them itch, 'and twenty other such pretty fancies'. It is unthinkable that he put itching-powder in Sarah's bed. One of his pretty fancies was to instal

* Christopher Morris (ed.): *Journals of Celia Fiennes*

distorting mirrors in his house so that gentlemen adjusting their wigs before dinner would go to the table looking like scarecrows; but it is hard to believe that the jape really came off. His least happy fancies, perhaps, were to hold a dinner at Bath at which all the guests were stutterers and another at which everybody had a squint. A great deal of work seems to have gone into a hoax on the unpopular opera manager, John Heidegger. With the aid of a wax cast taken from the victim's face when drunk, a 'double' of Heidegger usurped his rostrum and ordered the theatre orchestra, in the presence of royalty, to substitute 'Over the Water to Charlie' for the National Anthem, which they did. Both royalty and the orchestra had been alerted beforehand. The Duke's best-known hoax was to invite the public to the Little Theatre, in the Haymarket, to see a man put himself inside a pint bottle. As nobody emerged to perform this attractive feat the audience wrecked the theatre. They might have been better employed wrecking Montagu House, but at the time it was not known that the Duke was behind the hoax.

For all his buffoonery the Duke had many admirable qualities. He was known as 'Planter John' from his love of trees. Apparently he dreamed of planting an avenue of elms from Boughton to London, seventy-two miles long, but as the way-leave problems were not trivial he contented himself with creating seventy-two miles of avenues linking various villages near Boughton. The effect of all these trees, when fully grown, was to shut out the view from the house, which appeared to have sunk in a forest, as visiting critics complained. The Duke performed many generous acts, gave away a fifth of his income in pensions and built a hospital for old horses and farm animals; though this was doubtless regarded as further evidence of eccentricity. He could be kind to satirists too. When Pope regretted his inability to dine with the Duke because he could not afford to pay vails (tips) to the servants, the Duke sent an invitation with £5, a friendly gesture for which he was lucky not to be lampooned. Perhaps Pope was lucky not to find that all his fellow guests were cripples.

This unpredictable Duke had an eye for possibilities in trade. He owned another estate in Hampshire, and here, at Buckler's Hard, he proposed to build Montagu Town, a port where his own vessels would unload sugar from the West Indies. It was an attractive idea; but the Duke's first trading expedition of 1722 miscarried badly. Having been granted the governorship of St Lucia and St Vincent, he filled seven ships with 425 indentured servants, cattle, timber, and stores and sent them to start a colony. The chronicle of the voyage tells how French sloops arrived from Martinique to warn the settlers to vacate territories 'belonging' to the French King; how British warships were unable to offer protection; how the indentured servants began to desert to the French, who declined to return them; and how the ships dejectedly came home again. It was 'an undertaking truly worthy of the noble and generous disposition of His Grace of Montagu and the greatest ever undertaken by a subject at his own expense', with a potential to the nation of £200,000 a year.* As it was, the venture cost the Duke £40,000 and the British Government did not think fit to make an issue with France. It would be easier to sympathise with the Duke if he had taken the trouble to accompany his expedition. After his death Buckler's Hard became a prosperous shipbuilding yard which turned out more than fifty warships for the Fleet, including Nelson's *Agamemnon*.

A town house in London was an indispensability. Among ducal dwellings which were good enough for, and were later acquired by, royalty were Marlborough House, built by the first Duke, and Schomberg House in Pall Mall, which passed to the 'Butcher' Duke of Cumberland (and afterwards to Dr Graham, the humbug who invented the 'Celestial Bed'). These buildings were on prime sites, but the best site of all, as it was then and is now, was selected by John Sheffield, Duke of Buckingham and Normanby, at the end of the Mall. This fortunate nobleman, mocked as 'Lord Allpride', owed his elevation to a flirtation in Windsor Park with Princess Anne

* Anon: *A Relation of the Late Intended Settlement of St Lucia and St Vincent* (1725)

when she was fifteen. For this audacity he was packed off by Charles II to Tangier. On her accession Anne, remembering the poems and love-letters, created him a duke and personally chose him as Lord Privy Seal. He had by then been twice married, but, as Sir Winston Churchill says, 'romance received a belated dividend with compound interest'.*

The building of Buckingham House, forerunner of today's Palace, was attended by a touch of the drama that beset Blenheim. The story is that the architect, a Captain Wynne, took the Duke up to the roof to admire the view. He then locked the trapdoor by which they had ascended and threw the key over the parapet. 'I am a ruined man,' the architect explained, 'and unless I receive your word of honour that the debts incurred in this building are paid directly I shall instantly throw myself over.' When the Duke inquired, 'What is to become of me?' the reply was, 'Why, you shall accompany me.' On a promise being given, the trapdoor was opened at a pre-arranged signal, by a workman.† This costly dwelling was bought in 1763 by George III for his Queen and was known as the Queen's House. Nash later rebuilt it for George IV.

In his fine palace, which had a 'wilderness' with nightingales, the Duke wrote indifferent verse. Macaulay was indignant that 'to this day his insipid essays in rhyme and his paltry songs to Amoretta and Gloriana are reprinted in the company of "Comus" and "Alexander's Feast"'.‡ To demonstrate his genius the Duke took Shakespeare's *Julius Caesar* and split it into two plays, one of them called *Marcus Brutus*, rewriting them to conform with stricter disciplines and introducing love scenes. He wrote much miscellaneous work. Drawing on his experience as a volunteer in the Navy he urged sailors to watch out more carefully for approaching cannon balls and step smartly out of their path; also to be alert for bullets bouncing up from the waves. (It is not as silly as it sounds, since sharp-sighted boys were employed

* Sir Winston Churchill: *Marlborough*
† E. B. Chancellor: *The Private Palaces of London*
‡ *History of England*

at the Siege of Gibraltar to give warning of low-velocity cannon balls.)

As his third wife the Duke married a natural daughter of James II. Her former husband, Lord Anglesey, was beating her one day when she pointed to her housemaid and said, 'How much happier is that wench than I am!' Lord Anglesey thereupon kicked the maid downstairs, exclaiming, 'Well, there is at least one grievance removed.'* This Duchess, who outlived the Duke, suffered from the delusions of divinity which have affected so many widowed duchesses. She exacted from her waiting women a promise that, though she lay unconscious, they would never sit down until she was certified dead. She wrote to the Countess of Huntingdon remonstrating over the utterances of that lady's footman, David Taylor, who had gained fame as a Methodist preacher. His doctrines, said the Duchess, were repulsive and levelling. 'It is monstrous', she wrote, 'to be told that you have a heart as sinful as the common wretches that crawl on the earth.'†

---

* Horace Walpole: *Memoirs of the Reign of George III*
† Countess of Huntingdon: *Life and Letters*

CAREERS FOR DUKES
7

The careers open to dukes in the eighteenth century were these: soldier, sailor, courtier, minister of the Crown, diplomat and viceroy. Being a duke was almost a career in itself, if the duties of estate management, coupled with those of lord lieutenant, were taken seriously. It was assumed, however, that a duke would wish to make some reparation for his wealth, and to justify his high rank, by giving service in a conspicuous capacity to his country, or at least to his party. Those dukes who became ambassadors to France or viceroys of Ireland often paid huge sums to maintain the extravagance demanded by Paris and Dublin, with perhaps only a riband afterwards as reward; though Dublin offered a useful chance to find places for relatives. Only a financially strained duke would consider the governorship of Jamaica, an unhealthy post acceptable only for the salary and allowances. The first Duke of Portland, who set off to Kingston after losing his fortune in the South Sea Bubble, was felt to be demeaning himself and there was even talk of a whip-round on his behalf.

Few doubted that a duke, whether newly created or hereditary, was as capable of directing the affairs of the nation, or of running Ireland, as he was fit to be trusted with men's lives in battle, or with the selection of rectors. At the worst a duke was a good stalking-horse behind which an ambitious statesman could advance his own plans. Like a guinea-pig

director on a prospectus he gave respectability to contentious
enterprises. Sir Robert Walpole and Henry Pelham employed
dukes as freely as did Disraeli and Gladstone in a later day.
The eighteenth century saw four ducal Prime Ministers:
Newcastle, Devonshire, Grafton and Portland.

A good example of the dukes who were content to be dukes,
to enjoy their privileges and indulge their tastes and eccentricities, was John Manners, first Duke of Rutland, who was
advanced to that rank in 1703 by Anne to mark 'his great
merits and the services of his ancestors'. His greatest merit
consisted of having powerful Whig friends. He disliked the
Court and the city, preferring to live in his ancient strong-
hold above the Vale of Belvoir, attended by 150 servants and
drawing a reputed £23,000 a year in rents. The diarist
Abraham de la Pryme wrote that he was 'a man mightily
loved round about'. Defoe envied the Duke his view over six
counties, his demesnes equal to those of some sovereign
princes and 'his immense subterranean treasure, never to be
exhausted—I mean the lead mines and the coal pits'.* This
Duke set the style for his successors, whom Sir Bernard
Burke has described as 'patricians, kindly men enough, with
fair capacities and few conspicuous vices, but still patricians,
doing something and enjoying much, without much confidence in their claims and therefore very apt to push those of
their order ...' Being English gentlemen was, thought Burke,
'a high service of its kind', for which Belvoir and its depend-
encies were ample recompense.† It was left to the fourth
Duke of Rutland to show what a glittering figure a Manners
could cut when given a kingdom to rule, even if the kingdom
were only Ireland. In his twenties he set out to dazzle and woo
that convivial land, which he did with heroic banquets and
a twice-weekly service of fruit boats to Dublin. After his
tour of office the exhausted patrician had to order his Duchess
to observe the strictest economy—'no superfluous clothes
beyond what is required to appear clean and decent'.

* Daniel Defoe: *A Tour Through England and Wales*
† Sir Bernard Burke: *The Great Governing Families of England*

The Dukes of Devonshire also chose to live the lives of country magnates. 'Their property was enormous, their credit great, and reputation truly honourable; but the talents of the race had never borne any proportion to their other advantages,' said Horace Walpole. 'The family had affected to drop all polish, and to wear the honours of plain English gentlemen, under an outside that covered considerable pride.' Sir Robert Walpole had taken advantage of their popularity as Whigs, but the second Duke 'had no sense at all and the third a very dubious portion'.* The third Duke nevertheless was a man of the highest integrity. Dr Samuel Johnson testified that 'If ... he had promised you an acorn, and none had grown that year in his woods, he would not have contented himself with that excuse. He would have sent to Denmark for it. So unconditional was he in keeping his word, so high as to the point of honour.'†

On the battlefields the heirs of the great commanders like Marlborough and Schomberg did not greatly distinguish themselves. Withdrawing hastily from an ill-conceived descent on St Malo, the third Duke of Marlborough left behind a set of silver teaspoons which were solemnly returned to him in a vessel of war, under cover of a truce flag, by the Duc d'Aiguillon. Whether this was an elaborate insult or an excessive courtesy is not clear; the Duc d'Aiguillon had enough sensibility to prohibit bell-ringing and rejoicing when English prisoners were marched through the streets. The Duke of Marlborough is thought to have pursued the soldier's life as a cure for boredom. At Dettingen he commanded a brigade with success. The most popular soldier of the mid-century was a son of the third Duke of Rutland, the Marquess of Granby, whose features adorned scores of public-houses; the most unpopular soldier was a son of the first Duke of Dorset, Lord George Sackville, who was disgraced for failing to obey an order at Minden. He was generally assumed to have been guilty of cowardice.

* Horace Walpole: *Memoirs (George III)*
† James Boswell: *Life of Johnson*

At sea ducal commanders tried to retain their dignity and status in the jealousies between 'Gentlemen' and 'Tarpaulins', the latter being the captains who had come up the hard way and knew their trade. A brave but unsuccessful captain was the second Duke of Leeds, whose error of judgment allowed a number of valuable East and West Indiamen to fall into the hands of the French. The affair roused such an outcry that he was not employed again, though he was consoled by promotion to admiral. The sixth Duke of Bolton, a quarrelsome fellow who charged a fellow captain with misconduct and was counter-charged with misappropriation of stores, failure to engage the enemy and gross cowardice, was appointed to command the ninety-gun *Barfleur* under Hawke. After vainly chasing a foreign sail, he was making for the appointed rendezvous when the ship's carpenter reported the sternpost loose and dangerous. The Duke thereupon returned to Spithead, where he was court-martialled for deserting the Fleet. A dockyard report showed that the carpenter's fears were much exaggerated. The idea got about that the Duke was himself the instigator of the alarm and he became known as Captain Sternpost. Like the Duke of Leeds he was not employed again, and like the Duke of Leeds he was promoted to admiral.

For dukes with a graceful presence and an absence of political ideas the Court offered a variety of posts, with modest salaries. These included Lord of the Bedchamber, Groom of the Stole, Lord Chamberlain, Lord Steward, Master of the Horse and Master of the Buck Hounds. Fortunately, under the Hanoverians, such duties as handing the monarch his shirt and small clothes were discharged by valets, but there was still much ceremonial to be performed, much gruelling attendance to put in, much desolating small talk to be endured. However, there were advantages in being close to the royal ear and the great offices of the Household were never in danger of going unfilled. The first four Dukes of Manchester have been mocked for possessing 'no ambitions beyond successfully discharging the onerous duties of Lord of the Bedchamber, the great house having apparently gone

permanently asleep after obtaining the dukedom.'* Lionel
Sackville, created first Duke of Dorset in 1720 for no over-
whelming reason, was described by the Earl of Shelburne
as

> in all respects a perfect English courtier and nothing else.
> A large grown full man ... he had the good fortune to come
> into the world with the Whigs and partook of their good
> fortune to his death. He never had an opinion about public
> matters ... He preserved to the last the good breeding,
> decency of manners and dignity of exterior deportment
> of Queen Anne's time, never departing from his style of
> gravity and ceremony.†

As a change from beds, wardrobe and stables the Duke served
twice as Lord Lieutenant of Ireland, which in many ways
was an appointment for a good courtier, with its high pomp
of Battle-Axe Guards and almost Castilian formality. Unless
he struck a troubled period, a lord lieutenant could hope to
coast through his term of office by blending magnificence and
conviviality, leaving the business of the island to the resident
'undertakers' and jacks-in-office, and trying not to think about
the peasants who, as Lord Chesterfield feared, were treated
worse than negroes.

Perhaps the most notable courtier of the time was Charles
Fitzroy, second Duke of Grafton, who served the first two
Georges as Lord Chamberlain. As such he was responsible
for palace state and ceremonial; he had to keep order among
ambassadors squabbling for precedence; and his lesser chores
included censoring plays and choosing the Poet Laureate,
the sort of thing any nobleman could take in his stride. The
Duke of Grafton was never weighed down by his responsibilities. For the Georges it must have been a titillating
experience to be waited upon by a half-Stuart with that all-
too-recognisable *rusé* air and sardonic scowl; an unsettling
experience, perhaps, in times of Jacobite unrest. In the reign

---

* Howard Evans: *Our Old Nobility*. The Manchester title derived
from Godmanchester, in Huntingdonshire
† Lord Fitzmaurice: *Life of the Earl of Shelburne*

of George I he was not the only walking reminder of Charles II at Court. One day his uncle, the Duke of Northumberland, accidentally jostled the Prince of Wales who exclaimed pettishly, 'One can't move here for bastards!' But when that prince became George II the Duke with his easy manner was able to handle him skilfully, telling him hard truths wrapped in jest; he was even able to twit the Queen on her love life, or rather lack of it, and survive unrebuked, though sometimes only just. Royalty knew just how far to go with royalty.

Horace Walpole probably ascribed to Grafton more guile than he possessed:

> With very good common-sense and knowledge of mankind he contrived to be generally thought a fool and by being thought so contrived to be always well at Court and to have it not remarked that he was so ... He had a lofty person, with great dignity; great slowness in his delivery, which he managed with humour. He had the greatest penetration in finding out the foibles of men that ever I knew and wit in teasing them ... As he had no opportunity for forsaking the Royal Family for a family to which he was more nearly related, one must not say he would have forsaken them; betraying was never his talent; he was content to be ungrateful ...*

Lord Hervey, a jealous fellow courtier, attributed Grafton's success to never giving a direct answer to any question, while always being entertaining. 'By living perpetually at Court he had all the routine of that style of conversation which is a sort of gold leaf, that is a great embellishing where it is joined to anything else, but makes a very poor figure by itself.'†

In middle age the Duke is credited with having been the lover of Princess Amelia, daughter of George II. The two hunted together in Windsor Forest three days a week and on one occasion, having lost their attendants, they stayed

* Horace Walpole: *Memoirs (George II)*
† Lord Hervey: *Memoirs of the Reign of George II*

late at a house in the forest, which led the Queen to fear the worst. The King seems to have objected on humanitarian grounds to the Lord Chamberlain's hunting. According to Hervey, he told the Duke that it was 'a pretty occupation for a man of quality, and at his age, by spending all his time in tormenting a poor fox, that was generally a much better beast than any of those that pursued him.' The King's compassion also extended to the Duke's horse, which had to carry his 'great corps of twenty stone weight'. When the Duke replied that he hunted for health, the King suggested that he should walk, or ride post, for that purpose. All this did not mean that the King disliked his Lord Chamberlain. On the Duke's death he was desolate without his favourite Stuart.

Of the ducal Prime Ministers there is not much to be said, since, with one exception, they were reluctant performers advanced to the highest office as cover for the activities of abler men. The exception was the Duke of Newcastle (Chapter Eight), who was always avid for power; but even he was latterly used as a cover by Pitt. The other three Prime Ministers—Devonshire, Grafton and Portland—added little lustre to the office. They deserved credit for the sense of duty which propelled them upwards against all their natural inclinations.

The fourth Duke of Devonshire, then in his thirties, took office in 1756 on Newcastle's first fall. The Seven Years War was looming and Pitt was the obvious man to wage it, but the Whigs would not tolerate him as Prime Minister and he would not serve under Newcastle. Devonshire, as the head of the greatest Whig family, was therefore persuaded to lead the Government. His capacity was not high, but he was upright and conscientious; too honourable, perhaps, for his day. As soon as Pitt came to an agreement with Newcastle the young Duke resigned and, somewhat surprisingly, accepted the post of Lord Chamberlain. Under George III the heirs of the Revolution found themselves distrusted and despised; and the Scots favourite, Lord Bute, made it his business to humiliate them. In 1762 the Duke of Devonshire was dismissed as if he had been a thieving footman. Returning from the country, he called according to custom at the palace back stairs and sent a page to the King to say that he wished to pay his respects. The King, suspecting Devonshire of political plotting, instructed the page, 'Tell him that I will not see him.' As the page hesitated, the King (or possibly Bute) said, 'Go to him and tell him those very words.' The Duke kept his temper sufficiently to send back a message asking what was to be done with his gold key and the answer came, 'Orders will be given for that.'* In a fury the lord of Chatsworth resigned and his relations gave up their offices in sympathy. The King then compounded the insult by striking the Duke's name from the list of Privy Councillors. It was a sombre and brutal lesson for the Old Whigs. Two years later the Duke died at Spa, aged forty-four, the shortest-lived of Prime Ministers. Dynastically, he served his family well, for his marriage to the Earl of Burlington's daughter brought the Cavendishes a wealth of estates in England and Ireland.

The third Duke of Grafton, grandson of the courtier Duke, took office in 1767 on Pitt's resignation, leading an irresolute Government for two years. His ability was small, his ideas were few and his stamina was weak. 'Junius', the anonymous letter-writer, caught him trafficking over a Customs post; which enabled Lord Mansfield to rule, hypothetically, that a minister who sells offices to raise revenue out of them 'basely betrays the King'. The Duke's notoriety, apart from that derived from serving as a butt for 'Junius', stems from his association with the courtesan Nancy Parsons (Chapter Fourteen). He was happiest on the racecourse or on his estates at Euston Hall.

Like the Duke of Grafton, the third Duke of Portland suffered much abuse in his public life. The peak of his popularity was achieved in the rowdy election year of 1768 when his candidates took on, and partially defeated, those of the abominable bashaw of the north, Sir James Lowther, son-in-law of Lord Bute and later Earl of Lonsdale. The Duke's territorial, and hence electoral, influence in Cumberland stemmed from his interest in the Honour of Penrhyn, vested

* Horace Walpole: *Memoirs (George III)*

in his family, as he thought, by William III; but half way through the election battle Lowther claimed that there was a defect in the title. In truth, the Duke's claim to this northern province was distinctly shaky; however, popular sympathy was with him. To celebrate the Duke's electoral victory church bells were rung and ships dressed in harbour. The bill was somewhere between £30,000 and £40,000, though this was far from being an electoral record; the accounts from the innkeepers of Cockermouth alone came to almost £6,000.* Lowther boasted that he was ready to spend £20,000 against the Duke's £15,000 and would keep on doing it, knowing that his purse was longer. It took the Duke ten years of litigation to establish his title.

The Duke was no orator and was famous for his silences. He displayed what has been called a hereditary crotchetiness. In 1783 after much political bargaining he was chosen to head a coalition in which Lord North and Fox were linked; he knew, and everyone knew, that he was there only as a cloak. After two decades on his estates at Welbeck and Bulstrode he was called back, almost from the dead, to serve as a figurehead for Castlereagh and Canning, who were far from being Whig. He should have been the last ducal Prime Minister, but that dubious honour falls to the Duke of Wellington.

* A. S. Turbeville: *A History of Welbeck Abbey*

THE MACHINE MINDER

8

How was it possible for a jealous, agitated, procrastinating, garrulous, intriguing old woman of a duke to stay in high political office for nearly half a century? Why was the butt of the people, the senate and the Court twice appointed Prime Minister? Why was he honoured with *two* dukedoms? Why was a man who lacked all the parts of a great statesman indispensable to those endowed with fire, eloquence and vision? The short answer is: somebody had to mind the machine.

Thomas Pelham-Holles, first Duke of Newcastle of the third creation, was the Whigs' borough broker and controller-in-chief of patronage. He knew every man's secret and every man's price. His indispensability was due primarily to his birth and inheritances. As the head of a nexus of great Whig families he personally influenced a dozen Parliamentary seats. The shadow of democracy had not yet fallen. Eighteenth century Britain was ruled by an oligarchy of landowners who packed the House of Commons with their eldest sons. The Duke of Newcastle did not invent Parliamentary corruption, but since it existed he felt it might as well be regulated by him as by anyone else; in doing this he performed both a Party service and a public service (which he regarded as the same thing) and atoned for his wealth. He also enjoyed the game.

In his youth the Duke was outrageously blessed by fortune. As Thomas Pelham, son of Baron Pelham, he was eighteen when, in 1711, he inherited the huge estates, but not the title, of his uncle John Holles, sole Duke of Newcastle of the second creation. He was now Thomas Pelham-Holles. A few months later the death of his father brought him a new avalanche of estates, along with the title of Baron Pelham. He now held land in more than a dozen counties, but chiefly in Nottinghamshire, Sussex and Yorkshire. His rent-roll was put at anything between £25,000 and £40,000. It was not surprising if he felt, in Chesterton's words,

> That the fixed system that our land inherits,
> Viewed from a certain standpoint, has its merits.

On Anne's death in 1714 the young magnate graciously recognised the House of Hanover and was rewarded with a viscountcy, an earldom, two lord lieutenancies, the steward-ship of two forests and the appointment of Vice-Admiral of the Coast of Sussex. That was the year in which he bought the Claremont estate from Vanbrugh. In 1715 he helped his brother Henry Pelham to raise a troop of horse against the Pretender. For this, and such additional services as inciting the London mob to bay at Jacobites, he received a marques-sate and the dukedom of Newcastle-on-Tyne. By the age of twenty-five he had played host to his Sovereign, accepted the gold key of a Lord Chamberlain, sworn the oath of a Privy Councillor and decked himself in the Garter. There had been no such profligate, even idiotic, rain of honours since George Villiers captivated the heart of James I. This young Duke had none of the Villiers charm and address, but he was already showing a talent for politicking. Not everyone loved him. When George I tried to foist him on the Prince of Wales as godfather to his first-born there was a furious royal quarrel and the Prince was put briefly under arrest, the King mis-takenly thinking that he had challenged the Duke to a duel. The Duke, in the son's view, was unfit to be a chamberlain at a petty German court; but when the son mounted the throne he was to have this 'impertinent fool' as Prime Minister.

The Duke served as Secretary of State under his kinsman Sir Robert Walpole, who valued him for his borough influence, and in Lord Hervey's words, 'looked upon his understanding to be such as could never let him rise to be a dangerous rival'. As Walpole's power waned, Newcastle was suspected of negotiating with the Opposition, despite all he owed to the Whigs. He continued in office under his brother, Henry Pelham, on whose death in 1754 he became Prime Minister for the first time. In 1756 he fell and was created Duke of Newcastle-under-Line (*sic*). This trumping of titles was necessary because he had no heir to his peerages; the second dukedom (the only one created by George II) had a special remainder to his favourite nephew, Henry Clinton. In 1757 the Duke of both Newcastles was Prime Minister again, handling the Treasury bribes and the Secret Service money while William Pitt (later Earl of Chatham) performed the shining deeds of statecraft. The Earl of Chesterfield said the two were like a man and wife, the one jealous, the other imperious; 'as things are constituted, they must go on together, for it is ruin to both to part'. By 1762 the reign of the old Whigs was over. George III was living up to his mother's advice, 'Be a king!' and his favourite, Lord Bute, threw out the Duke of Newcastle.

It is easy to forget that, thanks to the efficiency of the Duke's political machine, honest men of high talents were able to rise swiftly in the nation's service. The mere fact that they entered the halls of Parliament through a shabby door marked Influence, sometimes with a bribe to the doorkeeper, did not mean that they left their integrity and their patriotism in the cloakroom. This having been said, it is hard to look without a shudder at a long public life devoted to the nominating, manipulating and sweetening of Members of Parliament, the infiltration of importunate Whigs into every branch of the Church, the Army, the Navy, the Law and the Excise. On the Duke's recommendations to the King flowed peerages, bishoprics, ribands, pensions, places and sinecures; and on his own initiative went bribes, dinners and the meanest *pourboires*, all given in the hope of purchasing or sustaining

loyalty. This exercise of patronage called for the striking of
some deplorable bargains; as when electors near Chichester
let the Duke know they would vote the wrong way unless
one of their number detained in Horsham Gaol on smuggling
charges was freed—and freed he was. Yet the Duke could
enforce discipline too. To punish the town of Lewes he
evicted tenants who had failed to support his candidates and
withdrew employment from offending tradesmen. Unlike a
later Duke of Newcastle, he did not have to justify this act
in Parliament with a plaintive, 'Shall I not do as I will with
mine own?'

The Duke revelled in business, enjoying bustle for its own
sake. 'His levees were his pleasure, and his triumph,' wrote
the Earl of Chesterfield, a near relation.

He loved to have them crowded, and consequently they
were so. There he generally made people of business wait
two or three hours in the ante-chamber, where he trifled
away that time with some insignificant favourites in his
closet. When at last he came into the levee room he
accosted, hugged, embraced and promised everybody, with
a seeming cordiality, but at the same time with an illiberal
and degrading familiarity.*

Both Lord Chesterfield and Horace Walpole make the point
that the Duke was as slow in dispatching business as he was
eager to engage in it; both say he never walked anywhere,
but ran. Chesterfield thought he resembled a courier who
carried letters rather than one who wrote them; Walpole said
he had the air of being one who solicited, rather than one who
was solicited by others.

Probably no statesman has conducted so much courteous
correspondence with the grasping and ambitious, or been
closeted so often and so long with the base and sycophantic.
According to the Earl of Shelburne the Duke was beset all his
life by toadies and intriguers who had been with him at

* John Bradshaw (ed.): *Letters and Characters of the Earl of Chesterfield*

Westminster School and never let go; they valued him as a man who could open doors for them.* The bigger fry were harder to handle, as the diary of George Bubb Dodington so clearly shows. Dodington, whose family controlled seats at Winchelsea, Weymouth, Melcombe Regis and—sometimes —Bridgewater, succeeded, by diligent befriending, besetting and betraying over a period of forty years in worming his way into the peerage, but enjoyed the style of Baron Melcombe Regis only for a few months. In 1753-54 he was in repeated attendance on the Duke, asking for livings, agreeing to bribe electors, pressing for reimbursement of his outlays and trying to extract something more than 'warm expressions of approbation'. Dodington claimed to have given the Duke six Members for nothing. The Duke reckoned five, but to show his gratitude took Dodington in his arms and kissed him twice, 'with strong assurances of affection and service'. At the Bridgewater election Dodington spent three days 'in the infamous and disagreeable compliance with the low habits of venal wretches', only to lose (as he said) through a trick by the returning officer. He assured the Duke that he was £2,500 out of pocket, which earned him only renewed professions of goodwill. There were, explained the Duke, no vacancies a man of Dodington's rank would accept; to which Dodington bravely said, 'I desire nobody to be removed, much less to die.' He added that he had no heir, and consequently 'a peerage was not worth the expense of new painting my coach'. If this was intended to bring the offer of a peerage, it failed. The Duke said, 'I suppose you will be disobliged if you have not the first fruit that falls', which Dodington pretended was a slur on his integrity. Time and again he called on the Duke to ask 'what I was to expect'. He became so bold as to ask 'if he imagined I would remain postulating among the common herd of suitors' for ever, and protested, 'I would as soon wear a livery and ride behind a coach in the streets.' In the intervals between snubs Dodington called on the Princess of Wales to tell her about 'the

* Lord Fitzmaurice: *Life of Earl of Shelburne*

wicked meanness, cowardice and baseness of the Duke of Newcastle'.*

The Duke could no more afford to spurn the Dodingtons of his world than his colleagues could afford to spurn him. To keep people dangling, and doing that little bit extra in the hope of reward, was part of his peculiar talent. Yet it is probable that he suffered real distress when he found he could not give his supplicants what they wished. Sir Benjamin Keene, serving as Ambassador at Madrid, coveted the Order of the Bath, which the King refused on account of Keene's humble birth. In long letters the Duke expressed his regrets. 'I own it goes to my heart to see you labour for us in a foreign country, separated from all your friends, in the manner you do, and to know that you are depressed the whole time, from your private disappointment.' Eventually the King conceded the Red Ribbon and the Duke wrote, 'You cannot conceive how happy the procuring of this trifle has made me.' The great Whig then sent his 'love and regard' to his humble, and peevish, envoy.*

The Duke himself had few political ideas, no large plans for the betterment of humanity. Innovations made him nervous. Lord Chesterfield's proposal to change the calendar seemed to him too bold an undertaking; he begged the Earl 'not to stir matters that had long been quiet'. He lacked any talent for waging wars, though Hervey says he 'always talked as his master [the King] talked, echoed back all the big words His Majesty uttered, and expatiated for ever on regaining Italy for the Empire, chastising Spain and humbling the impertinent pride of France.' When left with strategic decisions he was most unhappy, nor was his ignorance of geography much help ('Annapolis, Annapolis! Oh, yes, Annapolis must be defended; to be sure, Annapolis should be defended—where is Annapolis?'). He was no Demosthenes. The applause of listening senates rarely, if ever, reached his ears; and his idea of scattering plenty on a smiling

---

* H. P. Wyndham (ed.): *Diary of George Bubb Dodington* (1784)
† Sir Benjamin Keene: *Private Correspondence*

land was to drive *en prince* through Sussex debauching the electors at mediaeval-style feasts.

The Earl of Shelburne likened the Duke to the fly on the wheel that imagined it propelled the coach of government; but the Whig coach might well have been bogged down without him. Had he contented himself with the roles of paymaster and borough-broker there would have been fewer Cabinet collisions; but he grudged his more talented colleagues their acclaim and demanded a hand in destiny-shaping. For this they detested him, but could not afford to bully or antagonise him.

No one can read far through Horace Walpole's or Lord Hervey's works without coming across a well-polished passage, as rich in spite as in antithesis, at the expense of the Duke. Probably he was not quite such a figure of fun as the diarists make out. However, his fussiness of manner is well attested. A cruel Frenchman likened him to a body hanged in chains which was always fidgeting to be hanged somewhere else.*
His nervous sensibilities showed themselves in an effusiveness which could lead him not only to embrace suitors at his levees, but even to hug a Sussex soldier on parade. He cried easily. On solemn occasions all dignity vanished. Walpole's account in his *Memoirs* of 'Goody Newcastle's' behaviour at the funeral of George II is well-known:

> He fell into a fit of crying the moment he came into the chapel, and flung himself back in a stall, the Archbishop hovering over him with a smelling bottle—but in two minutes his curiosity got the better of his hypocrisy, and he ran about the chapel with his glass to spy who was or was not there, spying with one hand, and mopping his eyes with t'other. Then returned the fear of catching cold, and the Duke of Cumberland, who was sinking with heat, felt himself weighed down, and turning round, found it was the Duke of Newcastle standing upon his train to avoid the chill of the marble.

Westminster Abbey did not find the Duke at his best, for

* T. H. White: *The Age of Scandal*

at the Coronation of George III the Queen, withdrawing
to a specially prepared room with all conveniences, found
the Duke of Newcastle already making use of it.

Fear of catching cold was the Duke's obsession. His idea
of airing a bed was to detail a warm-blooded servant to sleep
in it the night before. On a journey across the English
Channel sailors performed this office, not only for the Duke
but for the Duchess. Once, in November, the Duke called
to discuss naval strategy with William Pitt, who was in
bed with gout and could not tolerate a fire. For a while the
Duke shivered in his cloak and then said, 'With your leave
I will warm myself in the other bed.' Without removing
his cloak he climbed into Lady Hesther Pitt's bed and
continued the discussion about Fleet movements.*

The Duke was proud of his plate and was always moving
it from one home to another. He even took it with him to
Hanover, whither couriers followed him with produce from
his Claremont farm; and on his return his tableware was
escorted from Yorkshire by cavalry. The plate may have
been the best part of his table. Once, bragging about his
Sussex puddings, the Duke asked a guest if he had such
puddings in his county. 'No, please your Grace,' was the
answer, 'and if we did we would need a Sussex man to eat
them.'† The palace of Welbeck, where previous Dukes of
Newcastle had lived in tremendous state, did not form part
of his inheritance. When he fell from power in 1756 he
withdrew to Claremont and, according to Walpole, bought
guns and green frocks and played at being a country gentleman; 'but getting wet in the feet, he hurried back to London
in a fright, and his country was once again blessed with his
assistance.'

Less prejudiced observers have stressed the Duke's ben-
evolence and genuine love of putting his wealth to work for
others. In 1760 he lent a sympathetic ear to the philosopher-
reformer, Jonas Hanway, who wrote a series of epistles to
him complaining of the tyranny of vails, as exacted by ser-

* L. Dutens: *Memoirs of a Traveller*
† John Byng: *The Torrington Diaries*

vants in great homes. Most hosts preferred not to know about the insolent rapacity of their servants. Hanway cited a supposed incident under the Duke's own roof, when Sir Timothy Waldo, leaving for his carriage, put a crown in the palm of the Duke's cook, who handed it back saying, 'Sir, I do not take silver.' Waldo retorted, 'Don't you indeed? Then I do not give gold,' and pocketed the coin. Hanway asked the Duke to consider the plight of a guest of low fortune, invited for his virtue and knowledge.

He entertains your Grace with his discourse and pays honour to your rank and condition, but he demands nothing for it. Your Grace entertains him at dinner and your servants make him pay for it ten times as much as it is worth to him. Can you enjoy the advantages of your high station, your great fortune and nobleness of mind with such an incumbrance?*

The Duke was sufficiently stirred to show the letters to the young George III, who tried to discourage the acceptance of vails under his own roof, thereby stirring up much domestic trouble for himself.

The Duke's private life provoked no scandal. His Duchess, a grand-daughter of the great Duke of Marlborough, though described by Walpole as mad, seems to have been a loyal partner, willing even to decipher crabbed official hand-writing for him. If at one time the Duke flirted with Princess Amelia, no one could have imagined her in danger of seduction. Once he apologised to her for being the worse for liquor, only to be told, 'My God! you were charming! You have never amused me so much in my life. I should like to see you always drunk.'† He was known at Court as 'Permis' from the diffidence with which he sought leave to speak (est-il permis?). Others called him 'Hubble-Bubble'.

The Duke is credited with a single witticism. After his fall almost all the bishops absented themselves from his levee, which drew the comment, 'Bishops, like other men,

* Jonas Hanway: *Eight Letters to the Duke of Newcastle*
† Lord Hervey: *Memoirs*

are apt to forget their Maker.' To Bute, who pretended to congratulate him on his retirement, he made the riposte, 'Yes, yes, my Lord, I am an old man; but yesterday was my birthday and I recollected that Cardinal Fleury *began* to be Prime Minister of France just at my age.'

The Duke's end came in 1768—'at last dead and for the first time quiet', wrote the Earl of Chesterfield. But the Earl stressed his better qualities. 'I knew him to be very good-natured, and his hands to be extremely clean, and even too clean if that were possible; for, after all the great offices which he had held for fifty years, he died £300,000 poorer than he was when he first came into them. A very unministerial proceeding!'* More than once the Duke refused a pension.

In a debate on election malpractices in 1780 Lord Nugent reminded Parliament how William Pitt had been elected for the borough of Aldborough 'owned' by the Duke of Newcastle. At that time the unsuccessful candidate complained about undue ducal influence which had given the nation 'the greatest man that ever lived'. The Duke, being naturally hospitable and generous, might have given a few dinners on that occasion, but Lord Nugent 'believed God never made a better man than the late Duke of Newcastle'.†

* John Bradshaw (ed.): *Letters and Characters of the Earl of Chesterfield*
† *Parliamentary History*, 2 February, 1780

DUKES AGAINST THE MOB
9

The Duke of Newcastle died in 1768, a year of tumult at the hustings, a year which shed not the least lustre on the electoral system. It was unnecessary to be an envenomed radical to see that reform of some kind was overdue.

The most sensational battle was the one which sent the mob baying outside the ducal homes of London. Their hero was John Wilkes, the profligate apostle of liberty, who had been lurking in France after his expulsion from Parliament, but had returned and won the seat of Brentford. Traditionally, the mob's way of celebrating was to force all householders to show illuminations in honour of whatever cause was animating them. The previous year they had joined the Spitalfields weavers in stoning and besieging the fourth Duke of Bedford for daring to advocate free trade, and had been driven off by cavalry, leaving Bedford House heavily garrisoned. After the Wilkes success at Brentford, with shouts of 'Wilkes and Liberty!' ringing through the town, the Duke of Northumberland (Chapter Eleven) was quick to set out candles at Northumberland House, after which he ordered the Ship Alehouse across the road to open up and serve the rioters with beer. He was then persuaded to join them in drinking to Wilkes.* Filling rioters with beer seems an odd way to discourage insolence, but the Duke saved his property.

* *Annual Register,* 1768

On that night ladies of rank were hauled from their carriages and made to shout for Wilkes. One of them defied the mob. She was the former Duchess of Hamilton, born Elizabeth Gunning, now married to the heir of the Duke of Argyll. Though her husband was absent in Scotland, though she was pregnant and surrounded by children, she forbade her house to be illuminated. On the second night of her defiance the mob tore up the pavement and broke the doors and shutters, but she was able to send out a messenger to the nearest barracks for help.

The Wilkes mobs were still rampaging in 1769. During this year the Dukes of Northumberland, Kingston and Bedford were all assaulted, Kingston by mistake for Bedford. Thanks to these and other tumults the Earl of Chatham was stung to give warning of the consequences of defying the people's will. He condemned the general corruption of the electoral system, demanded more seats for the counties and a widening of the franchise. It was one of the first powerful pleas for reform.

Ironically, it was at the height of the Gordon Riots, in 1780, when Protestant rioters inflamed by a duke's son (Lord George Gordon) were sacking London, that a duke rose in the House of Lords to present a Bill for the reform of Parliament. He was Charles Lennox, third Duke of Richmond. It is firmly embedded in radical teaching that dukes have always been the enemy of reform of every kind; consequently, in the popular pantheon, there is only the obscurest niche for this descendant of a royal bastard who had the impertinence to put the people's case half a century before the time was ripe.

All agreed that the Duke of Richmond had elegant manners and bearing. Some thought his much-talked-of beauty was an inheritance from Louise de Kéroualle. As a young man he quarrelled with George III, partly over the allocation of offices and partly over the King's youthful affair with the Duke's sister, Lady Sarah Lennox. His seat was Goodwood, where the second Duke, that amiable menagerie-keeper, had defied gangs of Sussex smugglers who subjected him to extortion demands and death threats. The third Duke was a soldier and fought well at Minden. In Parliament his exquisite manners occasionally failed him, as when in 1779 he mocked the new Lord Chancellor, Lord Thurlow, for his low birth. The Lord Chancellor, fixing on the Duke 'the look of Jove when he grasped the thunder', said in a loud, clear voice: 'The Noble Lord cannot look before him, behind him, or on either side of him, without seeing some noble peer who owes his seat to successful exertions in the profession to which I belong. Does he not feel that it is as honourable to owe it to these as to being *the accident of an accident?*'*† Edmund Burke laid flattering unction on the Duke in a letter (quoted at the beginning of this book) comparing him and his kind to 'the great oaks that shade a country'. Some of the wealth that Burke envied came from that inherited tax on coals shipped from Newcastle to London; a tax compounded in the Duke's lifetime to an annuity of £19,000. The Duke has been praised for his public spirit in declining to oppose a canal designed to carry Warwickshire coals to London, thus challenging his revenues. He explained that he did not wish to obstruct any measure likely to cheapen the cost of coals to the poor. The question of giving up his levy altogether did not arise. When the Earl of Shelburne mounted a Parliamentary attack on Crown patronage and sinecure offices, the Duke of Richmond made it clear where he stood. His emoluments came to him as a patrimony from his ancestors under a legal title confirmed by several Acts of Parliament. 'Were he even inclined he could resign no more than his personal claim, as others had an interest as well as himself.' He thought he was as well entitled as any man to enjoy a fortune transmitted from his forebears. If Parliament laid down that all such grants from the Crown were 'resumable whenever the exigencies of the State required it, he would submit on that condition,'

* Lord Mahon: *A History of England*
† This anecdote is sometimes wrongly told about the third Duke of Grafton

and not in response to the spleen of reformers.* Such was the man, a duke of royal blood, a major-general, an uncle of Charles James Fox, a supporter of the American colonists and an advocate of a 'union of hearts' (his own phrase) with Ireland, who in 1780 took up the cause of Parliamentary Reform; a course which his distrustful Sovereign was not alone in regarding as a 'strange conceit'.

The timing of the Bill which the Duke introduced in the Lords could not have been more disastrous. Even as he opened his speech the House could hear the howls of hundreds of rioters in Old Palace Yard. The Duke said he disapproved strongly of what was going on outside. Since he had been accused of being too ready to support the claims of the people, he wanted the House to know that, in his belief, distinctions between men had been ordained by Providence and that there was 'an eternal barrier in the human mind against the equal division of wealth and power'. His reason for opposing the electoral system as operated was that it made the King's will the rule and measure of government. He wanted to see the holding of annual Parliaments; the election of one hundred additional Members to represent the shires and to offset ministerial rotten boroughs; and the extension of the franchise to every man over twenty-one not disqualified by law. Hereabouts a peer interrupted to say that Lord Boston had been dragged from his carriage in the Yard and was being cruelly maltreated. After a brief discussion as to who should go to his rescue, if anybody, the Duke of Richmond suggested they should all go, with the Mace borne at their head. Lord Boston then burst into the chamber, his hair awry and his clothes covered with powder. Other peers staggered in, bearing similar marks of manhandling. The Archbishop of York had his lawn sleeves torn off and thrown in his face; the Bishop of Lincoln escaped from his smashed carriage and fled over some roofs disguised as an ordinary gentleman; the Duke of Northumberland was forced from his carriage, robbed and otherwise abused because his black-clothed

* *Parliamentary History*, 8 February 1780

companion was thought to be a Jesuit. In the House numerous dishevelled peers were all speaking at once, 'most of
them as pale as the ghost in *Hamlet*'. The House therefore
adjourned and their lordships nervously found their way
home in hackney carriages or on foot, under cover of dusk.*

Next day, in a calmer atmosphere, the Duke of Richmond
finished his speech. The system of boroughs he described
as the very sink of corruption. In some boroughs scarcely any
trace of a house could be found. In Midhurst were several
stones marked 1, 2, 3, 4 and so on in the park of a noble
lord—the Duke indicated Lord Montagu—which represented
voters and returned Members. It was obvious, said the Duke,
that these were very precious stones and the noble lord
would not part with them for a great deal. (Sixty years later,
fighting the same battle, Lord John Russell told the Commons of a green mound which elected two Members and a
wall with three niches in it which elected two more.) The
Duke complained that the constitutional right of election
had been taken from the many and given to the few. Not
more than 6,000 men returned a clear majority of the House
of Commons. Out of 1,625,000 men in England and Wales
only 210,000 had the right to vote.

The Duke cannot have been surprised that their lordships
scarcely bothered to discuss his Bill. The corruption of which
he complained was, after all, the livelihood of many of them,
though the measure could hardly be attacked for that reason.
Lord Stormont doubted whether the common people had
ever enjoyed the right to vote, so how could it be restored
to them? The Bill was thrown out.†

The Gordon riots gave the country a bad shock. It was
the mob's worst outrage of the century, even though the
impulses behind it were sectarian rather than political.
Was this the time to give the dregs of Alsatia the vote?
Undiscouraged, the Duke joined the Society for Promoting
Constitutional Information, founded by John Cartwright,
and attended propagandist meetings. When the Revolution-

* *Parliamentary History*, 2 June 1780
† *Parliamentary History*, 3 June 1780

ary Terror came to France the younger Pitt's Government
began to move against the constitutional and corresponding
societies, regarding them as covers for subversion. The wild
fringe of radicalism asked for trouble and got it. In this
climate the Duke of Richmond decided that the campaign
for reform must be put off. In 1792 he was bitterly attacked
in the Lords by the Earl of Lauderdale, who pointed out that
the Duke now commanded a large force at Bagshot designed
to overawe Reformist agitators in London. 'If apostasy could
justify promotion he was the most fit person for that command, General Arnold alone excepted,' said the Earl.* To
this the Duke took exception and a duel in the Edgware Road
was narrowly averted; the Earl later fought a bloodless duel
with General Arnold, the betrayer of West Point.

In the anti-Jacobin excitements of 1794, when the Government brought charges of high treason against Thomas
Hardy and John Horne Tooke, the defence were quick to
stress that the nefarious plans of which their clients stood
accused were first propagated by the Duke of Richmond.
His writings, argued Thomas (later Lord) Erskine, were
'the very Scripture' of the corresponding societies which
sought to change Parliament. It is unlikely that the Duke,
now Master General of the Ordnance and a Knight of the
Garter, relished his appearances in the witness box. Much
play was made with a letter which he had written, in 1783,
to a Lieutenant-Colonel Sharman, chairman of a group of
Irish Volunteers, who had asked what he thought the best
way of destroying that 'hydra of corruption, borough influence'. In his reply the Duke had stressed the disillusion
of the people with the electoral system, saying 'the people
have been so often deceived that they will now scarcely trust
any set of men ... it is from the people at large that I expect
any good.' The Duke had also ridiculed the idea of 'a few
great families dividing a county between them and choosing
Members of Parliament from a house list, like East India
directors'.

Defending the erratic Tooke, Erskine assured the court

* *Parliamentary History*, 31 May 1792

that the Duke of Richmond, 'a highly intelligent and illustrious person', with no thought of overturning the Constitution or 'enervating its functions', had pushed the principle and practice of Reform very much farther than Tooke; yet it was Tooke they were being invited to consign to infamy and death. Against this argument the prosecution could do little.* Edmund Burke, who had likened the Duke to a great oak, could scarcely have imagined that the branches of that oak would so soon spread their protection over agitators threatened by the noose.

The acquittal of two mob heroes deeply embarrassed the Government; but little more was heard of reform until after Waterloo. As for the Duke of Richmond, by now an ill-tempered old field-marshal, he gradually withdrew to his Goodwood estates, began to build a new octagonal mansion, projected the famous racecourse and, on a magnificent whim, planted one thousand cedars of Lebanon.

* *State Trials* 1794

A BRACE OF BEDFORDS

10

It will be recalled that the first Duke of Bedford, having been raised to that rank in honour of his decapitated son, retired to Woburn and lived a withdrawn and frugal life. His income, according to Luttrell, was £30,000 a year and rapidly rising. The second and third Dukes died young, aged twenty-six and twenty-four respectively. In his brief span the third Duke contrived to gamble away much of the family property. If Lady Mary Wortley Montagu is any guide, this wastrel shirked his duties in the marriage bed, to which he arrived a virgin. 'He was so much disappointed in his fair bride ... that he already pukes at the very name of her, and determines to let his estate go to his brother, rather than go through the filthy drudgery of getting an heir to it.' Swearing that she tells the truth, Lady Mary says: 'This comes of living till sixteen without a competent knowledge either of practical or speculative anatomy, and literally thinking fine ladies composed of lilies and roses.'*

The estate duly passed to the younger brother, John Russell, fourth Duke of Bedford. With him the story of the ducal Russells gains some needed momentum. He used the marriage bed as dukes were expected to use it—for the increase of possessions. His first wife, Diana Spencer, a grand-daughter of the great Duke of Marlborough, brought him

* Lord Wharncliffe (ed.): *Letters of Lady Mary Wortley Montagu*

£30,000 down with a further £100,000 on the death of the Duchess Sarah.* His second wife was a Leveson-Gower, a family rapidly on its way to owning more land than any other.

The Duke's first Government appointment came in 1744, when he found himself one of eight dukes in Pelham's Cabinet. All the other members were noblemen. Before he could distinguish himself as First Lord of the Admiralty the 1745 rebellion broke out. It was expected of dukes that they should be able to raise regiments quickly and the Duke of Bedford enlisted at his own cost a force of a thousand men. He was prepared to march north at their head but an attack of gout prevented him; he joined them, however, at Edinburgh for the campaign which ended at Culloden. Back at the Admiralty he carried out some urgently needed dock-yard reforms. He was an anti-Walpole Whig and his followers were known as the 'Bedford gang' or 'Bloomsbury gang'. In 1756 the Duke went to Ireland as Lord Lieutenant, professing the highest intentions. He had resolved not to admit parasites on the Irish establishment and to force all absentees to return to their posts, including Army officers and chaplains. Soon the King and the Duke of Newcastle, as Prime Minister, were pressing him to bend the rules. 'The King is sensible how much the establishment is loaded and is therefore un-willing to lay any further encumbrance upon it,' wrote the Duke of Newcastle; nevertheless, His Majesty wished to know whether a pension of £6,000 could be found on the Irish Establishment for the Princess of Hesse and her child-ren, driven from home by the French. The Duke of Bedford sent back discouraging figures with an invitation to the King to judge for himself whether the pension list 'will not be rather overloaded', and suggesting that Parliament should find the money. If the King insisted, he would 'use utmost endeavours to make it as little unpalatable to the nation here as possible'. The King insisted; and his next request was for a life pension of £2,000 for Prince Ferdinand of Bruns-wick Wolfenbuttel. The Duke scored one petty victory over

* *Complete Peerage*

the King. The death of the King's sister, the Queen Dowager of Prussia, freed an Irish pension of £800, and the Duke, his good resolutions forgotten, begged this sum for his sister-in-law, Lady Elizabeth Waldegrave.*

No duke of the period had more clashes with the mob, or feared them less, than Bedford. They hissed and barracked him in London for the part he played in making peace with France in 1763. They demonstrated at his rule in Dublin. At Woburn Abbey he had to be protected by the Blues during disorders over a militia Bill. In London, as we have seen, Bedford House was garrisoned by horse and foot against the Spitalfields weavers. In both London and Devon the Duke was attacked by Wilkes mobs. At Exeter he was driven from church, hissed and stoned. By his own account the people of Honiton set twenty bulldogs at his horse, though none actually took a grip. To avoid stones he went everywhere at a gallop, the chaise which followed him being pelted and damaged. The Duke took it all calmly. On the day after the worst incident he inspected one of his farms as if nothing had happened. The vicious 'Junius' took an indecent delight in the Duke's misfortunes. 'Whither shall this unhappy old man retire? ... At every town he enters, he must change his liveries and his name. Whichever way he flies, the hue and cry of the country pursues him.'†

With the aid of the architect Henry Flitcroft, the Duke rebuilt much of Woburn Abbey, which had been fast crumbling. Furnishings and treasures were brought from China in East Indiamen bearing the names of Russell and Tavistock, which docked in the family docks at Rotherhithe. He bought up Bedfordshire on such a scale that one family called him Ahab, presumably after *1 Kings xxl* 2: 'And Ahab spake unto Naboth, saying, Give me thy vineyard, that I may have it for a garden of herbs, because it is near unto my house; and I will give thee for it a better vineyard than it; or, if it seem good to thee, I will give thee the worth of

* Lord John Russell: *Correspondence of the Fourth Duke of Bedford*
† *Public Advertiser*, 19 September 1769

it in money.' He was a great improver and planter. When he asked his head gardener to thin some experimental evergreens the reply was, 'Your Grace, I cannot possibly do what you desire. It would destroy the plantation and injure my reputation as a planter.' To this the Duke ordered, 'Do what I tell you and then I will take care of your reputation.' The gardener's fears were justified, but he was exculpated by a notice: THIS PLANTATION HAS BEEN THINNED BY JOHN, DUKE OF BEDFORD, CONTRARY TO THE ADVICE AND OPINION OF HIS GARDENER.*

The Bedford estates, being scattered, were not easily administered. In the Duke's correspondence are references to Fen embankments being carried away by floods, necessitating emergency measures to keep open the roads. Blankets were sent to Woburn for naked children driven from their cottages and consignments of cheap wheat were provided. Relief operations which today are carried out by the State or voluntary bodies were then the prime responsibility of the landlord.

The Duke's activities were multi-faceted. Even in his failing years he attended meetings of the Paving Board, Trinity House and Turnpike Trust, went to levees, cricket matches and dilettante dinners—with time out to sit for Gainsborough. He listened to agriculturists, inventors, developers and philosophers. He was always an advocate of inoculation against smallpox and had his own servants treated whether they liked it or not. At Dublin University, where he was installed Chancellor, the ode described him as 'the greatest and the first of Science's glorious train', and asked:

> Are there, who honest to their trust,
>   Stem strong corruption's swelling flood,
> Who love to be perversely just
>   Or dare be singularly good?

The answer was in the affirmative. Lord Chesterfield did not find the Duke perversely just or singularly good, but 'invincible obstinate', with 'exceedingly illiberal' manners.

* Lord John Russell: *Correspondence*

Horace Walpole had a private quarrel with the Duke, but praised his inflexible honesty and goodwill to his country. 'His great economy was called avarice; if it was so, it was blended with more generosity and goodness than that passion will generally unite with. His parts were far from shining and yet he spoke readily, and upon trade, well; his foible was speaking on every subject, and imagining he understood it, as he must have done, by inspiration ... If the Duke of Bedford could have thought less well of himself, the world would probably have thought better of him.'* Lord Hervey considered the Duke 'the best economist in the world ... of such a turn as to have been able to live within his fortune if it had been fifty times less; and the Duke of Marlborough to have run his out if it had been fifty times greater.'†

Francis Russell, fifth Duke of Bedford, grandson of the fourth, earned early and immortal fame by drawing upon himself a terrible blast by Edmund Burke. In his twenties he had been reluctant to speak in Parliament for fear that his poor command of English and general lack of learning might disgrace not only their lordships' house but his own; but he quickly acquired a fluency and power of argument which made him a debater not to be ignored. What he did not acquire was that modesty which is becoming in one of great inheritance. In 1795 the Duke and his friend the Earl of Lauderdale criticised the award of a substantial pension to Edmund Burke, then nearing his seventies; and the Duke compounded the offence by speaking favourably of Reform. The result took the form of *A Letter to a Noble Lord*, a classic of denunciation.

Burke began by saying that his pension was the fruit of no bargaining, no intrigue, no solicitation; rather was it 'the spontaneous bounty of the Crown' designed to 'assuage the sorrows of a desolate old man'. Referring to the Duke as 'Poor rich man!' and 'my youthful censor', he said: 'I was

* Horace Walpole: *Memoirs (George II)*
† Lord Hervey: *Memoirs*

not, like His Grace of Bedford, swaddled and rocked and dandled into a legislation.' If the Duke thought the pension excessive, out of all bounds, what of his own wealth?

The grants to the House of Russell were so enormous as not only to outrage economy, but even to stagger credibility. The Duke of Bedford is the Leviathan among all the creatures of the Crown. He tumbles about his unwieldy bulk; he plays and frolicks in the ocean of the royal bounty. Huge as he is, and whilst he 'lies floating many a rood', he is still a creature. His ribs, his fins, his whalebone, his blubber, the very spiracles through which he pours a torrent of brine against his origin and covers me all over with spray—everything of him and about him is from the Throne. Is it for *him* to question the dispensation of the royal favour?

Perhaps, suggested Burke, the Duke had forgotten that the Bedford estates were monastery spoils? 'The lion having sucked the blood of his prey threw the offal carcase to the jackal in waiting. Having tasted once the food of confiscation, the favourites became fierce and ravenous.' The founder of the House of Russell was 'the prompt and greedy instrument of a levelling tyrant, who oppressed all descriptions of his people, but who fell with particular fury on everything that was *great and noble.*' But, whereas the Bedford lands were 'surrendered by the lawful proprietors with the gibbet at their door' (a reference, presumably, to the hanging of the abbot on the Abbot's Oak at Woburn), Burke's grant was bestowed by a mild and benevolent Sovereign.

The Crown has considered me after long service; the Crown has paid the Duke of Bedford in advance. He has had a long credit for any service which he may perform hereafter. He is secure, and long may he be secure, in his advance, whether he performs any service or not. But let him take care how he endangers the safety of the

Constitution which secures his own utility or his own insignificance ...

It was Burke's boast that, by opposing 'the obscene harpies of Revolutionary France', he had tried to prevent British aristocrats going the way of the French—'I have strained every nerve to keep the Duke of Bedford in that situation which alone makes him my superior.' His Grace had lands more extensive and much more fertile than many of the Grecian republics; but only so long as the monarchy stood would 'the mounds and dykes of the low, fat Bedford Level ... have nothing to fear from all the pickaxes and levellers of France.' Savages and revolutionaries would 'no more regard a Marquess of Tavistock* than an Abbot of Tavistock; the Lord of Woburn will not be more respectable in their eyes than the Prior of Woburn.'

As a warning to rich young inheritors to control their tongues the *Letter* is hard to fault. Inevitably it drew attacks. *A Letter by Henry Duncombe Esq., Member for the County of York* complained that 'Mr Burke penetrated to the very extremity of the tomb to drag from his peaceful urn the ancestor of the Duke of Bedford.' This 'intoxicated dotard' with 'a mind debased, crippled and ulcerated even to a gangrene' had lodged objections to the House of Russell which might equally have been lodged against the great houses of Cavendish, Fitzwilliam and Bentinck; and so on. From this distance, it would seem a salutary thing that the apostle of conservatism should have reminded a few proud families of the origins of their wealth.

Happily, the fifth Duke of Bedford did perform services to justify his 'advance'. Forsaking the senate, he turned to the pasture and the plough. At Woburn he started a model farm and conducted experiments in soils, grasslands, stockbreeding and mechanisation. His famous 'Woburn Shearings', partly modelled on 'Coke's Clippings' at Holkham, were the forerunner of the county agricultural show and gave belated status to the arts of cultivation and stock-

* The title borne by the eldest sons of the Dukes of Bedford

rearing. Arthur Young, who visited Woburn in the 1790s, said: 'The Woburn Sheep Shearing was by far the most responsible agricultural meeting ever seen in England, that is in the whole world, attended by the nobility, gentry, farmers and graziers from various parts of the three kingdoms, from many countries in Europe and also from America.' Sheep shearing was only one activity; there were ploughing contests and competitions for stock and produce of all kinds (one year there was a hog weighing one hundred stone). There were awards for the labourer who had worked longest on one farm, and for the man who had brought up the largest family unaided by the parish.* The Bedford farm workers were always well housed, in cottages with a 'B' and a coronet emblazoned above the door (the Duke of Northumberland put his coat-of-arms on his bothies). In more recent times the eleventh Duke of Bedford built cottages without front doors in an effort to prevent housewives from gossiping on their doorsteps.

The fifth Duke called in Henry Holland to extend and remodel Woburn Abbey. Not all the improvements on the estate were to the taste of that captious traveller, the Hon. John Byng. For one thing, the axe was being used far too freely. In 1794 an unabashed agent showed Byng an avenue a mile long, containing a thousand trees, all due to be felled. 'The Duke is a leveller,' complained Byng; he was even levelling old manor houses for the materials, instead of offering them as school-houses or homes for French *émigrés*. 'What a mean, stingy gull must this Duke of Bedford be!' exclaimed Byng on finding that an Inigo Jones mansion, Houghton House, was being broken up to build a new inn. Nor did Byng approve of the Duke's domestic life. 'At his own seat (the school of folly and prodigality) nothing but waste and intemperance are to be seen; from which only flattery and villainy can prosper.'†

At the time of his majority the Duke's 'housekeeper' at Woburn was that tireless befriender of dukes, Nancy

* Lawrence Meynell: *Bedfordshire*
† John Byng: *The Torrington Diaries*

Parsons (Chapter Fourteen), who was more than twice his age. She is reputed to have driven his grandmother out of the Abbey. After Nancy's departure he kept various ladies at Woburn without going to the fatigue of marrying them (it would have been little trouble, since the Dukes of Bedford enjoyed the privilege of issuing marriage licences). The Duke was a member of the Prince of Wales's set and in 1795 was one of the two unmarried dukes who held up the drunken Prince at his wedding to Caroline of Brunswick. Earlier he had bought up many horses from the Royal stud when the Prince had dispersed it after a racecourse scandal. He won the Derby three times, once with a horse anachronistically named Skyscraper. In the *Sporting Magazine* he does not always appear at his best. In 1788 Lord Barrymore 'betted his Grace £500 to £400 that he produced a man who should eat a live cat, which was performed at the time appointed by a labouring man of Harpenden, near St Albans.'

In 1795 the Duke was one of the Whigs who, in opposition to Pitt's tax on hair powder, met in solemn session at Woburn and cut off their queues. As a leader of fashion, however, he was hardly in the front rank. Beau Brummell, when the Duke asked for an opinion on his new coat, said, 'Bedford, did I hear you call this thing a coat?'

The Duke's sudden death in his prime, from hernia, released a wave of eulogy which, in the view of Arthur Young, that righteous agriculturist, was excessive for one who had shown contempt for morals and religion; good farming, beneficence and an even temper were simply not enough. Though Young had dined at Woburn he preferred the local inn to the Duke's 'great table which might as well be spread for a company of heathens as English leaders and men of fashion.'*

The funeral at Rickmansworth drew an exceptionally irreligious throng. A strong force of pickpockets drove down from London in their own chaises, 'made a crowd of themselves' and robbed the crowd trying to force their way into the church. Such was the pressure that some of the 'mourners'

* Arthur Young: *Autobiography*

broke the church windows in order to enter the building. Among those robbed was the dead Duke, whose escutcheons were stolen from the hearse.*

Both the fourth and fifth Dukes deserve the highest credit for the drive and inspiration they brought to the creation of Bloomsbury. It was a speculative enterprise which took the best part of a century to complete, an astonishing feat to be carried through by one family. For the early residents, the din and mess of building must often have been unbearable, but the final result was dignified and harmonious: a Georgian town on the edge of a city. Bedford Square, started by the fourth Duke about 1775, was the magnificent centrepiece; in the middle of each side was a mansion of exceptional stature. Hardly had the Square been completed before it was sealed off to non-residents and through traffic by a system of gates and beadles. No errand boys were admitted; the tradesman was required to call in person. The fifth Duke initiated work on Russell, Tavistock, Woburn and Gordon Squares, leaving their completion to his successors. Like the Grosvenors, who built up Mayfair and Belgravia, the Russells granted long leases, on the expiry of which the property reverted to the landlord, by which time the value of the area had increased enormously and higher rents could be charged. As a long-term method of moneyspinning it was greatly superior to planting trees. During the nineteenth century the system came increasingly under radical attack. The Russells also drew fat revenues from Covent Garden, made up of levies on every sieve of fruit and bunch of vegetables. This toll was later compared to the exactions of Rhine barons in the Dark Ages.†

---

* *Annual Register*, 1802
† Frank Banfield: *The Great Landlords of London*

A NEW LINE IN PERCYS

11

The great days of duke-making ended with George I. Horace Walpole says that on the fall of his father's government dukedoms were offered by George II to the Earls of Ailesbury and Northampton, but each declined because he had no son. In such circumstances Garters were often preferred. In 1748 the Earl of Chesterfield also refused a dukedom. Under George III the highest rank was hard to come by. Aspirants found themselves fobbed off with the title of marquess, which the old nobility tended to think of as a recent Gallic import. The Leveson-Gowers and the Grenvilles were among the families which had to be content with the lesser honour.* As a natural result the rank of duke became infinitely more desirable. One man who, with unusual confidence or unusual effrontery, spurned a marquessate and demanded a dukedom —and this without having shown any exceptional public merit—was Sir Hugh Smithson, who in 1766 became first Duke of Northumberland in the third creation, having already assumed the ancient name and arms of Percy.

In 1739 this Yorkshire baronet, more polished than some of his kind, wealthier than many and more ambitious than most, met Lady Elizabeth Seymour, grand-daughter of the 'proud' Duke of Somerset. In her veins ran the blood not only of

* F. M. L. Thompson: *English Landed Society in the Nineteenth Century*

Seymours but of Percys. She told her parents of Smithson's attentions, saying, 'I shall not scruple to own that I have a partiality for him.' Her fortune was then £10,000 a year and Smithson's about £4,000. Much pressure was exerted to persuade the proud Duke to agree to the match; and only after much grumbling over this squandering of ancient blood on an upstart did the old man give way. After her marriage Lady Elizabeth became heiress to the vast Percy properties, through the death of her brother from smallpox. This was just the sort of thing her grandfather had feared and he now tried unsuccessfully to disinherit her. In 1748 he died and Lady Elizabeth's father became Earl of Northumberland. When the latter died in 1750 that title passed to Smithson, who changed his name to Percy. In his new rank he went as Lord Lieutenant to Ireland, where he displayed a natural talent for magnificence.

The shame of owning great lands without being a duke began to rankle. There were precedents for reviving dukedoms when ducal estates had passed to daughters and the daughter concerned had made a suitable marriage. The Earl of Northumberland was not the only nobleman with similar expectations. George Brudenell, fourth Earl of Cardigan, had married the co-heiress of the second Duke of Montagu, the practical joker, whose dukedom had expired. He had taken the name and arms of Montagu and let it be known to George III through the favourite, Lord Bute, that he would not object to being created Duke of Montagu. Both aspirants would doubtless have argued that they did not seek dukedoms for themselves but only to perpetuate ancient family honours and to please their wives.

After his tour in Ireland the Earl of Northumberland was being considered for a Cabinet post when he heard that a prized Court appointment was being offered to Lord Hertford. He at once protested that the King had offered him no such mark of favour for his services at Dublin Castle. Faced with this difficulty, the Prime Minister, the Earl of Chatham, suggested to the King that the Earl of Northumberland be advanced in the peerage, perhaps to a dukedom. The young

King is said to have coloured and looked embarrassed, explaining that he would have to consider what other obligations he owed, instancing the Earl of Cardigan. Later the King described to Chatham his interview with the importunate Percy:

> I told him that his request for a dukedom was new to me, that I could give no other answer than that I would consider of it; that I had thought he only looked up to a marquessate. He said that was a more modern rank in the English peerage; that what he asked me was the old title of Lady Northumberland's family; that if he succeeded he would never be an applier for public employments. Undoubtedly few peers have so great an estate in point of income, and scarce any in point of extent; therefore if you will co-operate with me in declaring I don't mean by this to open a door for the creating many dukes I will consent to it.*

Horace Walpole fills out the story, making it appear that the Earl's impudence was matched by that of his fellow aspirant.

> Lord Cardigan, on an old promise, obtained by Lord Bute, that he should be a duke whenever one was made, was raised to the same rank [as Smithson]; but Lord Chatham, coupling it with a condition to both, that one should take no employment, and the other resign the government of Windsor Castle, Lord Cardigan refused the increase of title, saying he thought titles were honours and rewards, not punishments. Lord Northumberland acquiesced and obtained the precedence. The other, being firm, carried his point, kept his place and got the dukedom.†

The elevation of the upstart Smithson, on the wings of

---

* Quoted in E. B. de Fonblanque's *Annals of the House of Percy*
† Horace Walpole: *Memoirs (George III)*. At the same time as Northumberland and Montagu received their honour, James Fitzgerald, Irish politician and grandee, was created first Duke of Leinster, there being then no Irish dukes.

charm, wealth, impertinence and smallpox, was taken exceedingly amiss by the old nobility, over whose heads he
passed. It was clear then, and is clearer now, that he was
raised to a dukedom not for anything he had done but for
what he owned. Edward Barrington de Fonblanque, a
historian of the Percys, writes:

> There is perhaps no other instance in modern history of a
> private gentleman acquiring such an accumulation of high
> honours and dignitaries as fell to his lot. To the merits
> which commonly open the avenues to high social and
> official advancement, such as commanding statesmanship,
> great powers of debate, military achievement or legal pre-
> eminence he had no pretensions; nor, although his estates
> were large, could he claim that Parliamentary influence
> which enabled a few great owners of boroughs to turn the
> scale of Party and dictate terms to Courts and Cabinets.
> The day had gone by when a successful courtier could
> aspire to the highest place under the Crown and George III
> was chary in the bestowal of his favours and fastidious in
> the choice of his ministers.

This writer attributes Smithson's success to great personal
merit, resolute will to charm and 'ambition kept under
control by commonsense and sound judgment'; and, perhaps
more important, a capacity to take at the flood the tide that
leads to fortune.

Two years after his elevation the Duke was still taking the
tide at the flood. He had promised the King he would not
solicit public employment, but he saw fit to demand a regiment for his son and threatened to resign his Middlesex lord
lieutenancy if it were refused. The King gave in, angrily; had
he, instead, sent an insulting message by a page, Horace
Walpole for one would not have complained.

Walpole was clearly jealous of the Northumberlands. He
acknowledged that the Duke was 'exceedingly popular with
the meaner sort'. At gaming table his conduct was 'sordid
and illiberal' (meaning perhaps that he did not choose to
throw away his Hotspur castles at the cast of a dice). However,

Walpole graciously concedes that 'in an age so destitute of intrinsic merit his foibles ought to have passed for virtues'. The Duchess was 'a jovial heap of contradictions'—'the blood of all the Percys and Seymours swelled in her veins and in her fancy'. She surrounded herself with pipers, drummers and 'obsolete minstrels', and her 'buxom countenance at the tail of a procession gave it all the air of an antiquated pageant or mumming'. When the Queen went to the theatre the Duchess would follow with an even longer train of domestics; a practice which earned her an unheeded royal rebuke. She had a passion for shows, crowds and junketings. 'She was familiar with the mob, while stifled with diamonds; and yet was attentive to the most minute privileges of her rank, whilst almost shaking hands with a cobbler.'*

Alnwick Castle, the Duke's main Northumberland strong-hold, had long been a prey to owls and bats. It was the Duchess's idea to Gothicise it and the Duke did not resist. He assigned Robert Adam and James Paine to restore the interior, which they did with great distinction; and Capability Brown attended to the landscape. A ninety-foot folly called the Brislee Tower was raised to enable the Duke to survey his realms. It bore the self-congratulatory inscription, in Latin: 'Look around! I myself have measured out all these things. They are of my ordering. Many of these trees have been planted by my own hands.' At Syon House, Middlesex, which the Duke thought ruinous and inconvenient, Robert Adam again gave of his best and Brown opened up the views. In London that target of mobs, Northumberland House, con-tained a picture gallery open to the public, an unusual courtesy for those days. The Duke was reputed to pay £500 even for a copy of a picture.

Walpole's prophecy that sheer extravagance would wipe out the estates was wildly wrong. The Duke's lands prospered under his management. He was a great improver and is credited with planting 1,200 trees annually for more than twenty years, for which alone the sin of pride can be forgiven.

---

* Horace Walpole: *Memoirs (George III)*

Louis Dutens, his chaplain-companion (Chapter Twelve) estimated that in 1774 the Duke received £40,000 in rents and £10,000 from minerals. In 1775 the outgoings were swollen by £7,000 for election expenses. The Duke's table was the least of his extravagances. Butcher, baker, poulterer and fishmonger received no more than £1,200 a year and the candlemaker only £400. The whole expense of his table, including domestics, was £5,000. Upkeep of Syon cost £2,000 a year, Northumberland House £2,000 and Alnwick Castle £3,000. 'He was not generous,' says Dutens, 'but he bestowed his pecuniary favours so judiciously that he at least passed for being so.'*

When the Duke died in 1786 he was laid in the Percy vault in Westminster Abbey, where his Duchess had preceded him ten years earlier. Her funeral had been a calamity. It was one of the last to be held by torchlight and the spectacle always drew large crowds. Many onlookers perched on the screen of St Edmund's Chapel, which collapsed, burying people under three tons of debris. After nearly three hours' delay the service was resumed in the small hours, to shouts of 'Help!' and 'Murder!' from those still trapped.

By long tradition, the Percy family enjoyed the right to burial in Westminster Abbey. The Duke stretched his privilege by burying two natural daughters there along with his other children. They are not listed on the Percy tablet. A natural son, James Smithson, emigrated to America and founded the Smithsonian Institute.

The second Duke enjoyed some repute as a military commander, but his heart was not in the fight against the American colonists. His popularity with the men of the 5th Foot was such that they asked to change the regiment's name to the Northumberland Fusiliers. Though described as cheerful in demeanour he kept up the tradition of high pomp and ancient ways. The Royal Academician Thomas Phillips complained that the Duke never invited him to sit except when he was actually at work on a portrait, but he was not the only duke who found it necessary to keep Academicians

* L. Dutens: *Memoirs of a Traveller*

in their place. When the Duke and his Duchess travelled they set off separately, leaving a few days between departures. This was because their respective suites were so large that no accommodation could be found for both on the road. The second Duchess was said to be humble to her inferiors, very proud to those of equal rank. Her daughters were liable to rebuke if they conversed with guests at table beyond a simple question and answer. The Duchess spoke in such low tones as to be almost inaudible—'another mode of throwing coldness upon table intercourse'.*

Mary Mitford, dining at Alnwick in 1806, was ready to be unimpressed.

> After passing through three massy gates you alight and enter a most magnificent hall, lined with servants who repeat your name to those stationed on the stairs; these again re-echo the sound from one to the other, till you find yourself in a most sumptuous drawing-room of great size, and, as I should imagine, forty feet in height. This is at least formidable; but the sweetness of the Duchess did away every impression but that of admiration.

The Duchess presided over her sixty-four dinner guests in a 'helmet' of diamonds, supposedly worth £11,000, with more diamonds on her bosom, neck, arms and wrists.

Five years later Miss Mitford heard of the near-divine aura surrounding an auspicious birth at Alnwick. The father was a son of the Duke of Atholl and the mother was one of the Percy daughters. 'No bells were rung in the castle for a month. The servants all wore list shoes, and the Duke resigned his accustomed airings for fear of disturbing the young stranger. In short no child (except the King of Rome) ever excited such a ridiculous commotion ...'†

In Alnwick town is a tall column known as the 'Farmers' Folly' erected to the second Duke in 1816 by 'a grateful and united tenantry'. The popular story is that it was a gesture of thanks for a reduction of rents in times of stress; whereupon

* Sir Joseph Farington: *Diary*
† A. G. L'Estrange: *Life of Mary Mitford*

the Duke, surprised that his tenants could afford such a monument, raised their rents again. A less popular explanation is that the column was erected by estate Volunteers who stood ready to repel Bonaparte, in tribute to the Duke's leadership.

On the Northumberland estates there was a strong whiff of feudality lasting into Victorian times. To qualify for a one-room cottage, numbered and inscribed with the Percy emblem, a man had to serve as a 'hind'. He was paid £4 a year and was given keep for a cow, a prescribed amount of fuel and corn and was allowed to grow a few potatoes. In return he agreed to work for the Duke and furnish a woman labourer at one shilling a day during harvest and eightpence a day for the rest of the year. Hence the gangs of women workers to be seen tilling the Northumberland fields. Mostly they were strapping young girls who ate heartily at the hind's expense and did no more domestic work than they could help.* The system prevailed also in the Scottish Lowlands. Under a harsh landlord it could be oppressive to a degree, though in the main it produced no more misery than was to be found in rural areas of the south of England.

* William Howitt: *Rural Life in England*

CHAPLAINS AND TUTORS

12

In 1751 the Rev. Dr Joseph Warton, rector of Winslade, set off on a tour to the south of France with his patron, Charles Paulet, third Duke of Bolton. The circumstances called for exceptional broad-mindedness. Accompanying the Duke was his mistress, Lavinia Fenton, who had dazzled the town as Polly Peachum in *The Beggar's Opera* and by whom the Duke had three sons. On her deathbed in England lay the estranged Duchess, said by Lady Mary Wortley Montagu to have been 'crammed with virtue and good qualities'. The reason for having the learned and agreeable Dr Warton in the ducal party was so that he could marry the Duke and his mistress immediately news was received of the Duchess's death. Preferment in the Church was the prize for the clergyman who might be at hand to conduct this ceremony. Dr Warton may not have been swayed entirely by hopes of promotion; he already owed his rectorship to the Duke and may have felt that one good turn deserved another. Unfortunately the Duchess was a long time dying and Dr Warton, with regrets and apologies, returned to England. Only a month after his defection the Duchess died and the Duke was married by another clergyman at Aix-en-Provence. Dr Warton's career was not wholly blighted, for he became Headmaster at Winchester.

It seems only fair to follow with a story about the Rev.

John Young, a forthright cleric (and brother of Arthur Young, the agriculturist) who had been a frequent guest of the third Duke of Grafton at Euston Hall. One day he arrived unexpectedly in the late afternoon and went to dress for dinner in the room kept for him. When he reached the dining-room he found that the honours were being performed, not by his favourite duchess, but by the Duke's notorious mistress, Nancy Parsons, whom he had already thrust on London society. The Duke, seeing his visitor recoil and extend his arms in astonishment, said, 'Come, Jack, these things are always done in a hurry, without consideration. I had no time to make alterations or to inform you. I will explain later.' The rugged clergyman shook his head, withdrew and rode fifteen miles to spend the night under a more virtuous roof, that of his mother. His act probably lost him a bishopric.*

To serve a ducal master as well as a heavenly master was not easy. It was well understood that the post of tutor to a duke's sons led to a mitre (the radical *Black Books* of the 1820s are replete with examples). If the path to promotion meant accepting employment from rakes and dancing attendance on them, what was a virtuous man to do? Was he to remain a curate all his life and let the less scrupulous pass over his head to rule the Church? The fault lay with a system which made livings the spoils of Lord Chancellors and landowners.

Mere accident, as opposed to assiduous lobbying, could sometimes bring a clergyman promotion. James Butler, second Duke of Ormonde, when Lord Lieutenant of Ireland, was storm-stayed on the Isle of Man on the way to Dublin. There he became friendly with a curate called Joseph, whom he urged to call on him in Ireland. When the curate tried to do so he found the Duke difficult of access. The day came when Swift invited the young man to preach at St Patrick's in the Duke's presence. The text he chose was *Genesis xl 23*: 'Yet did not the chief butler remember Joseph, but forgot him.' At this point the Duke looked up and recognised his

* Arthur Young: *Autobiography*

companion of the storm. Shortly afterwards the curate was
advanced to a good living. When Ormonde went into exile
Joseph is said to have sent half his stipend. 'Unlike most
Irish stories,' comments Sir Charles Petrie, 'this reflects the
highest credit on all concerned.'*

Yet another way to ducal preferment was by way of the
hunting field. When the sporting fourth Duke of Grafton
was thrown by his horse into a ditch, a young curate riding
behind cried, 'Lie still, your Grace!' and leaped over him
to continue the chase. Remounting, the Duke swore to give
the young man the first good living that presented itself—
and later did so.† Had the curate stopped to offer sympathy
he would never have been forgiven. It is, perhaps, an English
story which reflects the highest credit on all concerned.

Once in ducal employ, a churchman had to beware lest
he became as much a part of the establishment as the steward
or the coachman. He would be under pressure to adjust to his
patron's whims. When the Duke of Newcastle (John Holles)
forgot to instruct his private chaplain to say grace at dinner,
and the chaplain reminded him, the reply was, 'If you cannot
take your salary without disturbing the family, leave it.'‡
To a chaplain who offered his views on matters which did
not concern him, the first Duke of Devonshire said, 'Sir,
remember you are to preach on Sunday next.'§ A sermon
which lasted too long, or which showed signs of original
thought, might provoke ducal rebuke on the spot.

The Duke of Northumberland (Hugh Smithson) had in
his entourage a French Huguenot cleric and man of letters,
Louis Dutens, who had been a chaplain and *chargé
d'affaires* at the Court of Turin. It was a curious association.
'The Duke was fond of the arts and sciences,' writes Dutens
in his *Memoirs of a Traveller*. 'I entered into all his tastes,
conversed with him upon every subject, and he found more
variety in my conversation than in that of any other person.'

* Sir Charles Petrie: *The Jacobite Movement*
† Bernard Falk: *The Royal Fitzroys*
‡ A. S. Turberville: *A History of Welbeck Abbey*
§ Joseph Grove: *Lives of Earls and Dukes of Devonshire*

Dutens also generously joined in the Duchess's 'small amusements' in the evenings. 'As I was not displeased with pomp and grandeur I was treated as a favourite in the house. I gave myself up to this family with all the attachment which the most decided fondness could inspire.' Unfortunately he showed little attachment to his Elsdon parishioners, who looked askance at his manners and accent. In 1768 Dutens set off on a tour of Europe as bear-leader to the Duke's son, Lord Algernon. 'We passed four years in the best understanding possible, without his entertaining any idea whatever of his being under my control.' For these services, which included a visit to Voltaire, Dutens was paid £1,000. He had been in hopes of a £1,000-a-year living from the Crown as some acknowledgment of his services at Turin, but the prospect faded when the Duke went into temporary Opposition. Eventually, when Dutens was offered a post at Naples the Duke made a counter-offer of '£500 and his table' to live at Alnwick, to be attached wholly to him and treated everywhere as his best friend. The Frenchman found this inadequate. A woman friend told him that the Duke was noted for 'doing nothing for those he liked, in order to keep them with him'. Now Dutens began to be ashamed of his simplicity. The Duke followed up with an offer of £500 a year for life. 'I was not at all surprised that a man who enjoyed £50,000 a year should sacrifice the hundredth part of it to have a friend always with him; but I could not take upon me to sell my feelings and to set a price upon my friendship.' Declining the offer, he continued to cultivate the Duke's company to the end. He claims that the Duke on his deathbed said to his son, 'I think we ought to do something for Monsieur Dutens.' The son agreed but no more was heard. How indispensable to the Duke was Dutens's company we have no means of knowing; but it seems probable that the chaplain would have been happy to sell his friendship for £1,000 a year.

A notable misfit in the role of ducal chaplain was George Crabbe, whose poems had brought him to public notice. As curate at Aldborough in 1782 he received a letter from

John Maitland, Duke of Lauderdale: he hated 'damned, insipid lies'

Equine homage to a master of dressage: William Cavendish, Duke of Newcastle. From the Duke's book, A General System of Horsemanship

The Duke of Newcastle exercises in front of his castle of Bolsover

James Scott, Duke of Monmouth: he suffered delusions of legitimacy

William Russell, first Duke of Bedford: the dukedom recognised the services of a martyred son

Thomas Pelham-Holles, Duke of Newcastle (right) with the Earl of Lincoln: the corrupter with clean hands

John Churchill, first Duke of Marlborough: 'never rode off any field except as a victor'

Blenheim Palace: 'too big for any British subject to fill'

Charles Lennox, third Duke of Richmond: a reformer ahead of his time

Hugh I.st Duke of Northumberland K.G.

Hugh Smithson, Duke of Northumberland: he rose on the wings of charm, wealth and smallpox

William Douglas, fourth Duke of Queensberry: a milk bath every morning

Richard Grenville, first Duke of Buckingham and Chandos: a Grand Tour by yacht to save money

George Granville Leveson-Gower, first Duke of Sutherland: the landlord who emptied the glens

Worksop Manor, seat of the Dukes of Norfolk in the Dukeries

Alnwick Castle, seat of the Dukes of Northumberland: 'Look around! I myself have measured out all these things'

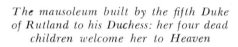

Charles Spencer Churchill, ninth Duke of Marlborough: two rich American wives

The mausoleum built by the fifth Duke of Rutland to his Duchess: her four dead children welcome her to Heaven

Edmund Burke saying that the fourth Duke of Rutland would welcome him as domestic chaplain at Belvoir Castle. This, as Crabbe's son explains, was an unusual offer of patronage, since such posts were usually filled by relations, friends, dependants or college acquaintances. Crabbe accepted the post; but soon, thanks to his own shortcomings, he was experiencing 'the acutest sensations of wounded pride'. The Duchess, a celebrated beauty, never failed to treat him kindly. The Duke, 'cordial, frank and free', would dismiss a splendid party from his gates and ride with the poet to some sequestered spot to talk on literature. Crabbe did not, however, 'catch readily the manners appropriate to his station', a failing which greatly displeased the servants. 'When the conversation was interesting,' says his son, 'he might not always retire as early as prudence might suggest; nor perhaps did he at all times put a bridle on his tongue, for he might feel the riches of his intellect more than poverty of his station.'* The local clergy were expected to show an interest in field sports, but Crabbe's first essay at coursing was his last: he was too upset by the cry of the doomed hare. In between preaching and arguing with the castle guests Crabbe finished *The Village*. In 1784 when the Duke was nominated as Lord Lieutenant of Ireland it was obvious that Crabbe was unfitted for the glittering life at Dublin Castle and he was allowed to stay on at Belvoir, where his first child was born. The servants made life so unpleasant that he took a nearby curacy. Then Lord Thurlow, the Lord Chancellor, invited him to dine and gave him two small livings in the West Country. On the Duke of Rutland's death in 1787 the Duchess asked the Lord Chancellor to exchange Crabbe's two livings in Dorset for two more remunerative ones in the Vale of Belvoir. 'No, by God, I will not do this for any man in England!' exclaimed Thurlow. Nevertheless, he did it for the Duchess, who stood over him until he agreed. Crabbe was on less easy terms with the fifth Duke, who apparently replied coldly when asked for permission to dedicate verses to him. Later the Duke found him a new

* *Life of Rev. George Crabbe, by his Son*

living at Trowbridge. Belvoir was soon to enjoy the distinction of a titled chaplain, the Rev. Sir John Thoroton, who helped to rebuild the castle (Chapter Twenty-four).

The posts of tutor and bear-leader on the Grand Tour attracted lay scholars as well as clerics. In 1763 Adam Smith, the political theorist, resigned his university chair in order to lead that young Etonian, Henry Scott, third Duke of Buccleuch, on a tour of Europe. Not every clergyman would have been happy to sit his susceptible charge at the feet of Hume and Voltaire, as Smith did. For the sacrifice of his academic career Smith received £300 a year plus travelling expenses and the same sum as a life pension. Many years later, when radical ideas were causing discomfort in high places, Sir Walter Scott became exercised by 'the very dangerous qualities which are sometimes found in the instructors placed round our noble youths'. These 'ingenious arguers upon speculative politics' encouraged young men to think it was generous and public-spirited to hold their privileges cheap.*

Temptations were fewer on a Grand Tour of Britain. The Rev. J. H. Michell has left a fascinating account of his travels through England and Scotland in 1795 with the twenty-year-old eleventh Duke of Somerset. It was a journey on which instruction and moral improvement were sedulously combined. At an early stage Michell was giving thanks in his prayers for being enabled 'to enjoy such scenes with such a companion'; but whether the young Duke rendered similar thanks is perhaps doubtful. They went to Birmingham and learned that it took forty men to make a bayonet. They descended mines and were covered with 'unctuous soot'. Michell was convinced that the Duke's introduction to the middle classes would not only inform his mind but raise his esteem in industrial areas. At Bala Michell was especially pleased with the respectful attitude of the inhabitants, who gazed on them 'with all the simplicity of uninformed admiration'. Chester gave the tourists a shudder when they visited the new gaol, 'a magnificent pile of wretchedness' built to

* J. G. Lockhart: *Life of Scott*

reformist plans. In the condemned cell were several prisoners in irons who implored, and received, ducal alms. At Liverpool the shudders were doubled. They went on board a 330-ton slaver and saw the quarters for five hundred slaves. A mate explained that good care was taken of the passengers' health and that it was rare to lose more than thirty on a voyage; on hearing which the young Duke expressed satisfaction. Nevertheless, they 'left the vessel in horror', and would have liked Liverpool better had it not been founded in blood.

Near Moffat, in Scotland, the travellers had an object lesson in ducal irresponsibility when they saw the hillsides denuded of trees by the fourth Duke of Queensberry (Chapter Fifteen). At Dumbarton the Duke walked among crowds of children who 'seemed disappointed in seeing a young man of common appearance, and courteous affability, without any extraordinary mark of distinction or chieftain hauteur.' Inveraray showed them a fine example of what a duke could do for his people. The Duke of Argyll had laid out the town with taste and utility and was finishing a double church, designed for worship in Gaelic and English. The people had been stimulated to catch vast amounts of fish; 'such an inexhaustible source of labour and wealth must enrich the inhabitants, if they are wise enough to adhere to their present frugality.' The two were guests at Inveraray Castle, where the noble ladies entertained them by dancing reels and singing at the organ; unfortunately, some of the party were addicted to cards, 'a sad but necessary resource where some employment is requisite for the vacant mind'. It is possible that the castle was not all that congenial, since Michell expresses the hope that the kindness of its lord to strangers might be rewarded by an increase of his domestic comforts. Several Scots towns made the visitors burgesses, with insignia to wear in their hats. At Aberdeen, the Duke found a regiment drawn up to salute him. The Duke of Atholl took his young guest to shoot the deer, leaving his guardian to comment that 'ferocity and usurpation over the beasts is dignified with the name of manly exercise and superior skill'. Under the

Atholl roof they sat and talked late 'in consequence of the abominable custom of Scotch conviviality, the only objection to their tables'.

Back in England the travellers stayed at Alnwick Castle, in all its new Gothic magnificence. But, sadly reports Michell, 'a young clergyman with a young wife, and four or five children, with many appearances of low circumstances, was an object that soon overpowered my admiration of Alnwick Castle and its princely lord, at whose palace the porters seem to be in a most enviable situation compared with that of my clerical brother.'

It says much for the young Duke that during five months with Michell there were no open clashes of temperament. The lesson of the tour was plain: 'The Duke will perceive from his own experience that the personal virtues of a great man may by the introduction of industry among his dependants be of infinite service to society and that he will assuredly consult his own interest and comfort by contributing to those of his inferiors.'*

In later life the Duke became keenly interested in science and mathematics and published two learned works: *The Elementary Properties of the Ellipse Deduced from the Properties of the Circle* and *Alternate Circles and Their Connection with the Ellipse*. He incurred some criticism by changing his family name from Seymour to St Maur, a foreign affectation tending to obscure the historical link with the mother of King Edward VI. It showed an inconsistency in a man who had given all his daughters the name of Jane. His Duchess seems to have been unusually economical. When the Duke invited the new minister of Berry Pomeroy to dine, the table was bare save for a leg of mutton at one end and a dish of potatoes at the other. Perhaps they were testing their guest's humility.†

One ducal tutor achieved a most unusual reward for good service. William Ogilvie had taught at Buck's School in Dublin for £30 a year and resigned when his employer de-

* J. H. Michell: *The Tour of the Duke of Somerset*
† Sir Joseph Farington: *Diary*

clined to pay him in guineas. Setting up as a private tutor, he was recommended to the first Duke of Leinster, who paid him handsomely to teach his four sons. The Duchess became very fond of him. Shortly after the Duke's death in 1773 she married her tutor and gave him an income of £4,000 a year and a sum of £10,000. There were two sons of the marriage. Ogilvie's conduct was such that he was on good terms with the Duchess's brother, the Duke of Richmond, and with the new Duke of Leinster, her son.*

* *Ibid*

THE CANAL DUKE

13

'The history of Francis Egerton, Duke of Bridgewater, is engraved in intaglio on the face of the country he helped to civilise and enrich,' wrote a proud collateral descendant, Lord Francis Egerton. How truly fortunate, thought Lord Francis, that men 'born to coronets on their cradles and scutcheons on their coffins' could sometimes 'descend from the dignity of doing nothing to the office of thinking and acting for the benefit of their fellow creatures'.*

It was only by melancholy good fortune that the third Duke of Bridgewater inherited his coronet. Born in 1736, he was one of a long string of consumptive children fathered by Scroop, fourth Earl of Bridgewater, a courtier-coalowner who married two daughters of dukes and was given a dukedom himself 'in consideration of his great merits', or in other words for being a Whig. By the death of an older brother Francis succeeded to the dukedom when eleven. Not only was he sickly but his mental capacity was such that there were serious thoughts of passing over him in favour of the next heir. His mother, a daughter of the second Duke of Bedford, took little or no interest in her moribund brood. On Scroop's death she had married Sir Richard Lyttelton, with whom she set out to charm society; Horace Walpole thought them 'the best-humoured people in the world'. The young Duke

* *Quarterly Review*, March 1844

Francis Egerton, third Duke of Bridgewater: his canal cut the price of coal

was abandoned to his own devices, but as Samuel Smiles points out, it was no bad thing to be left alone and 'to profit by the wholesale neglect of special nurses and tutors who are not always the most judicious in their bringing up of delicate children'.* When he became seventeen his guardians, the most conscientious of whom was the fourth Duke of Bedford, sent him on the usual foreign tour, under a scholar of charm and tolerance, Robert Wood. The gauche lad with the unstocked mind seems to have behaved reasonably well. There is a story that he bought a quantity of marbles in Rome and left them sealed in their packing cases all his life. Returning to England with some acquired graces, he plunged into the sporting life, consorting with, among others, the dissolute Earl of March who became the fourth Duke of Queensberry. He bought racehorses and even rode them himself. Such open-air activities may have strengthened his grip on life. After some minor affairs he fell in love with one of the excessively popular Gunning sisters, the dazzling but unendowed daughters of a Roscommon squire. Elizabeth, the younger sister, was already a duchess, having married and buried the rambunctious sixth Duke of Hamilton (they had wed at half-past midnight in Mayfair with a ring of a bed curtain as token). The young Duke of Bridgewater was now personable enough to be accepted by this merry widow. However, on hearing that her elder sister, Lady Coventry, was behaving scandalously, he asked his bride-to-be to refrain from seeing her. With some spirit, the lady refused and the engagement was broken. Having wed one duke and rejected another, she went on to marry the Duke of Argyll and eventually became the mother of four dukes.† After this heavy tumble in the lists of love, the Duke of Bridgewater, at the age of twenty-three, is said to have resolved on bachelorhood. Faced with a similar rebuff, 'a Roman Catholic might have built a monastery, tenanted a cell and died a saint', or so Lord Francis Egerton thought.

* Samuel Smiles: *Lives of the Engineers*
† She was the duchess who refused to light up her house for the Wilkes mob

There is, however, an alternative explanation for the Duke's renunciation of women. According to the *Gentleman's Magazine* (June 1803), which did not vouch for the story, the Duke was visiting a friend who was about to marry and so stirred the interest of the future bride that 'forgetting her own dignity and her sacred engagement to another she made an early sacrifice of her virtue to him'. This distressing experience 'wrought so strongly on his Grace's mind as to have indelibly impressed on it an idea of general infidelity in the sex and to have determined him against ever entering the pales of matrimony'. Either story represents the young Duke as a bit of a prig. Whatever the reason, he gave a grand farewell ball in London and went off to cut canals and live in a coalfield.

Probably the Duke would have turned to canal building even if he had married. On his Grand Tour he had been impressed by the Languedoc Canal which linked the Atlantic with the Mediterranean. The French, as he must have realised, were far ahead of the British in the development of inland navigation, and so were the Dutch. In 1737 his father had secured the passage of an Act to authorise a waterway on his Lancashire estates, though it had not been followed up. His brother-in-law, Earl Gower, of Trentham Park, had also dreamed aloud of linking the Trent and Mersey. The young Duke thus had every reason to be canal-minded. How wide was his industrial vision at the outset we cannot know; probably his chief concern was to stimulate the revenues of his inherited coalfield. The starting point was a conversation at Worsley, in Lancashire, with his talented land steward, John Gilbert, at which the idea was hatched of cutting a canal to convey coals cheaply from the Worsley workings to Manchester.

That dismal town, soon to become more dismal, was suffering severe growth pains. Coal was carried in baskets on horseback over slippery tracks and the cost of it was doubled by the time it reached Manchester. The plan of the first Duke of Bridgewater had been to render the Worsley Brook navigable to the point at which it reached the River

Irwell, but the obstacles were great. His son's proposal was to cut a canal from Worsley Mill and carry it direct to Manchester. Thanks to the support of his powerful Whig relatives, two more enabling Acts—in 1759 and 1760—were pushed through Parliament. The Duke promised that his freight charges would not exceed 2s 6d a ton and that he would sell his coals in Manchester at not more than fourpence per hundredweight, the prevailing price being sevenpence. This scheme was loudly hailed except by the vested interests affected.

It was to be a canal with a water supply largely independent of river or stream, the main source coming from tunnels, or soughs, which drained the ever-wet workings at Worsley. This was Gilbert's idea. The waterway was to dispense with locks and maintain the same level throughout. Where necessary it would be raised on embankments. It was to leap across the River Irwell on an aqueduct 200 yards long and thirty-nine feet high, leaving room for craft to pass beneath without lowering their masts. Carrying water over water was one problem; but in the treacherous Trafford Moss, which engulfed animals, water would have to be laid *on* water, and at various points streams would have to be sealed or diverted to prevent floods. It was the notion of boats sailing over boats which chiefly roused public scepticism, though it would have inspired no doubts in the French. A Parliamentary committee needed persuading that the water in the aqueduct and embankment troughs would not trickle away. They were given a demonstration with water, clay and sand by the knowledgeable James Brindley, now in the Duke's employment.

As a recent biography* of the Duke shows, Brindley has received more credit for planning the Duke's waterways than he merits, though this was no fault of his. Thanks in some measure to Samuel Smiles, Brindley has also been represented as an ill-paid serf, laying the basis of his master's fortune on a wage of 3s 6d a day; but he was paid a respectable, if not excessive, rate for the job and cannot be regarded as one of

* Hugh Malet: *The Canal Duke*

the Great Exploited. He was the sort of rough-hewn original, half-crank, half-genius, about whom legends greedily accumulate. The son of a hard-drinking father, born in the High Peak of Derbyshire, he had set up a millwright's business at Leek. Water fascinated him, whether as a source of power or as a bed for transport. He had already been consulted by Earl Gower on navigation plans. Over the next few years he was to serve the Duke of Bridgewater in many capacities, though never exclusively. He was happiest, perhaps, when conducting what he called an 'ochilor servey or ricconitoring'. He took charge of difficult operations and his rough improvisations saved much time and money. Arthur Young tells how Brindley's use of a local chalky limestone was worth £20,000 to the Duke, a sum which would otherwise have been spent on lime. He was unable to work from plans and could do mathematics only in his head. Faced with a difficult problem he would retire to bed to work it out. Though sub-literate he could expound his ideas clearly to doubting Parliamentarians, even if it meant bringing along a large cheese and modelling it with a knife.

The Worsley Canal was begun in 1759 and the first boatload of coals crossed the Barton Aqueduct over the Irwell two years later. On that day, according to Lord Francis Egerton, the Duke and Brindley had greater reason for pride 'than Agrippa and his architect, when from the last stone of the Pont du Gard they looked down on the savage ravine on which a freak of Roman vanity had chosen to exercise its art pontifical.'* In fact, there had been a nasty moment when the aqueduct was first flooded. Brindley, far from gazing on the scene with pride, had taken to his bed, unable to bear the excitement. It was as well that Gilbert was on hand, for one of the arches was threatened by the weight of water and quick remedial action was necessary. The monopolists who exploited the Irwell navigation would have been happy enough to see the aqueduct disgraced. If they had co-operated with the Duke at the outset its construction

* *Quarterly Review*, March 1844

would have been unnecessary. In Manchester the Duke improved on his pledge: he sold coals at threepence-halfpenny a hundredweight, or half the ruling price, and continued to do so for more than a generation. Soon the unfashionable coalfield was busy with the carriages of the rich, who had come to marvel at the ingenuities to which love unrequited could drive coroneted youth. Others, like Arthur Young, marvelled that at an age when most men thought only of pleasure and dissipation the Duke had chosen to give employment and bread to thousands.

The canal had cost the Duke about a thousand guineas a mile and in its later stages he had been much embarrassed by lack of ready cash. Though a shining industrial achievement, it was not an instant money-spinner. Yet already the Duke, still in his twenties, was grappling with the idea of an artificial waterway linking Manchester with its natural port, Liverpool. The existing route along the Mersey and the Irwell was full of maddening obstacles. What the Duke now proposed was a canal to run from Langford Bridge, near Manchester, to Runcorn, on the Mersey estuary, by-passing the river routes. This time Nature proved a less obstructive opponent than man. The 'Junto of Old Navigators' on the Irwell and Mersey tried to ruin the Duke's project by slashing their rates; the Earl of Derby, detecting a threat to his interests, encouraged his son Lord Strange to rally the Tories against this insolence by a Whig cub; and an 'environmental lobby' of landowners showed that they would fight to the last—or to the last penny of compensation—to prevent their vistas being spoiled by excavations. In Manchester, now reaping the benefit of ducal enterprise, the Duke was forced to pay £40,000 for a modest site on which to build warehouses and docks.

The Duke's financial state was now thoroughly alarming. Many of his estates were subject to legal restraints and could not be offered to moneylenders. The monthly bills were tremendous, the putative profits were far off. Closing down his London establishment, the Duke made a cash arrangement with a friend to provide him with dinner when he was in town. He dispersed his carriages, paid off his servants and settled down to live at Old Worsley Hall, admittedly no slum, on £400 a year, a laughable sum on which to sustain the magnificence expected of a duke. He kept only two horses, one of which was for his groom. From his wealthier friends or wellwishers he received sums against bonds or promissory notes, but many who could have helped did not see why they should subsidise this very singular sowing of wild oats. At one time the Duke was unable to cash a bill for £500 in Liverpool or Manchester. On Saturday nights there was scarcely enough to pay the navvies and the Duke was forced to adopt the traditional subterfuges of a man pursued by creditors. John Gilbert toured the estates borrowing £10 here and £5 there from loyal tenants. At length, in 1765, the Duke rode up to London and persuaded the banking firm of Child to accept his Worsley Canal as security for substantial loans.

Meanwhile, the Duke's manner was losing much of the polish it had briefly acquired. Sitting in public-house parlours with Brindley, arguing over pots of ale and puffing at a churchwarden pipe, he began to speak in a rough Lancashire accent and to use 'thee' and 'thou'. All too often, as Lord Francis Egerton points out, a man of birth and wealth, conscious of his lack of education and shrinking from self-improvement, tended to subside into low company and sensual indulgences. However, the passion that linked the three was of the purest: they had a mighty constructional challenge, they enjoyed overcoming the problems and they were determined to rout the monopolists. At times Brindley picked quarrels with Gilbert, but the Duke had dignity enough to stay clear of the bickering.

After prodigious obstruction, the last stage of the Manchester-Liverpool canal was opened in 1776. It had cost the Duke some £220,000, but the annual profits later in his life were to reach £80,000. Besides shifting manufactured goods to the sea the canal benefited farmers by ferrying their manures free. It also bore passengers and sightseers, who travelled in some style and sometimes found a spruced-up

Duke to welcome them. If he showed visible pride in his enterprises, he was fully entitled to do so, for his contribution to the Industrial Revolution was as big as that of any single individual. He could look with some amusement on the canal craze developing all over Britain, as capitalists lost their timidity.

The Duke did not neglect his responsibilities as a coal-owner and spent huge sums buying up more coal-bearing lands and honeycombing them with tunnels. Visitors marvelled how a mere lad could set in motion a 'gang' of twenty-one boats, each laden with seventeen tons of coal. The Duke's brown-coated, shabby figure was a familiar sight at Worsley. There were no constraints between him and his workmen. There is a story that he complained at the tardiness of drillers in returning to work after their lunch break. When they explained that they could hear the church bell strike twelve for knocking off, but could not hear the single stroke for returning, the Duke arranged for the clock to strike thirteen. The poor had first claim on his coal; their aprons and barrows were always filled before major loadings were undertaken. One of his beneficiaries asked him, not knowing who he was, for help in lifting a load, and received it.

On his excursions into polite society, as at Trentham Park, the Duke talked of little but canals. In later years his figure grew corpulent and clumsy. He was an explosive snuff-taker. In countenance he was said to resemble George III, in shabbiness Dr Johnson. He was not always 'nice to be near'. The usual bachelor eccentricities began to adhere to him. Though he drank a bottle of port a day he was never the worse for it. When travelling he always took his own wine with him. Perhaps because he had spent his best years cutting costs he had a dislike of fripperies. At Old Hall, Worsley, he would tolerate no conservatories or flower beds. Once, returning from London, he found that flowers had been planted against his orders and he whipped off their heads with a cane like any park vandal. This temptation he was able to resist in other people's gardens. In his own homes he would not allow himself to be served by women, though he did not object to them working in his Worsley mines.

The Duke acquired a late, and not wholly uncommercial, interest in art. He paid £43,000 for the Duke of Orleans's collection thrown on the market by the upsets in France. To house his treasures he built an extension to his London home, Bridgewater House. His family encouraged his new-found interest, if only to stop him talking about canals. Dealers found they could extract high prices from him by telling him that Lucien Bonaparte was among the bidders.

The Duke died in 1803 at Bridgewater House and the dukedom died with him. At the end he had been paying £110,000 a year in the new income tax. Most of his vast estate went to the Gowers, who were scarcely in need of it. Unhappily the canals which had been built to smash the monopolists in turn became a monopoly, but the 'd——d tram-roads', as the Duke described the early attempts at railways, stretched their rails over the Lancashire bogs and a new era of transport began.

'CHILDREN OF THE MIST'

14

It is popularly supposed that infidelity was inevitable in arranged marriages to which the bride brought estates and ready money and the bridegroom contributed a title; and that after ensuring the survival of the line husband and wife turned to mistresses and lovers. It happened, of course. As we shall see, ducal roofs were broad enough to shelter any resulting 'children of the mist'. But it did not always happen; and it would be extremely hard to show that marriages founded on romantic love were any more stable than money marriages.

The more raffish elements of society went their own way and saw no need to justify themselves to others. At no time have the laws of God and man weighed oppressively on the *haut ton*. The satirical author of 'Proposals for Amending the Ten Commandments' in the *Gentleman's Magazine* of February 1739 thought the Seventh Commandment 'ought by no means to be extended to people of Figure and Fortune, whose exuberancy of blood and riches may require ... expedients to reduce them to a sober degree of mediocrity and coolness.' Yet in the main people of figure and fortune endeavoured, if only in the interests of their class, not to create public scandal. It was important to avoid such *sottises* as bigamy (which the foolish Duchess of Kingston so conspicuously failed to do). It was also desirable to avoid being written up in the 'Tête-à-Tête' feature of the *Town and Country Magazine,* which flourished between 1769 and 1790; as it was, the Dukes of Grafton, Northumberland, Richmond, St Albans, Bridgewater, Dorset, Devonshire and Hamilton all had their indiscretions retailed in its pages, under titles like 'Palinurus and Arabella' or 'His Caledonian Grace and the Candid Wife'. The magazine in its heyday sold 14,000 copies a month.

The public, then as now, was fascinated by the goings-on of its betters. In the late 1760s mobs worked themselves into riot over the Douglas Case, in which the issue was: could a duke's sister have given birth to twins when over the age of fifty? In an eight-day judgment the Court of Session in Edinburgh decided that Lady Jane Douglas, sister of the first and last Duke of Douglas, did not achieve this prodigy, which meant on the evidence that the purported twins must have been bought or stolen in France. The decision led to wild window smashing in Edinburgh and intimidation of justices. Two years later the House of Lords reversed the judgment and it took troops two days to quell jubilantly vindictive mobs in the Scots capital. Modern jurists tend to the belief that by this judgment the House of Lords made itself look silly. The Douglas Case was to the eighteenth century what the Tichborne Case was to the nineteenth: an example of mass hysteria caused by solicitude for other people's birthrights.

In the life of government it was most desirable that virtue should not be openly flouted. Kings might parade their mistresses, but kings were incorrigible. Not surprisingly it was a duke of royal blood, Augustus Henry Fitzroy, third Duke of Grafton, who chose to squire his mistress in public while holding the office of Prime Minister. (Horace Walpole, referring caustically to the Duke's 'whore', does not seem to have rebuked his father, Sir Robert, for installing a mistress under his roof.) Grafton's 'whore' would have attracted less notice had it not been for the malevolent letter-writer 'Junius'. She was the notorious Nancy Parsons, daughter of a Bond Street tailor, who had taken up with a Jamaica merchant and fled

from him to the arms of many others. When the Duke first
met her in 1763 she was still good-looking, by no means un-
polished and of a ready intelligence. The Duke, who left his
Duchess in 1764, at first tucked away his new love in a cottage
in Epping Forest, later promoting her to a house in Whittles-
bury Forest, of which he was Ranger. He was still in his
thirties, elegantly saturnine, with enough conscience to urge
him towards public service but enough laziness and irresolu-
tion to make him threaten to resign when the going was
rough. Chatham used this Stuart as his Prime Minister from
1767 to 1770. It was in the second year of office that the Duke
sat with Nancy Parsons in the Opera House, in the presence
of the Queen, afterwards escorting her to her carriage. She
also accompanied him to the races and—as we have seen—
played hostess at his seat of Euston Hall.

The anonymous 'Junius' moved in to the kill in 1769.
Listing the Duke's many lapses, he regretted that 'the wildest
spirit of inconsistency should never once have betrayed you
into a wise or honourable action.' London had been left open
for two days to a Wilkes mob 'while the Prime Minister of
Great Britain, in a rural retirement, and in the arms of faded
beauty, had lost all memory of his Sovereign, his country and
himself.' Who was this Duke to censure Wilkes's morals?
'Is not the character of his presumptive ancestors as strongly
marked in him, as if he had descended from them in a direct
legitimate line?' *

Though affecting a high gallantry, 'Junius' kept harping
on Nancy Parsons's decayed appearance. 'For the sake of your
mistress, the lover shall be spared. I will not lead her into
public as you have done, nor will I insult the memory of
departed beauty.' His most lethal passage was this:

There are some hereditary strokes of character by which
a family may be as clearly distinguished as by the blackest
features of the human face. Charles the First lived and died
a hypocrite. Charles the Second was a hypocrite of another
sort and should have died upon the same scaffold. At the

* *Public Advertiser*, 24 April 1769

distance of a century, we see their different characters happily revived and blended in your Grace. Sullen and severe without religion, profligate without gaiety, you may live, like Charles the Second, without being an amiable companion, and, for aught I know, may die as his father did, without the reputation of a martyr.*

This was powerful poison to be disseminated in the public prints, but the Duke decided not to reply to it. He was about to leave Nancy Parsons and re-marry. A purported correspondence between Duke and mistress appeared in the *Gentleman's Magazine* in April 1769. The Duke reminds the lady that he 'connected himself' with her in the belief that her personal and mental qualifications would lighten his domestic troubles. He has no complaints on that score, but has never disguised his feelings that 'such a course of life was unseemly both in my moral and political character and that nothing but the necessity could justify the measure.' Now that he is able to enter into chaster connections their ties must end. He will make such establishment for his mistress as will put her in easy circumstances for life, 'chargeable only with this proviso, that your residence be not in these kingdoms; the rest of Europe lies at your choice; and you have only to send me word on your arrival where you are and the next post shall carry you your first quarterly payment.' He ends by professing great esteem and friendship.

The mistress in her reply finds it hard to believe that on the dissolution of her dear lord's marriage his affections 'could so mechanically abate in an instant to sacrifice the lover to the sordid considerations of interest or public opinion'. She can understand his desire for a change, but why must she go into exile? 'Am I to attribute it to malevolence or ill nature? ... I will call it the lapse of heart, the fault of constitution or any other softer name. Though my pride won't permit me to sue for the recovery of a heart ... yet, my Lord, suffer me this poor consolation to live in the same kingdom

* 30 May 1769

as you. Give me some time to mitigate a passion you first inspired me with; and though I find I must bid adieu to the transports of love, let me hope for the calmer delights of friendship ... May every hour of your life be brightened by prosperity; and may the happiness of your domestic character ever keep pace with your public one, prays the unfortunate ———.'

No names appear on the correspondence as published, but it is indexed under 'Grafton, Duke of'. Many of its phrases look like the work of the model letter-writers of the day and it could have appeared as 'A Nobleman Dismisses His Mistress' and 'The Mistress Replies to the Nobleman'. If the second letter is Nancy Parsons's own work, it shows marked clemency and sensibility.

The 'chaster connection' referred to was the Duke's remarriage in 1769 to the plain but amiable twenty-four-year-old Elizabeth Wrottesley, niece of the Duke of Bedford, who was to bear him twelve children. His long-suffering ex-Duchess in the meanwhile had eloped with the second Earl of Upper Ossory, nephew of the Duke of Bedford, whom she married as soon as the law permitted. 'Junius' saw nothing chaste in these arrangements. 'Is there not a singular mark of shame set upon this man, who has so little delicacy and feeling as to submit to the opprobrium of marrying a near relative of one who had debauched his wife? In the name of decency, how are these amiable cousins to meet at their uncle's table?'*

The laxness of the Duke's morals did not prevent Cambridge University from electing him Chancellor in 1768, nor did it discourage Thomas Gray from composing an ode which referred to the Chancellor's 'inborn royalty of mind', attributed to him 'a Tudor's fire, a Beaufort's grace' and contained the lines:

> Thy liberal heart, thy judging eye,
> The flower unheeded shall descry ...

* *Public Advertiser*, 12 June 1769

which was not thought to be a reference to Nancy Parsons.

In later years the Duke could be heard lamenting in the House of Lords the dissipation of the age. He turned theologian and wrote *The Serious Reflections of a Rational Christian* (1797), directing that copies should be given to all his children. This work expresses regret that he wasted his best days 'in the pursuit of every senseless dissipation of the times or in an indulgence in the fashionable vices'. He refuses to blame his ill behaviour on inborn or inherited wickedness. The Duke had taken to worshipping in a Unitarian chapel off the Strand. His renouncing of senseless dissipation did not apply to the turf, for his horses won the Derby three times after his *Rational Thoughts* were published. In piety and good fortune on the racecourse he had no rival until the first Duke of Westminster.

How long did Nancy Parsons take to mitigate her passion for the Duke? Not long, it seems. She was already in correspondence with a younger duke, John Sackville, third Duke of Dorset. Horace Walpole says that Grafton's spies intercepted her letters to her new lover, who 'had made impressions that seldom disturb the reason of professed courtesans'. The twenty-four-year-old Duke of Dorset, who succeeded in 1769, was handsome, well-built and wore 'an air of sentimental melancholy' which fascinated women. With Nancy Parsons he set off on a wild parody of a Grand Tour accompanied by singers, actors and buffoons. At a ball in Venice he seems to have been in peril of losing her to a noble Venetian, who was willing to remove her by force.* But Nancy was not to wear a Duchess's coronet. The Duke dropped her (this time there was no published correspondence) and moved on to break a succession of hearts and households. Nancy finally married the second Viscount Maynard, in 1776; but in the years 1784-86 she was to be found as a species of *châtelaine* at Woburn Abbey, looking after the young fifth Duke of Bedford, an arrangement unopposed by her husband.

* Victoria Sackville-West: *Knole and the Sackvilles*

The Duke of Dorset became notorious, less for his association with Nancy Parsons, than with the dancer Giannetta
Baccelli, whom he brought back from Paris, and whose
recumbent white nude statue intrigues visitors to Knole. In
Paris, where the Duke served as ambassador from 1783 until
the Revolution, she caused scandal by dancing at the Opera
with her protector's Garter wound round her forehead. At a
ball in Sevenoaks she caused further scandal by wearing the
Dorset family jewels. Her installation in a tower at Knole,
attended by a Chinese page, did not appeal to the servants;
there might be 365 rooms in that ancient house, but there
was no room for the master's trollop. She bore the Duke
several children, all but one of whom died in infancy. Sir
Joseph Farington's *Diary* in 1797 refers to a Mr Sackville,
the Duke's son by Baccelli, who while an ensign in the Army
had married the daughter of a pastry-cook. The Duke urged
him to seek promotion in the West Indies, where he died
from yellow fever.

In 1789 the Duke broke with his dancer and soon afterwards married the good-natured Arabella Cope, daughter of
an Oxfordshire baronet, who brought him £140,000. This
should have ensured a contented late middle age, with leisure
for the Duke's favourite pastime of cricket (he helped to
draw up the rules for the Marylebone Cricket Club); but his
temperament, possibly as a result of earlier excesses, was fast
degenerating. Georgiana, Duchess of Devonshire, who had
once pronounced him 'the most dangerous of men', would
have found him the most tedious. He grew both tetchy and
stingy, troublesome at cards and tiresome at table. He could
not bear to hear praise of other noblemen's seats and would
maintain that Knole possessed everything. According to
Farington, he still employed many artists, one of whom, an
Academician called Humphrey, occupied a room without
the Duchess's permission and tried to sell her copies of portraits she denied having commissioned. In his last years the
Duke had little to say to his family or anybody else and could
be solaced only by two musicians playing in an adjoining
room. His widow, who later married an earl, tried to retain

her duchess's rights of precedence, but was rebuffed by the Prince Regent.*

The 'children of the mist', or natural children, found under aristocratic roofs often enjoyed the affection not only of the nobleman who had sired them but of his wife, whose attitude could be summed up as: 'let by-blows be bygones'. In 1796 Farington, a close student of the habits of dukes, wrote: 'Nollekens showed me his bust of Miss Le Clerc, natural daughter of the Duke of Richmond. She is about twenty years old, is tall and handsome. She lives at the Duke's and the Duchess is very fond of her. She has been introduced at Court. The Duke comes with her sometimes to Nollekens and seems very fond of her.' This was the third Duke of Richmond, who fought prematurely for Parliamentary Reform. His Duchess was praised by Horace Walpole for her 'sweet temper and unalterable good nature'. According to the *Annual Register* (1807), the Duke had three natural children by his housekeeper and settled £50,000 on each of them, with another £50,000 to the housekeeper for her trouble; but such sums seem improbably high.

At Devonshire House and at Chatsworth the natural children of William Cavendish, fifth Duke of Devonshire, enjoyed the same privileges as his legitimate brood. The precise nature of the goings-on under these all-sheltering roofs has provoked endless and anxious speculation. The lethargic Duke was married to the dazzling, exasperating Georgiana, beside whom he made a sorry appearance. Yet even Georgiana could make a sorry appearance. Two years after they were married Fanny Burney saw her in the park, on the Duke's arm, with her curls tumbling, her jacket trimming unstitched, her cap awry, her cloak dusty and half off. 'I think her very handsome and she has a look of innocence and artlessness that made me quite sorry she could be so foolishly negligent of her person,' writes Miss Burney. The Duke was 'ugly, tidy and grave ... like a very mean shopkeeper's journeyman'.

* The widow of the third Duke of Leeds, who also married an earl, tried to walk as a duchess at the Coronation of George III. She too was rebuffed

Behind this unalluring pair stalked a servant in superb livery.*

Anecdotes about the Duke abound. He was said to have cut a clown-like figure as he slouched up to his Sovereign to receive the Garter. Seeking for words to describe the New Inn at Skipton, the Hon. John Byng described it as 'a gawky, dismal, ill-contrived thing, built by, and resembling, the Duke of Devonshire'.† The Duke's gaucheness and bored indifference are well exemplified in Fanny Burney's story of how, at a private reception, he lolled back against a very fine glass lustre. When it fell and shattered, he looked coolly at the wreckage and remarked, 'I wonder how I did that'; then, quickly forgetting what he had done, he leaned against the twin lustre and broke that too. With a 'philosophical dryness', he exclaimed, 'This is singular enough', and moved elsewhere without apology.‡ It is said that when woken in the night at Chatsworth to be told there was a fire, he expressed the hope that they would put it out and went back to sleep. Taciturnity was a Cavendish trait. On the way to Yorkshire the Duke and his brother stayed in a three-bedded room at an inn. Before entering their respective four-posters, each brother had sufficient curiosity to peep through the curtains of the third bed. Next day in the coach one said to the other, 'Did you see what was in that bed last night?' The answer was a nod and a 'Yes'. What they had seen was a corpse.

Before he married Georgiana in 1774 the Duke had fathered a daughter on a milliner, thus achieving a belated notice in the *Town and Country Magazine* in 1777. Georgiana, herself a great patron of milliners, found a governess for the child, Charlotte, in her close friend, the daughter of the eccentric Earl-Bishop of Derry, Lady Elizabeth Foster, whose marriage had collapsed. She was one of the wicked Herveys. Like Georgiana, she was talented and beautiful; Gibbon, who proposed to her, said, 'If she chose to beckon the Lord

---

* A. R. Ellis (ed.): *Early Letters of Fanny Burney*
† John Byng: *The Torrington Diaries*
‡ Austin Dobson (ed.): *Diary and Letters of Madame d'Arblay*

Chancellor from the Woolsack in full sight of the world, he could not resist obedience.' The Duke needed no beckoning. His relations with Georgiana, who had produced him no child and was squandering his rents at the tables, were strained. There is some evidence that she refused him marital rights, out of loyalty to an earlier lover whom she would have married, had her mother allowed her;* but other accounts say she was perfectly happy to become mistress of Chatsworth. Whatever the reason, the Duke turned gratefully to his wife's best friend, by whom he had a girl in 1785 and a boy in 1788. They were born abroad, given cover names and brought up in Devonshire House. Georgiana had daughters in 1783 and 1785. The parties to these *liaisons dangereuses* remained on the best of terms, even when the Duke was breeding from both women. If, just conceivably, Georgiana was unaware of her friend's infidelity, it is clear that her long-suffering mother, Lady Spencer, knew what was going on; she saw things she wished she had not seen at Chatsworth and did her best to avoid Lady Elizabeth. Georgiana's letters to Elizabeth are full of expressions like 'My dearest, dearest, dearest Bess, my lovely friend' and 'Oh, love, love, love me for ever', which seem to thrust at the permissible bounds of gush.† Why did Georgiana start having children by the Duke? One explanation, not wholly without support, is that the Duke paid her gambling debts only on the understanding that she performed her duties as wife and duchess, and that the birth in 1790 of an heir, the Marquess of Hartington, cost him £150,000.‡ There was a nasty shock for the Duke when, in 1791, he found his wife pregnant by the young Charles Grey, the future Prime Minister. Georgiana was banished to Italy, where Elizabeth went to join her. After two years Georgiana was forgiven by the Duke, but the child did not qualify to be brought up in Devonshire House and was handed over to

* Hugh Stokes: *The Devonshire House Circle* (1917)
† Earl of Bessborough (ed.): *Georgiana; Extracts from Correspondence* (1955)
‡ Hugh Stokes: *The Devonshire House Circle*

Grey's parents.* The triangular relationship continued until Georgiana died in 1806. Three years later the Duke married Lady Elizabeth, who was eager enough to be his Duchess.

'Was Georgiana a dupe, was she indifferent, or was she a consummate hypocrite?' asks Violet Markham, author of a book about the sixth Duke of Devonshire. She concludes: 'It is more credible that she was the victim of an astonishing innocence.'† Much has come to light since that was written and it now needs an equally astonishing innocence to believe in that innocence. In 1972 the unexpurgated Fanny Burney *Diaries* were published.‡ It appears that in August 1791 Miss Burney met the Duchess, her mother and Lady Elizabeth at Bath. With them was a 'little French girl', called Caroline, mincing and affected. 'To the tales told about her, *scandal* is nothing—INFAMY enwraps them,' exclaims Miss Burney. She has heard that the Duke is Caroline's father, but tries hard not to believe all the 'terrible stories' circulating at Bath. She is cold towards Lady Elizabeth and almost convinces herself that the Duchess secretly resents her rival. Drily, Joyce Hemlow, who edits the diaries, comments: 'Fanny Burney would have been surprised to know that at this time the Duchess was carrying Charles Grey's child.' Miss Burney passes on a conjecture that the Duchess was forced by the Duke to consent to 'this unnatural inmating of her House' as a punishment for her extravagances, under threat of separation.

Throughout her life the 'artless' Georgiana kept rackety, dissolute company. She was an intimate of the worldly Prince of Wales (George IV) and of Charles James Fox, in whose election campaign of 1784 she lavished kisses on voters. She gambled at every table, not least at Spa, which until the Revolution had an infamous reputation. Her lust for distraction and her feather-headedness—well expressed by the tall ostrich plumes she made popular—drew continual mockery in print. Financially, she was incorrigibly devious and treated

* Francis Bickley (ed.): *The Diaries of Lord Glenbervie*
† Violet Markham: *Paxton and the Bachelor Duke* (1935)
‡ Joyce Hemlow: *The Journals and Letters of Fanny Burney*

the loyal banker, Thomas Coutts, badly. At this distance, and on her record, it is hard to see what was so entrancing about her; yet contemporary writers insist on her omnipotent charm and we are told that at news of her death crowds stood stricken. Her servants were no less prostrated. One who had cause to be grateful to her was the young footman who made off with the family jewels in 1778. Not wishing to incur the odium of having a footman hanged, Georgiana persuaded the Duke to intercede and the indictment was so framed as to allow the culprit to be transported.*

After the Duke died in 1811 his second Duchess tried to have her son, Augustus Clifford, recognised as legitimate, only to meet predictable opposition from the Cavendishes. Clifford and the young sixth Duke had gone to Harrow together and they remained friendly all their lives. Clifford became Admiral Sir Augustus Clifford and, at the Duke's instance, was appointed Usher of the Black Rod. Both of them doubtless knew of the popular legend that the sixth Duke was in fact the son of Elizabeth, who had exchanged her babe for a daughter of Georgiana's born at roughly the same time.

At Blenheim the sight of a natural child at the dinner table aroused a perilous ferment in the breast of that rising young politician, Lord Ashley, the future seventh Earl of Shaftesbury. He was related to the Marlboroughs and had been found a Parliamentary seat at Woodstock. In 1828 he wrote: 'I dined with the Duke of Marlborough. Never did I feel so touched as by the sight of his daughter, Susan—his natural daughter. She is Charlotte, our dear Charlotte, over again, in voice, in manner, in complexion, in feature, in countenance. I could hardly refrain from calling her *Sister*. O Great God, have compassion upon her forlorn state! What will become of this poor girl? What danger is she beset with? May *I* have the means of doing her some real lasting service? Father of mercies, grant Thy protection and keep her from the awful perils that are on every side.'

Edwin Hodder, who quotes this passage in his biography of Shaftesbury, does not say what happened to Susan, or what

* Earl of Bessborough: *Georgiana: Extracts from Correspondence*

were the awful perils that threatened her. In the view of A. L. Rowse, the best service 'this young prig' could have done would have been to marry the girl.* Instead he married the legitimate daughter of an earl.

Shaftesbury's fellow Member of Parliament for Woodstock, the Marquess of Blandford, later sixth Duke of Marlborough, had a guilty secret which was not to be revealed for another ten years, when it came out in court. According to his own evidence, early in 1817, when he was still Earl of Sunderland, he became friendly with Susannah Law, the daughter of a Dublin provision merchant, and they cohabited in London as Captain and Mrs Lawson. He insisted that he did not represent her as his wife, or as Lady Sunderland or Lady Blandford, or allow her to be so described. On a visit to Scotland he travelled in one carriage with a valet, and she in another with her baby and servant. She was never received in society and their association ceased when he decided to marry, which he did in 1819.

The lady's story was that Lord Blandford had expressed the most ardent affection for her. For family reasons, he explained, their wedding would have to be private. Fortunately he had a brother who was a clergyman and willing to conduct the ceremony. Susannah, then sixteen, consented to this plan, and the service was held in her parents' house in London. After they had lived together she discovered that the 'clergyman' had been an Army officer, a friend of her husband. When she protested the Marquess admitted deceit and consented to take her to Scotland where, by publicly acknowledging her as his wife, she would become so legally. Back in London she learned that he was to marry a daughter of the Earl of Breadalbane. His allowance to her of £400 a year had later been halved by the Duchess of Marlborough.

All this was revealed in the Queen's Bench in 1838 after a scandalous organ, *The Satirist*, having learned about the Scottish escapade, alleged that the Blandfords' marriage was bigamous and the heir therefore illegitimate. Counsel

* A. L. Rowse: *The Later Churchills*

addressed themselves to such questions as: if Susannah was deceived by the marriage, was it likely that her parents were? Lord Denman thought there was a 'strong imputation' against the Marquess; however, some of Susannah's statements invited suspicion and he could find no evidence of a real marriage.* The case, involving as it did the validity of titles and the destiny of a great birthright, was just the sort of thing the Victorians loved.

Duchesses sinned from time to time, as did Georgiana with Charles Grey, but the skilful ones were able to cover up. One of them was the Duchess of Gordon, wife of the fourth Duke. Like Georgiana she was ready to distribute kisses indiscriminately in a good cause, which in her case was that of raising recruits to the Gordon Highlanders by proffering the King's shilling between her lips. This redoubtable beldam, at one time a popular Tory hostess, succeeded in marrying three of her four daughters to dukes (Richmond, Manchester and Bedford) and a fourth to a marquess. According to Augustus Hare, who got the story from a member of the Cleveland family, one of the girls had been intended as a bride for Lord Brome, but his father, Lord Cornwallis, objected on medical grounds. The Duchess sent for the father and said to him with impressive candour: 'I understand that you object to my daughter marrying your son on account of the insanity in the Gordon family. Now I can solemnly assure you there is not a single drop of Gordon blood in her veins.'† The wayward Duchess eventually broke with her family, led a wandering life and died in Pulteney's Hotel, in London, where her lying-in-state for all to see caused the final scandal of her life.

Eight years later her Duke married a village woman, Jane Christie, by whom he already had several children. She declined to establish herself at Gordon Castle, saying his friends would cease to call on him. This Duke held the dukedom for seventy-five years and was the builder of Gordon Castle. Though something of a feudal lord, he is noted as the author

* *Annual Register* 1838; *The Times*, 10 and 23 November 1838
† Augustus Hare: *The Story of My Life*

of a popular song 'There's cauld kail in Aberdeen'. The first
verse runs:

> There's cauld kail in Aberdeen
> An' custocks in Strabogie,
> Whaur ilka lad maun hae his lass,
> But I maun hae my cogie.
> For I maun hae my cogie, sirs,
> I canna want my cogie,
> I wadna gie my three-girr'd coq
> For all the wives of Bogie.*

The message of the song appears to be that whatever is consumed from a cogie is of more account than a woman.

By the rules of the times, it was socially acceptable for an
elderly nobleman to marry a young woman for her money.
Although he was appropriating her birthright, he was giving
her a title and her children would be born to high estate. It
ceased to be universally acceptable, however, if a young man
took as bride a rich woman well beyond the age of child-
bearing; which is what happened in 1827 when twenty-six-
year-old William Aubrey de Vere Beauclerk, ninth Duke of
St Albans and a descendant of Nell Gwynn, married the
fifty-year-old widow of Thomas Coutts, the banker, possibly
the richest man of his day.

   The incivilities which greeted this romance were heightened by the fact that 'Ma Coutts' had been an actress since
infancy. She was born Harriot Mellon, her mother being an
Irish strolling player turned milliner and her father a
lieutenant in the Madras Light Infantry. At a very early age
Harriot played child parts in Shakespeare. Though not in
the first flight of actresses she was thought to fit Byron's
words:

> Being rather large, and languishing, and lazy,
> Yet of a beauty that would drive you crazy.

Her first stroke of fortune was supposedly to win £10,000 in

* Custock: a cabbage stock. Cogie: a bowl. Girr: a hoop

a public lottery, but the worldly said the money came from Thomas Coutts, who cherished her company. It certainly did not come from the Duke of York, who also admired her. Coutts's first wife had been his brother's nursery maid, an alliance which upset his relatives. After her death he pleased them no better by marrying Harriot Mellon. When he died in 1822 he left her all his wealth, including 'personal property within the province of Canterbury ... sworn under £600,000'. Harriot was now regarded as a 'universal Croesus'. Writers looked to her for patronage; that is, they pressed her to buy up the scurrilities they hastily put together, purporting to be accounts of her life. Harriot refused and the scurrilities were published under titles like *The Memoirs of Miss Harriot Pumpkin*. She was a cheerful, friendly and kind-hearted woman who liked to give lavish hospitality, but many who accepted it went only to sneer.

Lockhart in his *Life of Scott* describes a visit to Abbotsford by the Duke and Mrs Coutts in 1825. The lady was making a 'progress' through Scotland in seven coaches, but considerately used only three four-horse carriages when calling on the Scotts. They contained, besides the Duke and his sister, a *dame de compagnie*, two physicians (in case one was incapacitated), various menials and two bedchamber women (one to perform the toilette, the other to watch by night and ward off ghosts). Lady Scott was in a flutter at this invasion, especially as she already had several guests of high rank. Scott had accepted Mrs Coutts's hospitality in London and was anxious that she should be well received; but the remarkable entourage plainly amused some of his guests, and they showed it. After dinner Scott cut the gentlemen's session short, took aside the youngest, cleverest and gayest of the ladies, a marchioness, and read her a curtain lecture on behaviour. He reminded her that they had all been told days before that he had accepted Mrs Coutts's visit and could have left if they had wished. To this the beautiful marchioness said: 'Thank you, Sir Walter—you have done me the great honour to speak as if I had been your daughter, and depend upon it you shall be obeyed with heart and goodwill.' One by one

the ladies engaged in amiable conversation with Mrs Coutts
and the marchioness sang a song in her honour. Soon the
victim of the 'evil eye' was rattling away with comical anecdotes of the stage and joining in the chorus of 'The Laird of
Cockpen'. Lockhart acquits Scott of deferring unduly to
wealth; he was kind to Mrs Coutts because, like Pope's
Timon, she helped to clothe the poor and feed the hungry,
and he would have protected her even if she had arrived in
the role of comic actress. Such vast wealth, he thought, could
hardly be enjoyed without a measure of ostentation.

At Abbotsford the Duke's suit 'throve but coldly'. Mrs
Coutts told Scott she had refused him twice—'he was merely
on the footing of friendship'. Scott was not against the match.
'If the Duke marries her,' he said, 'he ensures an immense
fortune; if she marries him, she has the first rank. If he marries a woman older than himself by twenty years, she marries
a man younger in wit by twenty degrees. I do not think he
will dilapidate her fortune—he seems good and gentle; I do
not think she will abuse his softness of disposition—shall I
say, or of head? The disparity of age concerns no one but
themselves; so they have my consent to marry, if they can get
each other's.'

The good and gentle Duke was Hereditary Grand Falconer
and as such had no thought of abandoning his prey, if prey
she was (he was by no means penniless). The marriage took
place in the bride's home in Stratton Street, Piccadilly. 'She
gives him £30,000 as an outfit! The rest to depend on his
good behaviour,' exclaimed the envious Creevey.* Prince
Pückler-Muskau was at the reception at the Duchess's Highgate villa, where garlands of fresh flowers strewn on the
bushes produced 'an indescribably rich effect'. The Prince
wrote: 'Perhaps there never was a woman who had the art
of appearing more innocent and child-like; and certainly
this captivating sort of coquetry is the greatest charm, though
not perhaps the greatest merit, of women.'† That was one of
the kindest comments on the alliance. Almost instantly, says

* Sir H. Maxwell: *The Creevey Papers*
† Prince Pückler-Muskau: *A Regency Visitor*

the *Gentleman's Magazine* (October 1837), 'the sluices of slander were opened upon her ... No woman in any age or country was ever assailed with half so much acrimony. She wisely bore it in silence, and malignity, having nothing left to feed it, exhausted itself.'

According to the same source, the union was a very happy one and the Duchess was well received by the most exalted of the nobility. Yet Creevey noted in 1830 that Queen Adelaide would not let 'old mother St Albans' attend a ball at the Brighton Pavilion, though more than eight hundred others were invited.

Tattlers said the Duchess bought a house at Brighton in order to eat prawns facing the sea; used bank notes for curling papers; and admitted a cow with gilded horns into her dining-room to give fresh milk for syllabubs. Despite a sumptuous way of life her income exceeded her expenditure by £40,000 a year; and on her death, in 1837, she had nearly doubled her first husband's capital. Throughout she retained personal command of her wealth. Most of it was left to Angela Burdett, grand-daughter of Thomas Coutts, better known in later life as the Baroness Burdett-Coutts. A sum of £10,000 a year went to the Duke along with her two houses. When 'the most noble Harriot' was buried at Redbourne Hall, the Lincolnshire seat of the Beauclerks, there was a big turnout of tenants to honour her. The Duke married again, had two children and died aged forty-eight when hunting.

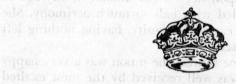

TWO VOLUPTUARIES

15

During the years of the Regency died two ducal voluptuaries, two old reprobates linked by sensuality, love of the turf, contempt of public opinion and a general air of 'You be damned'. Both grossly insulted George III, both were cronies of the Prince Regent. They were Charles Howard, eleventh Duke of Norfolk ('the dirty Duke') and William Douglas, fourth Duke of Queensberry ('degenerate Douglas').

The Duke of Norfolk has achieved peculiar fame by his practice of paying the mothers of all his numerous bastards on the same day at the same time at the same bank. One authority has it that the variety of the Duke's tastes was attested by 'blue eyes, Jewish noses, gipsy skins and woolly black hair ... grafted on to the unmistakable Howard features of the infants'.* Some of his offspring were still babes in arms, others were sturdy children wheeling up their mothers to collect the Duke's dole. In Henry Angelo's account of the ducal pay-day, which was a quarterly occasion, 'the great and illustrious Whig' sat in a back parlour from which he could 'peep at his old acquaintances'. As each woman applied for the wages of shame, a clerk would bring him a cheque for verification. At his elbow was a 'confidential person' to whom he would exclaim, 'What a dowdy!' or 'What an old hag!' or, occasionally, 'I'faith, she looks as young as twenty years

* Sir Osbert Sitwell and Margaret Barton: *Brighton*

ago.' If sufficiently moved by compunction or caprice, he would call in one of the mothers and urge her to live a respectable life.*

The whiskery, barrel-bellied Duke was a dirty old man in the most literal sense. When he complained of rheumatism, a sympathiser said, 'Pray, my Lord Duke, did you ever try a clean shirt?' His dislike of soap and water was such that his servants waited until he was dead drunk before washing him. On the imminent onset of unconsciousness the Duke would cause a bell to be rung three times, at which signal four footmen skilfully loaded him on to a litter made of strong belts and bore him away, like a trophy of the chase, swinging slightly. The whole thing was performed with practised skill and in silence. It was an age in which refinement was still at war with coarseness. In 1784 François de la Rochefoucauld complained to the Duke of Grafton of the English habit of providing chamber-pots on the sideboard so that gentlemen could relieve themselves while the rest were drinking (judges also used chamber-pots on the Bench). In such society the Duke of Norfolk was no misfit.

Roman Catholic tutors have been blamed, perhaps unfairly, for many of the Duke's shortcomings. According to a censorious obituarist in the *Gentleman's Magazine* (January 1816) his talents 'were not softened or liberalised by early education or the native and inestimable gift of tender or moral feeling'. The Duke renounced his Roman Catholicism in the year of the Gordon Riots. Politically he was a Whig with a leaning towards Republicanism and he opposed the American War. He had no fear of Jacobins under the bed. In some ways the wearer of the oldest ducal coronet was more radical than the third Duke of Richmond. He loved the rowdiness of electioneering, which brought out his down-to-earth eloquence; and the public rallied to an old world anti-beau who so plainly cared not a fig for Court or Cabinet. At a political dinner at the Crown and Anchor Tavern, off the Strand, in 1798, in the presence of two thousand people, the Duke proposed an oddly worded but clearly inflammatory

* Henry Angelo: *Reminiscences*

toast: 'Our Sovereign's health—the Majesty of the People!'
George III swiftly deprived him of his West Riding lord
lieutenancy and the colonelcy of his militia.

The Duke's seat was Arundel Castle, Sussex, from which
every year he drove to the Pavilion at Brighton to dine two
nights running with the Prince of Wales. In 1804 the Prince
became seriously ill after drinking bottle for bottle with 'the
Jockey', as the Duke was called, so the following year Mrs
Fitzherbert, the Prince's mistress, suggested a ruse. After the
first corks had popped 'important' letters were brought to
the Prince, who withdrew to answer them, leaving his guests
drinking with the Duke of Clarence (William IV). When the
stratagem was repeated the next day Norfolk took offence.
'Stay after everyone is gone tonight,' said the Prince to the
ubiquitous Thomas Creevey. 'The Jockey's got sulky and I
must give him a broiled bone to get him in good humour
again.' All four sat down to 'broiled bones', after which Norfolk and Creevey fell asleep. When Creevey was roused by
the Duke's snoring, the two kings-to-be were discussing a
wig worn by George II.* On another occasion the Duke,
having drunk deeply at the Pavilion, called for his carriage
to go back to Arundel. The royal dukes pressed him in vain
to stay. As he fell asleep in his carriage the coachman was
persuaded to drive him round and round the lawns. When
he woke next day he was in bed at the Pavilion—very angry,
and very probably clean.

The Duke moved freely in high, middle and low society.
He loved to gormandise by himself in chop-houses, where
people were entranced by the spectacle of an old-fashioned
duke eating his way through a rump of beef. Charles Marsh
watched him in action at the Beefsteak Club. 'Eyes, hands
and mouth were all intensely exercised; not a faculty played
the deserter.' After devouring two or three steaks he would
rub a clean plate with a shallot and then pause for about ten
minutes, nursing his expectations even as he regathered his
forces; then he would tackle the next portion of the rump.†

* Sir H. Maxwell: *The Creevey Papers*
† Charles Marsh: *The Clubs of London*

He was often seen at cock-fights, garbed in such a way that he was once greeted with, 'Come, my honest butcher, I'll take your bet!' In the theatre an attempt was made to have him ejected from the stalls by someone who thought he was a servant keeping a seat for someone else. The Duke could also be found in Holland's caricature shop, buying up the scurrilities of the day; but, says Angelo, he took offence at seeing a caricature of himself being 'drummed out of the regiment' and with a 'So, Mr Holland' left the shop never to return. His extraordinary bulk was a gift to caricaturists. Gillray showed him casting the shadow of Silenus.

Yet the Duke was conscious enough of being a duke to live in the grand manner when the occasion required it. He went to great expense to make Arundel a worthier seat (he also had houses in Cumberland, Yorkshire, Nottinghamshire and Hertfordshire). At Arundel the main London road ran under the ramparts, and privacy was further impaired by the presence of a bowling-green and houses. The Duke bought up extra land, eliminated the coach road and built another at his own expense. He then enclosed 11,000 acres and into this New Park introduced one thousand head of deer. In his refurbished castle the Duke gave entertainments in which the exuberance of old English hospitality was 'chastened and refined by the graces of modern elegance'. Such refinement owed nothing to his Duchess, who lived in seclusion at Scuda-more House, Hertfordshire, 'in consequence of occasional mental derangement'. Robert Smirke, the architect, visiting Arundel in 1811, reported that the Duke's habit at dinner was to drink three or four glasses of wine and fall asleep; then, occasionally waking, he would take another glass and pass the bottle. This went on from six until ten. The conversation, such as it was, was about families and property.*

That crusty obituarist in the *Gentleman's Magazine* ('no severity shall mark this article') harped on the degree to which the Duke's mind was 'engrossed by the phantom of the exclusive greatness of the Howards ... he had a lively and

* Sir Joseph Farington: *Diary*

never-sleeping jealousy of other families; he watched their pretensions with a severe and prejudiced solicitude ...' Pride in the Howards even impelled him to try to trace the family links of an 'unhappy madman' of that name who often beset his door. The tone of this obituary stung a reader to say that accusations of family intolerance were ill-founded; the Duke, as Earl Marshal, deserved credit for opposing silly claims to dormant peerages. That the Duke was proud of his Howard blood is not disputed. The *Complete Peerage* says he wanted to hold a grand tercentenary entertainment for all traceable descendants of 'Jockey of Norfolk', who fell at Bosworth, but regretfully abandoned the idea on finding that the total of guests would run to 6,000. It is questionable whether he would have been proud of the thirteenth Duke of Norfolk who, in the 1840s, advised the hungry poor to take a pinch of curry powder to warm their empty bellies.

Of William Douglas, fourth Duke of Queensberry, a Victorian biographer has said: 'To exist for close on ninety years in enjoyment of rank and wealth, without accomplishing anything worthy of a nation's praise or gratitude, is a feat still achieved by many; but to be the "observed of the observed" for over sixty years and enjoy as much notoriety as an eminent statesman or hero is accorded to few.'*

This crafty old lecher had to wait fifty-four years for his dukedom, which came to him on the death of his cousin Charles, the third Duke; until then he was the Earl of March.† There was a fearful skeleton in the family cupboard. The third duke should have been Charles's older brother James, known to history as the 'cannibalistic idiot'. This monster was normally detained in a cell at Holyrood, but in 1707 his keepers wandered off to watch the riots in Edinburgh and he escaped to slay a cookboy left on duty in the kitchen. When discovered he had the boy on a spit and was roasting him. Insanity, as we have seen, was no bar to a ducal coronet in

* J. R. Robinson: *Old 'Q'*
† The Dukes of Queensberry used this title as well as the Dukes of Richmond

the house of Howard, but the house of Douglas wisely passed over James in favour of Charles, who had all his senses and a good deal of charm as well.

This third Duke was married to the notorious Duchess Kitty, as hare-brained a duchess as ever went to Court in an apron or sat her guests on dung heaps. She adopted the poet-playwright John Gay after his clash with the Court and all three of them—Duke, Duchess and poet—used to sit writing composite letters to their friends, apologising for each other's facetiousness and disclaiming responsibility for blots. As *ménages à trois* go, it lacked turpitude. The Duchess, both of whose sons had died, tried to keep an eye on the fatherless William Douglas, Earl of March; but he proved to be a self-contained ingrate determined to go his own way, which was the way of stews and hells, of White's, the Haymarket and Newmarket. His wealth was not unlimited, but what he had he conserved by selfishness and enlarged by cunning. The sporting world at that time revelled in absurd, sometimes ingenious and often heartless wagers. Noblemen did not themselves ride horses to death, or sit down to eat live cats or fox cubs, but they were willing to produce men to do these things and to wager large sums on their prowess. The Duke (it is more convenient to call him by his later rank) showed his crafty streak when, at the age of twenty-five, he undertook, jointly with the Earl of Eglinton, to build a four-wheel carriage, to be drawn by four horses, capable of travelling nineteen miles in an hour. The stake was a thousand guineas. Coaches in those days did not bowl along; they lurched from pot-hole to pot-hole, and if they were noblemen's coaches there were running footmen to remove obstacles. The Duke set about constructing a coach which should be little more than four wheels linked by the lightest of structures. Two or three were built and found wanting; numerous high-bred horses died in practice; but eventually, in the area of Newmarket Heath, a contraption made of wood, whalebone and silk completed the prescribed course with over six minutes in hand. The Duke had driven a coach-and-four through the regulations. Another of his wagers drew the admiration of

'Nimrod', the sporting writer. The undertaking was to carry a message fifty miles in an hour, a feat which was achieved at no cost in horses. Standing in a wide circle, twenty-four cricketers threw a ball containing the message from one to another until the distance was covered. In an eating contest, the Duke's candidate is supposed to have defeated Sir John Lade's entrant by 'a pig and an apple-pie'. The Duke and his cronies entered wagers at White's on the life expectations of ailing public men, or of each other, or on how soon their friends would be married or catch the pox. The Duke was not ashamed to sue when he thought he was being cheated. He had taken over a bet as to whether Sir William Codrington or a Mr Pigot would die first. Pigot died on the morning the bet was laid, which encouraged his son, a party to the bet, to claim the wager void, likening his father to a horse which dropped dead before it could come under starter's orders. Lord Mansfield, who adjudicated on this nonsense, was unsympathetic to young Pigot; and the Duke, who sat beside the judge after giving evidence, had the pleasure of hearing the jury decide in his favour.

If, as some would argue, the prime function of a nobleman is to support the Turf, to provide it with runners, and to lend dignity by his presence to an otherwise unhallowed rabble, then the Duke of Queensberry did something to fulfil that role. Though strongly suspected of sharp practice in his early years, he became a steward of the Jockey Club. 'Nimrod' calls him 'one of the most distinguished characters on the English Turf', with the quality of being 'wide awake'. When his jockey reported an offer of a large sum to lose a race, he said, 'Take it', and then rode the horse himself to a win.*

It is hard to censure a man for not letting himself be shot dead by quarrelsome Irish duellists. The Duke when insulted preferred to apologise, even to a challenger who reputedly picked him up by the ears in a gambling hell and called him a contemptible little cock-sparrow. On the racetrack an Irishman who suspected him of trickery turned up, ready to duel, with a coffin bearing the ducal arms and the date of

* 'Nimrod': *The Chase, the Road and the Turf*

decease. It would have raised the Duke into the first rank of heroes if he had dispatched this confident adversary; but he politely declined the challenge. One of his descendants attributes his refusal, not to cowardice, but to 'chronic disinclination to engage in a gamble in which the odds were not in his favour'.*

Of the Duke's morals much has been written. On first arriving in London he became sufficiently enamoured of Frances Pelham, daughter of the Prime Minister, to buy a house in Arlington Street, next door to her father, and build a special bay window in order to ogle her. Frances was impressed, but Henry Pelham knew a rake when he saw one. Eventually the rake lost interest, though Frances never did. Duchess Kitty gave up hope of marrying off her kinsman to a virtuous woman. Less fastidious match-makers, demireps and adventuresses all pursued the Duke, but he was that untrappable quarry, the cold sensualist. His manners were adequate to his status and he cut a spruce figure, very different from 'Jockey' of Norfolk. For a time he was a member of the 'Hell Fire' brotherhood of libertines and legislators which met in the Dashwood caves at Medmenham, there to indulge in sexual exhibitionism before unholy altars, but his taste was for private, not public, defloration. He was partial to Italian opera girls, partly because they had, or could affect, social graces; being essentially fastidious, he abhorred foul-mouthed sluts. One of these Italian mistresses was the Marchesa Fagniani, who became pregnant either by her husband or the Duke. Possibly suspecting a financial trap, the Duke thought of his witty and wealthy friend George Selwyn, who had two great loves: playing with children and watching executions. Selwyn, the Duke reasoned, would like the world to think he had fathered a child on a beautiful woman, without having gone to the fatigue of bedding her; and as it turned out Selwyn was happy to accept the little girl, who was known as 'Mie Mie'. Her father was almost certainly the Duke, who showed an indulgent interest in her as she grew

* (Tenth) Marquess of Queensberry: *The Sporting Queensberrys*

into a merry baggage and found her a noble husband almost as lecherous as himself in Lord Yarmouth, later third Marquess of Hertford.

The nearest the Duke got to striking a blow for virtue and morality was when he denounced his fellow monk from Medmenham, John Wilkes, for writing the indecent *Essay on Woman* (a copy was obtained by trickery from the printer by the rascally Rev. John Kidgell, who held the improbable post of chaplain to the Duke). The nearest he came to heeding public opinion was when, after an outcry, he doubled his £1,000 contribution to the Trafalgar Fund for Nelson's sailors. His greatest feat of public service was to be a Lord of the Bedchamber for nearly thirty years; from this post he was summarily dismissed in 1789 when the King recovered from a bout of mental illness to find that the Duke, on reviewing the medical evidence, had decided he was incurable and had thrown in his lot with the Prince of Wales.

'Degenerate Douglas' was the label fixed on the Duke by Wordsworth, not in respect of his morals but for the gross insult he offered to the scenery of Nithsdale. In 1788, on succeeding to the dukedom, he inherited the huge, four-square, twelve-turreted castle of Drumlanrig, standing amid fine trees above the Nith. If he felt any temptation to settle down as a landed magnate, on his native soil, and attend to the wants of an industrious peasantry, the Duke resisted it. His greedy eye took in the forests and saw them only as timber. The order went out to ravage Nithsdale and Neidpath, which soon looked like a worn-out hairbrush. The third Duke of Queensberry had allowed decrepit horses to graze out their lives at Drumlanrig, and had excused decrepit peasants their rents; but the new owner, animated by the spirit of *noblesse exige*, ordered an end to lenity. Burns belaboured the Duke as a reptile in a ducal crown. Years later the Duke told a friend: 'I have been twice in Scotland since I have been Duke of Queensberry. The first time I was popular and the people of the country took the horses from my carriage and drew me home. The second time I was pelted with stones, mud and execration and G—— d—— me, I

liked the last, by G—— better than the first reception, d——
my blood.'*

Along with Drumlanrig the Duke of Queensberry inherited estates at Amesbury, in Wiltshire, with a mansion
designed by Inigo Jones, but the rural life made no appeal.
To reinforce his status he bought a villa at Richmond, Surrey,
reasonably close to the pleasures of the capital. A Lord
Mayor of London, Sir William Beckford, had reported the
air of Richmond to be so bad that twelve of his natural
children had died there,† but this consideration would hardly
have weighed with the Duke. Soon he was extravagantly
bored with his villa, because the Thames (like the Nith) did
nothing but 'flow, flow, flow' past his windows. He preferred
to spend his last years on the balcony of his mansion in Piccadilly, under an awning, watching the flow of pretty women.
Here his shrivelled hulk enjoyed the attraction of an old
performing clock which periodically jerks into life. Women
who knew of his reputation (and who did not?) enjoyed a
frisson if the ogre looked at them. Some of them were eager
enough to attract his attention. If the Duke reciprocated
their interest he would send a message by way of his groom,
Jack Radford, who sat on horseback under the window. The
same groom trotted behind him when he rode out in his
vis-à-vis, bony hands encased in a muff. At this time, if
Thomas Raikes is right, the Duke was 'a little sharp-looking
man, very irritable' who 'swore like ten thousand troopers'
and was 'enormously rich and selfish'.‡

The old roué inspired many rhymesters and caricaturists.
It may be that he aroused disapproval not so much for the
number of women he seduced as for the length of time he
went on seducing them, as a recent biographer has suggested.§
He took great care of himself. A contemporary journal
printed a purported account of a typical day in the Duke's
life. At seven a.m. he had a warm milk bath, perfumed with

* Francis Bickley (ed.): *The Diaries of Lord Glenbervie*
† Horace Walpole: *Memoirs (George III)*
‡ Thomas Raikes: *Journal*
§ Henry Blyth: *Old 'Q'; The Rake of Piccadilly*

almond powder, in which he took coffee and a buttered muffin. After this he retired to bed again until nine, when he called for *café au lait* with a newly laid egg. At eleven they brought him two warm jellies with rusks. By one he was ready for a veal cutlet *à la Maintenon*; by three he was consuming more eggs and jellies; by five it was time for a cup of chocolate and rusks. All this fortified him for the main meal of the day at seven, a heavy dinner of high-seasoned dishes, with claret and madeira. At ten came tea or coffee with muffins. Midnight was signalled by a roast pullet with lime punch. At one the Duke went to bed, in good spirits, and slept until three, when a male cook produced a hot savoury veal cutlet which, with wine and water, prepared him for further sleep until seven, when he was ready to bathe in milk.* The neighbourhood knew all about the Duke's ablutions; some households were said to be unwilling to drink milk, fearing it might have furnished the old goblin's bath. It sounds an improbable regimen for an octogenarian with fading senses and no teeth, and can scarcely have commended itself to Père Elizée, former physician to the French Court, who was paid a retainer for every day the Duke stayed alive, terminable on death.

When they heard that the Duke was nearing his end the members of White's began to lay bets on his chances. Would he outlast his pious colleague of the Turf, the Duke of Grafton? The Duke himself wagered that he would be dead by a certain hour on a certain day and had to pay out £500. When he expired in 1810, in his eighty-sixth year, his bed was covered with begging letters and proposals from 'frail daughters of Eve'. What was to be done with the body of this impious nobleman? There was a vacant space under the communion table of St James's, Piccadilly, so they laid him there. He was followed to the church by all his male domestics who had ensured that no tastes had gone ungratified. For once his running footmen walked.

His will caused scandal and, one would like to think, hilarity. To the Earl of Yarmouth and 'Mie Mie', now Lady

* Quoted in J. R. Robinson's *Old 'Q'* and elsewhere

Yarmouth, went £150,000, along with his mansion in Piccadilly and villa at Richmond (Selwyn had already left 'Mie
Mie' a fortune). Père Elizée and the Governors of the Lock
Hospital received £5,000 each. There were bequests of £1,000
each to 'three French ladies of some celebrity', but no gifts
for any female servants. Jack Radford, the groom, received
all the horses and carriages and a pension of £200. The clerk
at Coutts who kept the Duke's account, and a good many
confidences as well, was left £600 a year.* John Fuller, an
apothecary who latterly had slept at the Duke's bedside,
claimed £10,000 from the estate for 9,340 visits and attendance on 1,700 nights. Lord Yarmouth and others testified
that they thought the claim reasonable. He was awarded
£7,500.

The title of Duke of Queensberry passed, as a second title,
to the Dukes of Buccleuch. Sir Walter Scott's friend, the
fourth Duke of Buccleuch, restored the ravaged hillsides of
Nithsdale, rebuilt the neglected castle of Drumlanrig and
soothed the ruffled tenants, charging a rent 'high enough to
forbid idleness, but not to overpower industry'. Writing in
1817, Scott said that the public-spirited Duke had absented
himself from London and its costly pleasures and was employing some 950 labourers on his Scottish estates at a cost of £70
a day. It was wonderful, Scott thought, what a small sum
would support a Scots labourer.†

Such a renunciation of the fleshpots, and such a pampering
of the peasantry, would have scandalised the man whom
Scott described as 'the late abominable Q'.

* *Gentleman's Magazine*, February 1811
† J. G. Lockhart: *Life of Scott*

THE VULTURE'S BEAK

16

Early in the nineteenth century the British taxpayer had to find huge sums to buy out a variety of noblemen who enjoyed the right to impose levies on goods they did not produce and never saw, or who drew pensions which neither they nor their ancestors had done anything to earn.

The royalty of one shilling levied by the Dukes of Richmond on every chaldron of coals imported to London from Newcastle was converted in 1799 to an annuity of £19,000. A few years later this arrangement was terminated by payment of a lump sum of almost £500,000.* In similar fashion the Dukes of Grafton lost their right to exact duties on imported wines and were paid an annuity of £6,870, later commuted to a payment of £135,000.

In a class of his own came John Murray, fourth Duke of Atholl, who in 1828 exacted a sum of over £400,000 for the loss of his forebears' 'sovereignty' over the Isle of Man. It was the culmination of an impudent campaign sustained for over half a century.

The island was taken over from the House of Atholl by the Crown in 1764. It had been for generations a sanctuary of smugglers, supported by the sort of high-living riff-raff and outlaws who used to infest Port Royal, Jamaica before an avenging earthquake buried them under the sea; but the

* Bernard Falk: *The Royal Fitzroys*

Isle of Man remained obstinately above the waves. Its inhabitants ran goods to the mainland in the finest and fastest of clippers. They heaped indignities on the King's revenue men, not hesitating to assault, kidnap or confine them. The only duties imposed on goods entering and leaving the island were modest ones, payable to the Lord of Man; but the ever-growing volume of illicit trade meant that the island revenues waxed steadily year by year.

'Sovereignty' over Man had been awarded by Henry IV, in a moment of culpable gratitude, to the Earls of Derby, but in 1736 the island passed by female descent to the Dukes of Atholl. In 1764 Parliament authorised the Prime Minister to approach the third Duke and his Duchess with a view to buying their rights over the island. Here was the Duke's chance to get rid of an inherited cesspool and in so doing to demonstrate his loyalty to the Crown, but the Duke did not see it that way. He was so tardy in replying that the Government informed him that immediate action would be taken to suppress smuggling in his realm; this took the form of a Mischief Act, entitling revenue officers to search all ships entering Manx ports. The Duke then named a sum of almost £300,000, of which the bulk was in respect of customs duties and £42,000 for 'regalities', the rest being for church patronage. To this the Crown replied that it wished to buy regalities and customs rights only, and awarded compensation of £70,000, the Duke to reserve his landed interests. As a sop the Duke and Duchess were granted a joint annuity of £2,000. Faced with a dismal future of agriculture and fishing, the men of Man expressed loud abhorrence at the proposed infringement of their status, but a Revesting Act was passed in 1765 and Man was annexed to the Crown. Frustrated greed led to riots and troops were sent over to keep order.

The third Duke's life was soured by grief at the thought of the bad bargain he believed he had made. In 1774, in his forty-sixth year, he drowned himself at Dunkeld 'in a fit of delirium'. His son John, the fourth Duke, now began a dogged campaign for increased compensation, brushing aside the argument that the lost revenues had been swollen by illegal traffic. In the island he fell foul of the House of Keys, the members of which suspected he would do his best to recoup himself from the island's resources. They deprived him of his taxes on herrings and turf and denied his right to free labour; he in turn fought back in high feudal fashion, one of his demands being the right to search houses for dogs which threatened his game. At Westminster his first two petitions to amend the Revestment Act came to nothing. By 1794, however, he had nagged and jockeyed himself into the post of Governor-General. There was support for him among his fellow dukes. If an Atholl could be forced to sell an inheritance, might not Russells and Devonshires be called on to disgorge their monastery lands? The fifth Duke of Rutland, visiting the island in 1797, sighed over 'the most proud circumstance' of a nobleman having enjoyed 'so unlimited a command', with power of life and death, and authority to coin money; rights which were by no means enjoyed at Belvoir. It was the Duke of Rutland's belief that the Atholls had sold out for a trifling sum. He thought Castle Mona, built by the Duke of Atholl as a Governor-General's residence, was somewhat humble for its purpose and that the Governor-General's pay and income from his estates were inadequate. 'All the hills are his,' he noted, 'but the people by paying 1½d a year have liberty to send their horses on them.'*

The more the Isle of Man prospered, by natural increase, the more the Duke determined to wrest his 'share'. In 1805, after a third petition, he succeeded in getting a Compensation Bill before Parliament. The second reading in the Lords was a stormy one, in which the Lord Chief Justice, Lord Ellenborough, gave one of his more apoplectic performances. For the Duke, the Earl of Westmorland said: 'The royalty and dominion of the family over the island was a distinction such as no subject of the Crown enjoyed or ever had enjoyed; and the then noble owner had expressed in most unqualified terms his utter reluctance to deprive himself or his descendants of it.' He had, however, deferred to the wish of his

* (Fifth) Duke of Rutland: *Journals of Three Years' Travels*

Sovereign and the public good. 'It would be injurious,' argued the Earl, 'for this great country to reap the immense benefit it has reaped from the bargain and refuse further compensation out of a part of that gain.'

Lord Ellenborough began his tirade against the Bill by insisting on the indecency of hurrying it forward without giving the House a chance to study the evidence. They had only just had thrust into their hands a huge folio volume 'so reeking from the press' that it was dangerous to life. He sat down to allow a Government spokesman to make some concession, but since none was forthcoming, he rose again. Though he had had no time to read the volume it appeared that he had no doubts about the law on the subject. The proposition in the Bill, he said, was untrue in fact and in law. The Isle of Man was not a sovereignty; it was a lordship and not a dominion. He could find no words to convey his contempt for the reasoning by which the Duke sought to obtain a large sum of public money. The nation was indeed under the beaks of vultures. 'Perhaps the vengeance of Heaven hangs over the nation! Let their lordships prepare to meet it with some mitigation of the evil by returning to the practices of honest times.'

Among others who opposed the Bill was Lord Suffolk, who said his family had owned 60,000 acres in America, worth £200,000, and had lost all in the War of Independence. His mother and sister had received £200 compensation. If the Atholl Bill went through, promised the Earl, he too would lodge a claim for redress.

In the Commons several Members described the Bill as a 'job'. Sir William Young said an ancestor of the Duke had farmed the revenue of the island to a Liverpool merchant for £1,000 a year and the Duke had no right to claim additional compensation 'in consequence of the increase of that revenue under the fostering care of the British legislature'. The Chancellor of the Exchequer was convinced that the Duke had that right. Sheridan described the Duke as 'an injured and oppressed man' (which later earned him an invitation to shoot in Glen Tilt, where he developed a liking for Atholl Brose).* The Bill was approved and the Duke was allotted a fourth part in the island's revenues.

As Governor-General he had increased powers of patronage and had filled lay and clerical posts with his creatures, including a stiffening of Murrays. His least popular appointment was that of a kinsman, George Murray, to a bishopric. No sooner was Bishop Murray installed than he was demanding tithes on a variety of crops, and in the ensuing riots his palace narrowly escaped being burned down.

By 1826 the Duke was so angry with the island that he ceased to visit it. His bishop was translated to a happier see at Rochester. However, the Duke did not relax his campaign for further compensation. In 1828 the Government offered to buy out all remaining rights for the astonishingly high sum of £417,414, swollen by a claim for £100,000 in respect of lost patronage. The sum was handed over to the less than grateful Duke, who retained his Governor-Generalship until he died. No citizen ever received, or can hope to receive, a higher reward for the loss of a corrupt income.

The Duke began to use the compensation money to build a large castle at Dunkeld, but died after one year when it was half built. To family consternation, no trace could be found of the Manx windfall, and since the heir could afford neither to finish nor maintain a castle of that size it was pulled down and served as a quarry. Joseph Mitchell, the railway builder and occasional guest of the Duke, who interested himself in the mystery, says an accountant spent six months vainly searching for the money.†

As a road builder and planter in Scotland the Duke had a good reputation. He afforested some 15,000 acres. In response to a poem by Burns, he provided trees at Bruar Water to protect basking trout and courting couples. His appearance in the streets of Dunkeld, according to Mitchell, impregnated the air with awe and reverence. However, his people had wounded him deeply on occasion. In 1783 the Atholl Highlanders he had raised to fight in America, but who served

* *Parliamentary History*, 7 June and 8 July 1805
† Joseph Mitchell: *Reminiscences of My Life in the Highlands*

only in Ireland, mutinied on being embarked at Spithead for service under the East India Company; the Government acknowledged this grievance by taking no action. The Duke had another humbling experience in Perth during the fervour arising from the French Revolution. Townsmen erected a Tree of Liberty at the town cross, forcing the churches to ring their bells and the middle classes to light up. When the Duke went among them he was called upon to cry out, 'Liberty and Equality!' This he did 'in a very prudent manner'.*

* T. C. Smout: *A History of the Scottish People*

THE GOOD GREY HEAD

17

The Duke of Wellington, as he himself complained, was 'much exposed to authors'. He cannot be omitted from this book on the grounds that his deeds and his idiosyncrasies are too well-known. For a week in June 1815 his shoulders held the skies suspended. Nations can rub along for generations, for centuries even, without any one man being called upon to take such awesome decisions, on such a desperate stage. His function here can only be to serve as a yardstick against which other dukes must stand to be measured; and for those who secured their advancement by solicitation, marriage and inheritance the comparison must needs be odious. If there had been a loftier rank than duke, declared *The Times*, then Wellington would have been awarded it; as it was, 'the highest rank of our ancient nobility was at the same time ennobled and diminished by the gigantic proportions of its new member.'*

The man who, against prodigious odds, out-generalled Napoleon's marshals and drove them from Iberia, then, with the aid of the Prussians, routed the Emperor in pitched battle and occupied his capital, has been hailed as a dazzling advertisement for privilege and influence. As an earl's son he was found seats in the Dublin and Westminster Parliaments. His brother's money won him promotion in a string

* 17 September 1852

of regiments, but it was a long time before the 'fool of the family' heard the clear call of military duty. In India, again thanks to his brother, he became a major-general at thirty-three. In a hard and realistic school he learned the arts of high command and faced the burdens of civil administration. Here, as his *Dispatches* show, he first became an executioner. As Colonel Wellesley at Seringapatam he sent a message to General Harris: 'I wish you would send the provost here, and put him under my orders. Until some of the plunderers are hanged it is vain to expect to stop the plunder.' At forty, hard and without illusions, possessed of great powers of judgment and anticipation, blessed with an uncluttered mind, following no compulsion except the call of duty, confirmed in the habit of victory, he was ready to take on the armies of Revolutionary France. Like Marlborough, he learned while plucking the eagles what it was to be abused by strategists at home. Unlike Marlborough, he did not have to stand by and watch his victories being betrayed. Marlborough did no more, in the end, than check the power of France; the Battle of Waterloo broke it utterly.

Generalship of that order is the rarest of flowerings. 'He is such a man as Europe has not seen since Julius Caesar,' wrote Sir Walter Scott, with all the confidence of a quartermaster in the Volunteers. Yet Wellington was no warlord, no dedicated conqueror; he detested talk of glory and despised all gasconading and heroics. He did not regard his generals as 'a band of brothers'. The last sound he wanted to hear was the cheering of his soldiers. Sir John Fortescue, historian of the British Army, has written: 'It cannot be said that Wellington was an ideal leader, for he commanded no such adoration from his men as had Marlborough. To speak plainly, he was not a lovable character. He was in fact never loved in his life by man or woman; and one has a suspicion that, after all, a military career was not that which he thought to be really best suited to him.' In Fortescue's eyes, the Duke's fame was due to 'that penetrating insight into the heart of things which is called genius'. If he was not loved, he was trusted; 'without Wellington the Allied line [at Waterloo] could never have endured to the end and he was in a modest way aware of it.'*

Although Wellington did not receive the key to a mighty palace like Blenheim, his rewards—as Byron keeps pointing out—were far from meagre. His Indian campaigns brought him £40,000, which included £25,000 from the Mahratta Wars, £5,000 prize money from Seringapatam and £5,000 from the East India Company. In the Peninsular War, after the passage of the Douro and the victory of Talavera, he was created Baron Douro and Viscount Wellington, thanked by Parliament and granted an annuity of £2,000 for himself and two successors. During the next two years he received, not the thanks, but the criticism of Parliament and of stay-at-home generals; then, in 1812, after the seizing of Ciudad Rodrigo and Badajoz, he was created Earl of Wellington, with an additional £2,000 a year, and Parliament found it possible to thank him again. As yet these were modest rewards for singularly hard slogging; but before 1812 was out Salamanca and Madrid had fallen and he was created Marquess of Wellington with a supporting grant of £100,000. Parliament, which had starved some of his operations, was beginning to take the keenest pleasures in his victories. In 1813, after the great French rout at Vittoria, he dispatched Jourdan's baton to the Prince Regent, who sent him a specially designed baton for himself. In 1814, with Napoleon confined to Elba, he was created Duke of Wellington and awarded an additional £400,000 to buy estates. His share of the Peninsular prize money came to £50,000. In five years he had ascended through all the degrees of the peerage; and when he took his seat in the House of Lords the patents of all his creations were read together, an episode without precedent. In the Commons he was received in the style accorded to the Duke of Schomberg. All stood as the one-time Member for the pocket borough of Rye entered, arrayed in the Garter, the Fleece and a blaze of foreign orders. The Duke thanked the House for the noblest reward ever given to an individual and said he was ready to serve them again with the same zeal. The

* J. W. Fortescue: *History of the British Army*

opportunity to do so was all too near. Napoleon escaped from Elba, reassembled his armies and on the field of Waterloo saw them cut to pieces by Wellington and Blücher. There was now no higher dignity to award, but the Duke was given a further £200,000. He waived half his £60,000 share of the Waterloo prize money, the rest of which was divided in the ratio of £1,250 for a general, £9 for a sergeant, £2 10s for a private. A grasping commander could have exacted far more prize money in respect of captured ships. As it was, the rewards of high command, over his lifetime, must have reached £1,000,000.

The full roll-call of the Duke's honours is not only majestic but faintly comical. Like Marlborough he became a prince —a Prince of Waterloo, with the estate of La Belle Alliance, presented by the King of the Netherlands. As well as the dukedom of Wellington he held those of Ciudad Rodrigo, Brunoy and Vittoria; on top of the marquessate of Wellington he held those of Douro and Torres Vedras. He was a Count of Vimiera in Portugal and a Grandee of Spain of the First Class. He was a Marshal of Russia, Austria, France, Prussia, Portugal and the Netherlands, and Captain-General of Spain. He had more knighthoods than any warrior could be expected to remember; their names form a melodious catalogue in which Swords and Crowns, Saints and Conquerors, Lions and Eagles, Merit and Fidelity jostle with the Garter, the Bath, the Golden Fleece and the Holy Ghost. Of all his honours and trophies, his unhappy but loyal Duchess said: 'All tributes to merit—there is the value! And pure! pure! No corruption—ever *suspected* even. Even of the Duke of Marlborough that could not be said so truly.'*

The Duke was given estates by Spain, Portugal and the Netherlands. Louis XVIII, who owed his throne to the Duke, had intended to present him with the great *château* of Chambord. Instead he offered the estate of Grosbois, but even that proposal so antagonised the marshals of France that the King substituted the Order of the Holy Ghost set in diamonds. The Duke, at the French King's suggestion, had

* Christina Colvin (ed.): Maria Edgeworth's *Letters from England*

asked the Prince Regent's permission to accept Grosbois, but really 'did not care one pin about the matter'.*

After Waterloo a board was formed under the Speaker to consider building a palace for the Duke at a cost of about £150,000; but the idea of a second mighty monument adorned with lions mauling cockerels raised no great enthusiasm. Architects, remembering what had happened to Vanbrugh, were wary. At length the Duke settled for a modest second-hand property and in 1817 the Parliamentary Commissioners acquired for him the estate of Stratfieldsaye, in Hampshire, for £263,000. The mansion, which had belonged to Earl Rivers, was comfortable without being opulent. For a while the Duke contemplated erecting a new seat on higher ground, but eventually abandoned the idea. Agriculturally, Stratfield-saye was a bad investment, for the ground was wet clay and the Duke spread a thousand waggon loads of chalk from Basingstoke over it in an effort to improve it. He was a fair and conscientious landlord, but was fond of grumbling that the estate would have ruined any man but himself. In London he acquired another secondhand but imposing residence, Apsley House, overlooking two royal parks. As Lord Warden of the Cinque Ports he had the use of Walmer Castle near Deal.

One of the Duke's laconic comments after Waterloo was, 'I think we've done for them this time.' He spoke in a military sense only; for he was quick to oppose schemes by one ally or another for humiliating and dismembering the enemy, and he urged an early end to the occupation. During these years he shone both as statesman and economist. However, the French did not relish the sight of their conqueror, whose name they could not even pronounce, riding about Paris in the company of laughing, hero-worshipping women. A lieutenant called Cantillon who tried to assassinate him was left 10,000 francs by the ogre on St Helena. In *Don Juan* Byron accused the Duke of having 'repaired Legitimacy's crutch'. Echoing old Kaspar, he said

* (Seventh) Duke of Wellington: *Wellington and His Friends*

And I shall be delighted to learn who
Save you and yours, have gained from Waterloo.

Unfortunately the poet saw too little of the Long Peace to
discover the answer. When the Duke returned to Britain he
was everywhere a figure of wonder. On his visit to Fonthill
in 1822 the crowds who had come to look at Beckford's mighty
folly recognised him and followed him about, as if he were
the greatest curiosity on show. But as radicalism, long stifled,
began to reassert itself the Duke found himself increasingly
at odds with the King's subjects. His contempt for popular
enthusiasms and the pretensions of democracy, in whatever
lands, was enormous. He had seen what mobs could do. 'Rely
upon it', he said, 'that with all our civilisation and advantages
we are the nation in Europe the least disciplined and the
least to be trusted in a situation in which we are not controlled
by the strong arm of authority and law.' The mob which
yelled to him to cry 'God Save the Queen' in support of the
egregious Caroline stung him to his most crushing rejoinder:
'Well, gentlemen, since you will have it so, God save the
Queen—and may all your wives be like her!' (Perhaps he
would not have gone so far as the fifth Duke of Dorset who
turned a number of tenants out of their farms for drinking
to Queen Caroline with toasts like 'May tyranny waste away
like dew before the sun!')

The Duke can have derived little pleasure from serving
George IV in his fuddled decline; but the wail of 'Arthur,
the Cabinet is defunct' from a gross figure in a grubby night-
cap could not be ignored, and duty drove the Duke, as it
had driven earlier dukes, to accept an office he had always
protested he was unfit to fill. As Prime Minister his only
triumph, and that a bitter one, was to force through the
Catholic Relief Bill, but for which Ireland would have been
in revolution—and he would have had the task of pacification.

During his brief premiership the Duke twice took steps to
defend his honour. The Marquess of Winchelsea had accused
him in the *Standard* of 'harbouring insidious designs for the
infringement of our liberties and the introduction of Popery

into every department of the State'. Although the Marquess was a fool, he was a gentleman; the Duke therefore called him out and they exchanged shots at Battersea Fields. The editor and publishers of the *Morning Journal* could not be expected to stand fire as gentlemen; so, since the Prime Minister could hardly go after them with a horsewhip, he moved to prosecute them. They had published a letter from the Duke of Cumberland's chaplain describing Wellington as an ambitious, unprincipled and dangerous minister who kept the King under degrading and unconstitutional control (this was equally libellous of the King, in suggesting he could be so controlled). The Duke took further exception to a reference to his 'despicable cant and affected moderation' and his 'want of compassion'. By modern standards these last statements would seem hardly worth pursuing. The *Journal* was found guilty, but the verdict raised a popular outcry.

In the next political battle, over Parliamentary Reform, the Duke chose untenable country to defend. The run-up to the first Reform Bill was made exceedingly tense by the outrages of the Luddites and the adherents of Captain Swing. Some of the more resolute ducal landlords, the Duke of Wellington among them, found ways in the winter of 1830 of standing up to the rioters. The Duke of Buckingham and Chandos was guarded against marauding mobs by the menfolk of his own villages, who bivouacked outside Avington House for three nights and conducted sorties against machine-breakers, the rector of Itchen Abbas at their head. In West Sussex the fifth Duke of Richmond, a veteran of Waterloo, organised the countryside in the manner of a military occupation, with every four parishes under a leader and a system of alarms. Other counties copied his method. In Hampshire, of which he was Lord Lieutenant, the Duke of Wellington persuaded the magistrates to put themselves on horseback at the head of their servants, grooms, huntsmen and gamekeepers, armed with whips, pistols and fowling pieces, and to ride down the mobs. This was done 'in a spirited manner, in many instances, and it is astonishing how soon the country was tranquillised, and that in the best way, by the activity and spirit of the gentlemen.'* At Ringmer, where labourers were invited to voice their grievances to authority, a representative of *The Times* heard an old soldier 'descanting' on the fact that the Duke had come through the Peninsular campaign with a whole skin and had been given £60,000 whereas he, who had lost a limb in the same campaign, had difficulty in getting ninepence a day.† It was certainly something to descant about. The Duke later sat on the Special Commission at Winchester which capitally convicted one hundred men, leaving six for execution, of whom two were hanged. He helped to choose the six men.

The electoral battle now monopolised interest. Nearly half the Members of the Commons were still the creatures of the Lords. The land interest remained paramount. Vast areas in the industrial north were without representation, while in the south and west Members were returned by pocket boroughs and rotten boroughs. According to the *Black Book* (1820)‡ dukes controlled about seventy seats. Wellington was not one of them and it is impossible to see him in the role of electioneer standing drinks to the mob. Yet, as he saw it, the system returned good men to Parliament (it had returned him, in earlier days, to three seats). If representation was given to the new towns, this could lead only to universal adult suffrage, followed by the overthrow of the Constitution and loss of empire. For mass Reform meetings he felt 'the greatest contempt'; but there was one thing, he told his fellow peers, that he did fear—'I am afraid of revolution and of revolutionary measures brought in and proposed by His Majesty's Government.' He warned: 'There is not an important possession in the world, whether for the purpose of navigation, commerce or military defence, that does not belong to us. If this democratic assembly should once be established in

---

* *Dispatches*
† *The Times*, 25 November 1830
‡ John Wade (and others): *The Black Book, or Corruption Unmasked*

England, does any man believe that we should continue to enjoy these vast advantages?' Was it not the custom of democracies to declare war on property and oppose the payment of public debts?*

Lord John Russell's first Reform Bill passed the Commons with a majority of one, but the Government fell on another issue. The London mob revived its old sport of forcing the wealthy to light up their houses, this time to show sympathy for Reform. An obvious target was Apsley House, where the Duchess of Wellington had just died. The Duke had been at her deathbed but had left London. Even in less sad circumstances it is doubtful whether he would have lit up. The mob smashed his plate glass windows and began to tear out his railings, but a servant fired a blunderbuss over their heads and they moved on. The Duke, according to Mrs Arbuthnot, was convinced that revolution was certain. The lower orders, he believed, were 'rotten to the core', avid only for blood and plunder.† Later that year, when the Lords threw out the Reform Bill, mobs rioted everywhere. Once more they smashed the windows of Apsley House, a stone narrowly missing the Duke's head as he sat writing. In the garden armed men were standing ready to repel invaders. That night the Duke was burned in effigy in Seven Dials. On his instructions the firm of Bramah built bullet-proof shutters for his windows. They were not removed until four years after his death.

The Duke was called upon to prepare London's defences against Reform mobs. In the country his fellow dukes were again taking their own steps to put down revolution. It is surprising to see how many of them were able to deploy their own cannon, or to obtain access to the nation's cannon. At Belvoir the Duke of Rutland, who in normal times was never happier than when firing royal salutes, was preparing to discharge more than blanks. In 1832 he wrote to Lady Shelley: 'I am having all my labourers and servants drilled

* *Hansard*, 4, 5 October 1831
† Francis Bamford and Duke of Wellington: *The Journal of Mrs Arbuthnot*

to the use of the great guns here. I have an artillery sergeant residing here for the winter and we have drills every day. Last week I obtained a large supply of shot and ammunition from Woolwich. I am determined to make a good defence, if attacked.'* Nothing can give a clearer idea of the liberties accorded to, or taken by, the dukes of the day than the spectacle of a Manners drilling footmen and potboys to blow their fellow citizens to pieces. The Duke of Buckingham and Chandos brought ashore the cannon from his yacht to defend his possessions. This was the vessel in which he had fled from financial oppression; the cannon, which he does not mention in his diary of the voyage (Chapter Eighteen), were possibly intended for use against corsairs. On the Gareloch the seventh Duke of Argyll fortified his seat at Ardencaple against Clydeside mobs. Inspired by the spirit of his mother who had defied the Wilkes rioters, he armed all available menservants, and his son's tutor, with the assorted guns in his possession.†
The most uncompromising of all the dukes was the fourth Duke of Newcastle, whose castle at Nottingham was sacked by the mob (Chapter Twenty).

The Duke of Wellington, after much soul-searching, refrained at the last from voting against the Bill. His comment on the first Reformed Parliament is part of national folk-lore: 'I never saw so many shocking bad hats in my life.' It was as much a criticism of the quality of the headgear as of the wearers. The Commons was, of course, only partially reformed; it long remained the prey of 'influence'.

For much of the 1830s the defender of Throne, Constitution, Church and Property was deeply distrusted by the masses. He showed no penitence; indeed, he seemed to go out of his way to uphold the dingier practices of privilege. In the Lords he defended the Lord Chancellor of Ireland, Lord Plunkett, who was under fire for distributing lucrative posts among his family. It was a Chancellor's duty, maintained the Duke, to look after his friends and dependants, if their abilities and pretensions were adequate. Forthrightly, he

* R. Edgcumbe (ed.): *Diary of Frances, Lady Shelley*
† (Eighth) Duke of Argyll: *Autobiography and Memoirs*

condemned the 'senseless outcry against public men for not having overlooked the ties of blood and Nature in dispensing the patronage of office'.*

By the next decade the Duke had graduated to the role of non-party public servant, 'our chief state-oracle', 'the good grey head which all men knew', a man 'rich in saving common-sense' and 'in his simplicity sublime' (to quote Tennyson's *Ode*). Yet the air of authority was far from being extinguished. Disraeli left this impression of him in 1841: 'In the classic contour of your countenance, and at the first glance, we recognise only deep thoughtfulness and serene repose; but the moment it lights up into active expression, command breathes in every feature; each glance, each tone, indicates the intuitive mind impervious to argument, and we trace without difficulty the aquiline supremacy of the Caesars.'†

In that year the old Roman was 'literally hunted' by the crowd, in carriages, on horse and on foot, when he rode in the Queen's suite to Woburn Abbey; but it was a changed crowd. In Woburn town 'every creature' removed his hat and cheered. Fearing he was attracting too much attention, he disengaged and was chased at full gallop back to Woburn Abbey.‡ There were a dozen years of hero-worship yet to come; it was a bonus that Marlborough had never lived to enjoy.

Queen Victoria much esteemed her Duke and in 1844 determined to visit him at Stratfieldsaye. The house had no state apartments. With some difficulty the royal suite was squeezed into inappropriate rooms and the Duke personally took a candle to light the Queen to bed. Mary Mitford, who was in the neighbourhood, was critical of his hospitality. 'Our Duke went to no great expense,' she writes. 'One strip of carpet he bought, the rest of the additional furniture he hired in Reading for the week!' The ringers after four hours'

---

* *Hansard*, 12 March 1832
† William Hutcheon (ed.): *Whigs and Whiggism: Political Writings by Disraeli*
‡ (Seventh) Duke of Wellington: *Wellington and His Friends*

labour at the church sent an empty can to the house asking
for more strong beer, but it was returned empty. The band,
having played itself to a standstill, begged a meal and were
given bread and cheese. Or so Mary Mitford says. She com-
plains that the Duke has no open-heartedness. 'He is without
the high sense of what is due to his position which made
Napoleon, with all his spirit of order, so truly magnificent ...

'*The aquiline supremacy of the Caesars*'

The Duke of Wellington welcomes the Queen to Stratfieldsaye

The Duke looked relieved beyond all expression when he
had made his last bow to the royal visitors.'*

For high-spending fellow aristocrats with hordes of idle
menservants the Duke had every scorn. If he lagged behind
them in splendour and size of stables, he was ahead of them in
comfort, for he installed central heating in his house and was
able to boast of a temperature of sixty-four degrees throughout, even on stairs and in corridors. 'You would think yourself
in Russia,' he told Princess Lieven. In notable contrast,
Blenheim did not have central heating until the 1890s.

* A. G. L'Estrange (ed.): *Life of Mary Mitford*

Although enjoying his home comforts, the Duke hated 'playing Boniface' to visitors. He was the ideal guest rather than the ideal host. He once summed up the difficulty of conversing with the Queen with 'I have no small talk and Peel has no manners,' yet he moved easily enough in society and hostesses never ceased to compete for him. 'Towards the female nobility the Duke carried himself with a chivalry and punctilious courtesy, and with no small degree of enjoyment,' said the *Annual Register* (1853). He was sought after by the great Whig houses of Woburn, Chatsworth and Belvoir. Curiously, the Duke had no objection to dressing up for a fancy dress ball; his impersonation of the Duke of Cumberland must constitute the greatest posthumous honour the victor of Culloden ever received. 'The Duke goes to every lighted candle,' said Henry Greville, who was grateful enough to have him at his musical party.* Princess Lieven complained that the Duke tried to be the universal man. Society, knowing his inclinations, attempted to make him the universal godfather, and charities the universal subscriber; he complained that not a Hindu temple was built in the Queen's domains without a request to him for money. The Royal Family regarded him not only as godfather but as sick visitor, undertaker and executor. To him fell the task of burning George IV's love-letters and disputing his tailors' bills. There was a £600 bill for a blue silk coat which three men had been fitting to the King's gross figure ever day for three weeks, altering the seams after each session; and reluctantly the Duke had to recognise that a fashionable tailor was entitled to be paid more than a Minister of State.† All the minor chores that fell to other dukes fell on him a hundredfold. He warded off with suitable asperity all applications from strangers for advancement, and made it clear that the Army was not a refuge for society's protégés (though he himself had been one). 'Hands off the Army' was his rule. When he heard that the Bishop of Nova Scotia wanted soldiers to

---

* Viscountess Enfield (ed.): *Diary of Henry Greville*
† Christina Colvin (ed.): Maria Edgeworth's *Letters from England*

present arms to him, he directed, 'The only attentions the soldiers are to pay the Bishop are to his sermons.' He who had complained about the volume of paper work in the Army found himself deluged by letters from bored gentlemen, cranks and publicity-hunters. Some of his correspondents who received crushing snubs were merely seeking his autograph, as he must have suspected. Those who wrote for genuine reasons assumed that because the Duke was seen to be interested in so much he would be interested in still more. Certainly he liked to inspect new inventions and gadgets. Of an unsuccessful rocket he said: 'If this had been invented first and gunpowder afterwards, what a capital improvement gunpowder would have been.'*

For the eulogies of authors the Duke cared nothing and rarely bothered to correct their errors; for the press, which existed only to spread misinformation and licentiousness, along with reports of impostors claiming to be his nephews, he had almost total contempt. He grew impatient with artists and sculptors, for whom he was expected to parade, like a subaltern, in full uniform, or to sit for hours with his arms crossed, 'that they may profit by it'.† In particular he grudged ten sittings to an unestablished artist who wished to make a 'study' of him. This painter had the impertinence, not only to study him, but to interrupt his reflections with conversation. He then asked to borrow the Duke's clothes, which Sir Thomas Lawrence already had in his possession. 'The fact is I have neither time nor clothes enough for all the calls made on them,' he told Lady Shelley. When paying for Sir David Wilkie's picture of Chelsea Pensioners reading the Waterloo Gazette ('full sixteen months constant work', according to the artist), he counted out 1,200 guineas in notes, brushing aside the suggestion that a cheque would be acceptable with, 'Do you suppose I would let the clerks in Coutts know what a fool I have been?' The controversy in 1846 over Matthew Wyatt's giant equestrian statue of the Duke erected on the arch opposite Apsley House scarcely

* Alan St H. Brock: *A History of Fireworks*
† (Seventh) Duke of Wellington: *Wellington and His Friends*

heightened his regard for the world of art. The critics complained that the statue was too big for the site. It had been borne to the arch, in the presence of royalty, in the manner of a Roman imperial triumph, with an escort of videttes, bands, 'the members of the Committee in their carriages', riggers, pioneers and detachments of every Guards regiment. Was it to be removed in the same manner to an obscure site? Which were more important, the feelings of the Duke or those of his critics? The statue stayed on the arch until long after his death.

The Duke had no objection to being the inspiration of Thomas Moore's songs. During the Peninsular campaign he was shown a poem about Talavera by John Wilson Croker and reported, very civilly, 'I did not think a battle could be turned to anything so interesting.' But he would have been content to be remembered by his own *Dispatches*, of which he said, after their publication, 'Well, if these were to be written all over again I don't think I should alter a single word.' To a suggestion that they would be long remembered, he replied, 'It is very true. When I read them I was myself astonished and cannot think how the devil I could have written them.' This, Charles Greville says, was a typical response from 'a man who had not one grain of conceit in his disposition'. The really great 'are equally free from undue vanity or affected modesty and know very well the value of what they do.'* Anyone who has read the Waterloo Dispatch, written in the immediate aftermath of a great terminal battle, will be as puzzled as the Duke to know how the devil he could have written it. It is not hard to imagine how Napoleon would have opened such a dispatch. Wellington began his report to the Secretary of War: 'My Lord, Bonaparte having collected the 1st, 2nd, 3rd, 4th and 6th Corps of the French Army and the Imperial Guards, and nearly all the cavalry on the Sambre ...' The dispatch was clearly marshalled; it had all the available facts; it lacked vainglory; it conceded that 'such a desperate action could not be fought, and such

* Henry Reeve (ed.): *Memoirs of Charles Greville*

advantages could not be gained, without great loss, and I am sorry to say that ours has been immense'; it contained the necessary tributes; and it even mentioned that a General Pozzo di Borgo had sustained a contusion.

If the mob had forgiven the Duke in his old age, the Duke had not forgiven the mob. In 1848, the panic year of revolution in Europe, the Government called in their seventy-nine-year-old Commander-in-Chief to defend the capital against Fergus O'Connor, who was threatening to march on Westminster from Kennington Common with 400,000 Chartists. The Great Captain made his troop dispositions in his most incisive manner. To helpful suggestions by a Minister he snapped 'Done already' or 'Done three hours since'. All the Whitehall offices were protected, garrisoned, provisioned. Huge numbers of troops were deployed out of sight. Cannon commanded the bridges and artillery officers were authorised to open fire at their discretion. O'Connor abandoned the march and the petition was delivered, ignominiously, to the Commons in a hansom cab. The Duke had won a total, bloodless battle over the ranks of democracy. But, though his brain was still keen, his physical powers were fading. At Parliamentary ceremonies the great Sword of State, which he bore, was seen to assume 'a regicidal angle of incidence'.

It is the heroic stature of the Duke which makes his private life such a puzzling study. No natural children sat round his table at Stratfieldsaye, or were sealed in tombs in Westminster Abbey. If his friendship with the Arbuthnots constituted a *ménage à trois*, it was not the sort of threesome which made Nelson notorious. The Duke had always enjoyed female society. One of his fellow officers in India recalled that he had 'a very susceptible heart, particularly towards, I am sorry to say, married ladies'. But he was never one to be carried away. Badgered by officers' requests for local leave in Lisbon, he ruled that forty-eight hours was as long as any reasonable man could wish to stay in bed with the same woman. The courtesan Harriet Wilson claimed to have had him as a client, but it would have been odd only if she had failed to claim him.

The Duke's wife, born Kitty Pakenham, could not play the hostess, or the duchess, in the manner he required; their temperaments were wildly incompatible. For solace and support he depended on a succession of women (mediocre ones, complained Peel) by whom he was received and with whom he interminably corresponded. In return for their company he gave them sage advice. The Duke would probably not have quarrelled with the Rev. Cornelius Whurr, the anthologists' delight, who observes:

> What lasting joys the man attend
> Who has a polished female friend!

Inevitably gossip said he was the lover of Mrs Arbuthnot, but the lady indignantly denied that she ever received him outside visiting hours. She was politically minded and sought to provide him with that 'confidential intercourse' he could not obtain on his domestic hearth. Henry Greville thought the Duke's twenty years friendship with Mrs Arbuthnot was his greatest resource; 'I believe him to be equally attached to husband and wife, and that there was no matter, personal or political, that he did not freely discuss with them in the most unreserved manner.'* From her correspondence Mrs Arbuthnot does not emerge as the most likable of women and she had a spiteful scorn for the Duchess. Lady Shelley, for long one of the Duke's companions and correspondents, was convinced that the Duke was not Mrs Arbuthnot's lover. She affected to regard the Duke, Mrs Arbuthnot and herself as 'a perfect union, where no jealousy or littleness of feeling ever intruded'.† That was not the three-cornered relationship the scandal-mongers discussed. Elizabeth Longford takes the lenient view of the Arbuthnot affair; it was, she says, 'a most unusual, subtle and successful essay in triangular friendship'.‡ When Mrs Arbuthnot died both the Duke and her husband were badly shaken; but it was the Duke who nursed the husband through a breakdown. Arbuthnot had never

* Viscountess Enfield (ed.): *Diary of Henry Greville*
† R. Edgcumbe (ed.): *Diary of Frances, Lady Shelley.* 1818-73
‡ Elizabeth Longford: *Wellington: Pillar of State*

complained of the association. Nor had Sir John Shelley grudged his wife the pleasure of the Duke's company (for two years she was in disgrace with the Duke for allowing a military appraisal to be made public and it was her husband who, with a well-timed joke, restored the friendship).

The Great Duke attends divine service at St Mary's, Walmer

To the heiress Angela Burdett-Coutts the Duke wrote more than eight hundred letters. She proposed marriage to him when she was thirty-three and he was seventy-eight, but he explained to 'my dearest Angela' that his role must be that of friend, guardian and protector. He had to rebuke her for proposing to call on him uninvited, which would have threatened the reputation of both; and he was angry when she took lodgings near him at Walmer. Quite the oddest of the Duke's young women friends was Anne Maria Jenkins, a beautiful orphan who wished to attend to his immortal soul and invited his attention to certain passages in the Bible. It does not appear that she had any serious designs on his dukedom. He paid her visits. Over the years the correspondence faltered, was resumed and faltered again. It is possible to see in this relationship an avuncular *tendresse* rather than a senescent silliness.

As a family man the Duke suffered endless disappointments. He thought his sons lazy and too prone to seek idle company; as do most fathers. No one could fail to sympathise with his heir, the Marquess of Douro, who said after his father's death, 'Think what it will be when the Duke of Wellington is announced and only *I* come in.'*

* Augustus Hare: *The Story of My Life*

DISGRACE AND RUIN

18

The Long Peace after Waterloo brought with it the shameful spectacle of dukes going bankrupt. No one found this more reprehensible than the Duke of Wellington, who had strong views about those who lived above their means (his nephew, the seventh Duke of Beaufort, had to shut his houses, sell his horses and winter in Italy). In the main the causes of financial collapse were not agricultural depression or high taxes, but extravagance, dissipation and gambling.

On these counts, duchesses were sometimes more to blame than dukes, not all of whom had the resources of a Cavendish to meet a wife's table losses. The Duke of Wellington's hostess at the famous ball before Waterloo, the Duchess of Richmond, had much to answer for: her husband, the fourth Duke was hard put to find the £30,000 which his Duchess apparently lost to Marshal Blücher. 'She has ruined him by gambling,' says an entry in the Farington *Diary* in 1818. In that year the straitened Duke, father of fourteen children, went off to govern Lower Canada (the fifth Duke of Manchester was already governing Jamaica). On a tour of his northern territory in 1819 the Duke of Richmond fondled a pet fox which bit him and he died of hydrophobia. His widow later inherited the ample lands of her brother, the fifth and last Duke of Gordon.

In 1816 Captain Rees Howell Gronow, sometime Member of Parliament, man-about-town, duellist and gossip, journeyed with the Marquess of Blandford* in a singularly well-equipped carriage to the estate of White Knights, near Reading. The Marquess was the future fifth Duke of Marlborough. On the journey he opened a cupboard and produced a 'capital luncheon' with wines and liqueurs. On the touch of a spring a secretaire flew open, revealing writing materials and a large pocket-book. This, as the Marquess explained, held fifty Bank of England notes for £1,000 each. They had been borrowed in the City from a moneylender called Levy who had exacted in return a 'post-obit' on his father's death for £150,000. 'You see, Gronow,' said the Marquess, 'how the immense fortune of my family will be frittered away, but I can't help it. I must live.' His father, he explained, inherited £500,000 in ready money and £70,000 a year from land; but when his own turn came to live at Blenheim there would be nothing left but the £5,000 annuity on the Post Office.

The Marquess, in Gronow's eyes, had many good and amiable qualities, but was 'by far the most extravagant man I ever remember to have seen'.† His less amiable qualities had caused a family breach. While his parents, the fourth Duke and Duchess, lived at Marlborough House in London, he had been reduced to occupying lodgings at Triphook's, the bookseller's, in St James's Street. Since his allowance did not match his rank he had recourse, as Gronow tells, to 'the Jews'. Much of what he borrowed was spent on his obsessive hobby of flower-growing, practised on forty acres at White Knights. These regally kept gardens were not to everyone's taste, however. Mary Mitford in 1817 gained access to 'a certain wood, shut in with great boarded gates, which nobody is allowed to enter'. It turned out to be 'the very palace of False Taste— a bad French garden with staring gravel walks, make-believe bridges, stunted vineyards and vistas through which you could see nothing'. Since the Duke—'that notable fool'—was absent, 'we had the comfort of laughing at it as much as we chose'.‡ The furnisher of these costly pleasures, hidden and otherwise,

---

* Courtesy title of the heirs to the Dukedom of Marlborough
† Capt. R. H. Gronow: *Reminiscences*
‡ A. G. L'Estrange: *Life of Mary Mitford*

thought nothing of paying the Hammersmith firm of Lee and Kennedy £500 of his borrowed money for a rare shrub. In short, he was that happily rare phenomenon, an incontinent botanist. His indoor hobbies at White Knights were equally expensive, for he spent freely on rare books. He had acquired the famous Bedford Missal and had paid £2,260 for a 1471 edition of Boccaccio's *Decameron*, bought at the sale in 1812 of the third Duke of Roxburghe's great library (a famous event in the annals of bibliomania).

The Marquess's turn to live at Blenheim came in 1817. His father had retreated into that silent melancholy in which so many dukes have ended their lives. He refused to speak to anyone; but near the end, hearing that the dreaded Madame de Staël was at his gate, clamouring for an interview, he broke his silence with a tragic cry to his servants, 'Take me away! Take me away!' The fifth Duke was now tempted to fresh extravagance. In 1819 the bailiffs' men descended on White Knights and seized nearly everything but the Bedford Missal, which the Duke, according to Mary Mitford, abstracted from its locked case 'by an admirable feat of legerdemain unsurpassed since the escape of the man from the quart bottle'. Among items removed were two hundred pairs of leather breeches.

In 1821 the Duke of Wellington rode over from Stratfieldsaye with Mrs Arbuthnot and a party to view the horticultural folly, which they were informed had cost £50,000, with £10,000 still owing to the Hammersmith suppliers. Three years later the disapproving Duke and Mrs Arbuthnot paid a visit to Blenheim to see the State Apartments and anything the bailiffs might have left in that triumphal palace. It was an odd, and yet perhaps an inevitable, objective for a day's outing; possibly the Duchess would have enjoyed it too. Mrs Arbuthnot found herself wishing that her companion could have had his own Waterloo Palace. They did not make contact with the Duke of Malborough, whom Mrs Arbuthnot described in her *Journal* as a disgrace to his heritage and little better than a common swindler. In his desperation he was allowing people to shoot and fish at so much an hour and but

for the Court of Chancery would have sold off all his timber.*
(When his eldest son brought an action against him in 1818
for felling the Blenheim trees, the Vice-Chancellor expressed
the hope that the Duke's sense of family honour would prevent
him from wasting the estates.)†

Captain Gronow returned to Blenheim (he does not give
the date) and found that the Duke's earlier prophecy had
come true; he had little to live on but the Post Office annuity.
His other revenues were forestalled and many of his possessions entailed; he was unable to obtain credit either in Oxford
or London. Fortunately the estate yielded fish, game, venison
and mutton and there was still a good cellar. In such pauper-
dom the Duke ended his days, closing down room after room
of the palace until he became a hunted recluse in one corner,
though occasionally he escaped with a pair of breeches or two
to a watering-place.

Extravagance came all too easily to Richard Temple Nugent
Brydges Chandos Grenville, first Duke of Buckingham and
Chandos, whose name was a roll-call of great Whigs and a
record of rich marriages. In 1820, if Mrs Arbuthnot is right,
he expressed his thanks for the Garter and his hopes of a
dukedom in the same letter. The dukedom has been described
as a mark of personal friendship by George IV, but it was
basically part of a political accommodation in which the
Grenvilles lent support to a Tory Prime Minister and took
the side of the King against his Queen. The Duke came of
a family which had been most prodigally sustained from the
public coffers. In the *Black Book* (1820) is a reference to his
rotten borough of St Mawes, in Cornwall, said to consist only
of a few huts occupied by fishers, who had no right to vote.
On election days the Duke would 'create' a few electors for
the purpose of returning his candidate. He acquired a private
fortune by marrying a Brydges, heiress of the third Duke of
Chandos. By 1827 his open-handed patronage of literature
and the arts had brought him in sight of ruin; but a con-

* Francis Bamford and Duke of Wellington: *The Journal of Mrs
Arbuthnot*
† *Annual Register*, 1818

tributory cause was the hospitality he had extended to the
Court of France. 'Neither Louis XVIII nor Charles X took
the slightest notice of the obligation they had incurred—
apparently regarding such imprudent generosity as the natural acknowledgment of their exceeding merit,' complained the
editor of the Duke's *Private Diary*. The Duke therefore
decided to do what distressed aristocrats always did—to live
abroad until the estates recovered. His first necessity was a
yacht in which to leave the country, so a vessel, named the
Anna Eliza after his wife, was built for him. In this he prepared for a two years' cruise, starting in 1827, with only a
secretary, chaplain, surgeon and a few servants. The *Private
Diary* records the Duke's farewells. He took a last drive with
his Duchess, who wept violently and was consoled by the gift
of a rose; she wanted him to sell up Stowe. He rode round the
park with his son, telling him where to plant trees and how
to control the deer, but the son treated the father as if he were
a foolish boy. There was an old imbecile librarian who said
he had been turned away from the kitchen when he begged
for food; investigation showed that he had eaten a hearty
lunch and forgotten all about it. The Duke kissed this queru-
lous servant on the forehead, but there was no reciprocal
emotion other than greed.

The *Anna Eliza* was delivered in a disgraceful state and
the crew were dead drunk before they left Southampton. They
proved mutinous and ungovernable; but off Malaga the Duke
seized the ringleader and handed him over to the consul for a
taste of gaol. From time to time the Duke stayed at foreign
courts. He watched slaves toiling in Spain, saw an execution
in Sicily, was offered *una bella signora* by a tout in Italy
('I repulsed him vehemently and indignantly'), saw a prima
donna at the Rome opera spitting blood as she sang. In Rome
he picked up a few statues for the portico at Stowe. A King's
Messenger arrived from England charged by the Duke of
Wellington to collect all the peers' proxies he could find in
Italy, for a vote on the Roman Catholic question. In his spare
moments the Duke wrote poems. How much money was saved
by this self-inflicted Grand Tour we do not know. The Duke

returned in time for the uproar over the Reform Bill.

In 1839 he was succeeded by his son, who had earned the title of 'The Farmers' Friend' by his insertion into the Reform Bill of the 'Chandos clause' extending the franchise to £50 tenants. He was far from being 'The Railwaymen's Friend'. To frustrate the prospectors with their theodolites he formed his tenants into a *posse comitatus* to harass them and stretch sheets and tarpaulins across their lines of sight; but the engineer of the line raised his surveyors on ladders propped up by their mates. The chainmen worked by moonlight to avoid pitched battles. At length the engineer drove up in triumph in a chaise-and-four to his favourite inn shouting, 'I've done the Duke!' and ordered champagne for all.* This Duke was even more reckless, financially, than his father. His estates were heavily encumbered, yet he bought more and more land with borrowed money, even though the rentals due were less than the interest payable on his borrowings. By 1845, when Queen Victoria visited Stowe, it was rumoured that the Duke was in grave straits; yet there was no sign of it as the Queen and her consort, escorted by Yeomanry, drove through triumphal arches to the great Palladian mansion. Five hundred labourers in clean white smocks had been paraded to wave flags and five hundred tenants were drawn up on horseback. In this treasure-house touched by the hands of Vanbrugh, Robert Adam and Grinling Gibbons, set in grounds shaped and embellished by William Kent and Capability Brown, the Queen could expect hospitality as princely as that of Chatsworth or Belvoir; nor was she disappointed. There is a legend that the bailiffs were already in possession and were persuaded to wear the royal livery. In a woodland enclosure the Prince massacred a large number of cornered hares and was rewarded by the Duke's band playing 'See The Conquering Hero Comes'.

Soon the embarrassments of the Duke of Buckingham were common knowledge. Creditors were seeking powers to sell off the contents not only of Stowe but of Wotton Hall, Aylesbury. a mansion at Avington, Hampshire, and two mansions in

* J. K. Fowler: *Echoes of Old Country Life*

London. The press estimated his debts as in the region of £1,500,000 and passed on a rumour that the Government proposed to buy Stowe for the Prince of Wales; its proximity to Windsor was thought to be a recommendation.

The scene in Stowe Park in August 1848 was compared to Derby Day, a county picnic, the march of the mob on Versailles and the incursion of the Greeks into Priam's palace. A procession of barouches, flys, 'busses', traps and grocers' carts mixed with the carriages of the high nobility and the Rothschilds. Timber waggons were busy removing the ducal trees. Attached to a noble beech was a weighing machine for dispensing venison, prices for which—so much for a whole buck, so much for a haunch—were set out in a notice nailed to the front door. According to the *Morning Post*, a party who had arrived in a butcher's cart were highly indignant at being refused permission by Messrs Christie to eat their bread and cheese in one of the carpeted salons. 'Mr Christie referred the spokesman of the party to the Duke and Duchess of Bedford, who were partaking of luncheon under the colonnade of the house.' This example of good breeding quickly silenced the grumbler. Regrettably, catalogues were allowed to fall into the hands of 'improper persons', a swarm of whom, despite opposition, stormed into the mansion, breaking glass as they went.* Inside, only a slight attempt had been made to preserve the Duke's carpets from what *The Times* called 'excessive trituration'.

The attitude to the sale adopted by *The Times* was passionately wrong-headed. Its leader-writer appears to have made the journey to Stowe to lament over the dissolution of an empire. In the State Dining Room he watched the auctioneer's men weighing out the Duke's candelabra, his epergnes, his goblets, his trophies. Also for sale was Holbein's portrait of Charles Brandon, the Duke's Tudor ancestor. Such sights greatly inflamed the leader-writer. The sale was a 'disgraceful event', brought about by one whose extravagance had struck a heavy blow at the whole order to which he, 'unfortunately', belonged. The public were prepared to respect the House of

* *Morning Post*, 15 August 1848

Lords, but not a degenerate aristocracy; 'when dynasties are falling around and aristocracies have crumbled into dust, disgrace acquires the force of injury and personal ruin is a public treason.' This most noble and puissant prince, in the year of European revolution, had set a lamentable example, in the midst of fertile fields, to an industrious people. Scandalously, he had persuaded his son, the Marquess of Chandos, to sign away his birthright and divide it among the creditors. 'A ducal home is overthrown to atone for one man's folly and to give expensive tradesmen and extortionate moneylenders better security than they contemplated when first they sold their goods and lent their money.'*

Other newspapers were quick to trounce *The Times* for suggesting that the Duke and his heir should have sheltered behind the law of entail in order to cheat creditors. The *Morning Post* observed that its rival was now spilling on to the living the venom normally reserved for its obituary notices; in its view the Marquess of Chandos, in giving up the entail, had acted 'with a degree of hereditary high-mindedness which must ever redound to his honour'. The *Standard*, objecting to what it called a violation of 'the sacred rights of misfortune', accused *The Times* of the true Jacobin spirit.

The sale at Stowe lasted forty days. Some of the treasures went to other stately homes, some to 'hotels and the drawing-rooms of self-made men'. The prices were disappointing, but many of the treasures were themselves disappointing, having been accumulated by accident, bequest, marriage and public presentation rather than by the exercise of conscious taste. In the end the receipts just exceeded £75,000, a modest sum compared to the £262,990 received earlier that year from the sale of estates. The creditors were merciless and land sales went on for ten years, but Stowe and Wotton remained in the family, entailed on female heirs.

The hapless Duke, who had entertained so high an opinion of his capacity and importance, turned to authorship, gathering and editing the family papers from the reign of George III onwards. It was as useful a service as he had ever done. By

* *The Times*, 14 August 1848

a severe irony, the one-time foe of the railways ended his days in the Great Western Hotel at Paddington, the recipient of a £500 pension from his son, the Marquess of Chandos, who was chairman of the London and North-Western Railway.* He left a £200 will. 'Few men will have passed away less honoured in their life or regretted in their death,' wrote the diarist Henry Greville.

Plantagenet blood proved no handicap in running a railway. The Marquess, who became the third Duke, used to ride on the company locomotives studying performance and fuel consumption and even checking the use of cotton waste (the third Duke of Sutherland also drove locomotives and liked to ride on fire engines). This Duke strove hard to pay off the family debts. He held many State posts and, as Governor of Madras, performed a prodigy of famine relief. When he died in 1889 the dukedom to which he brought a belated worth became extinct.

* J. K. Fowler: *Echoes of Old Country Life*

THE GREAT IMPROVER
19

It was the responsibility of a landowner not only to improve
his land but to improve the habits and morals of his tenants.
Nowhere did such an endeavour meet greater opposition than
in Scotland, where—to the alien eye—pride, sloth, ignorance
and malice appeared to be as indigenous as bracken and even
harder to eradicate. The first Duke of Sutherland was dubbed
'The Great Improver' as if improving were a crime; and his
enemies claimed that the way this English inheritor carried
out his improvements, as by forced clearances, was indeed a
crime. Nevertheless the Duke strove to ameliorate the human
lot on lines that seemed to him both right and profitable. He
was not alone in the struggle. George Campbell, eighth
Duke of Argyll, who also bore the responsibility for vast
estates, considered that every single step towards improving
the family's lands, over a period of nearly a century and a half,
had been taken by the proprietor and not by the people; 'and
not only so, but every one of these steps without exception has
been taken against the prevailing opinions and feelings of
the people at the time.' He was a Scotsman talking about
Scotsmen.

Let us consider the Duke of Argyll's record first. He was
a great lecturer of his fellow men and something of a scold.
One of his many books* is a vigorous account of his family's

* (Eighth) Duke of Argyll: *Crofts and Farms in the Hebrides*

stewardship of the isle of Tiree, where endless sub-division of land, wasteful grazing and cropping, and an ever-growing population had resulted, by 1880, in a badly underemployed and overcrowded community, much given to drink. Emigration to America or Canada seemed the obvious solution, but agitators denounced such a course. A committee of the Highland and Agricultural Society recommended 'every conceivable expedient, each one more absurd than another, for preventing the people from seeking a land of greater abundance'. The idle crofters inherited an idle proprietor in the sixth Duke who was 'what silly people call an excellent landlord because he let the people do exactly as they liked'. Then came the potato famines of the 'hungry forties' and the seventh Duke had 7,000 starving mouths to feed, though it was his son who organised relief, which was given as wages in return for work on drainage schemes. It was still 'the epoch of fools', when demagogues preached that an excessive population ought to be 'rooted in the soil', but by now the folk of Tiree were petitioning for help to emigrate. The Duke enabled a thousand of them to leave, but when people began to look on emigration as a boon to the landlord he ceased to offer help except to those who asked for it.

The Duke fiercely criticised a Royal Commission on the Highlands which visited his lands in the mid-nineteenth century. He held that the members, instead of asking silly and offensive questions about ducal affairs, would have done better to cross-examine witnesses and rebuke them for selfishness, lying and slander of his deceased agents. In Edinburgh the Duke had seen a man hypnotised into believing a piano was a horse; only by some similar induced delusion, he thought, could the tenants have come to believe their grievances. The Duke never ceased to castigate fools and knaves. Here he is on drainage: 'The landlord invests his thousands, mainly underground, and the passing idiot thinks that his rental is some kind of spontaneous return for which the owner has done nothing.' On bounties, baits and bribes: 'The establishment of higher standards must come by exertion and by thrift, not by gratuitous benefits which dispense with both.' The

Duke believed that people had to be watched all the time and rendered subject to the authority that went with ownership; otherwise a tenant would ask for a byre to house a cow and then let a family move in instead.

In fifty years the Duke spent £500,000 on improvements to his various estates. It had not been in vain. The crofters in Tiree had prospered by the departure of their neighbours. Good husbandry had been dinned into them and the Duke was proud of their achievements. As for the fishermen, they had become as sober as they were industrious, thanks largely to his refusal to have a public-house on the island.

The problems of the Dukes of Argyll in Tiree were trivial enough compared to those faced in Sutherland by George Granville Leveson-Gower, Marquess of Stafford and first Duke of Sutherland, but the antagonisms aroused were of the same order. This territorial magnate acquired by marriage a vast tract of Scotland thinly peopled by proud wretches and left it a paradise of happy sheep, with the dispossessed natives—or what remained of them—clinging on at the edges, trying to convince themselves that they were better off. From time to time noblemen had pulled down English villages which offended the view from their mansions; they had driven parishioners from the commons and enclosed them; but if a Russell had set about driving upwards of five thousand of 'his' people from their Bedfordshire homes, for what he conceived to be their own good, with orders to build new homes and adopt new occupations, Woburn would not have stayed long unsacked. Yet, in the depressed north of Scotland, a wealthy Englishman was able to move aboriginal populations on this scale without serious opposition. He did what even the Crown, in theory, could not do; for the Earl of Chatham, in a famous pronouncement, said:

> The poorest man may in his cottage bid defiance to all the forces of the Crown. It may be frail—its roof may shake —the wind may blow through it—the storm may enter—

the rain may enter—but the King of England cannot enter—all his force dares not cross the threshold of the ruined tenement!

The most flattering things that can be said about the Duke of Sutherland were said after his death by a kinsman, Lord Francis Egerton:

> He tamed the torrent, fertilised the sand,
> And joined a province to its parent land.
> Recurrent famine from her holds he chased,
> And left a garden where he found a waste.
> A stranger from a distant land he came,
> But brought a birthright where he chose a name;
> And native accents shall his loss bewail
> Who came a Saxon and remained a Gael.*

In more prosaic terms, the achievements of the Duke in Sutherland were these: he laid down 450 miles of road where no roads existed, he built 134 bridges where there had been only one (the biggest was an iron bridge by Telford linking a spur of Ross-shire to the 'parent land' of Sutherland); he built twelve schools, three inns and several hamlets; he founded a fishing port with curing sheds at Helmsdale; and he rebuilt the old Dornoch Castle as a gaol, with a courtroom. In many of these operations he received Government grants. His task force included his wife's tenants, who were excused rent in return for labour. Thanks to his enterprise letters from London were enabled to reach Lochinver and Tongue on the fifth evening, the last lap being achieved by gig mail (until 1811 no mail had run north of Aberdeen). These were solid achievements; but it is a flight of fancy to pretend that the Duke 'left a garden where he found a waste'.

George Leveson-Gower was born in 1758, son of the first Marquess of Stafford. The Gowers originated in Yorkshire, moved to the Stafford area and married into the Levesons, whose coal-bearing estates had once belonged to the Church.

* Quoted in James Loch's *Memoir of Duke of Sutherland*

In three generations they rose from a baronetcy to a marquessate, 'without doing anything significantly worth-while to earn the elevation' (see Lord Ronald Gower in Introduction). As Earl Gower, the future Duke was sent as ambassador to Paris during the Revolution and achieved the difficult feat of writing dull dispatches about it. His grandson says he was 'hopelessly and lamentably' dull. 'Dull he looks as a youth, when he sat for his portrait to Romney; and dull he looks in his old age, when Phillips painted and Chantrey sculptured him ... nothing can be imagined less interesting than his career to whom Fortune had been so lavish.'* How then did he come to win the hand, in 1785, of Elizabeth, Countess of Sutherland in her own right and owner of most of that county? This presumably was the Leveson-Gower secret. The bride was beautiful and talented and it may have been she who moulded her husband into a discriminating patron of art. In 1803 he inherited from his uncle, the last Duke of Bridgewater, the famous canal and estates, along with a fine art collection. In the same year by his father's death he acquired Trentham in Staffordshire and Lilleshall in Shropshire. He was now Marquess of Stafford (as he remained through the years of controversy) and the largest landowner in Britain, with nearly 1,500,000 acres. None of his lands yielded high rents; the English estates were run down, badly drained, and a prey to greedy middlemen, and their reorganisation now claimed his attention. It was not until a dozen years after his marriage that he seriously turned his eye on his wife's coast-to-coast domains. By then he had realised that other Scottish landlords were greatly increasing their revenues by breeding sheep and selling the wool and meat to England.

The plenipotentiary assigned by the Marquess to civilise and develop his northern possessions was James Loch, an advocate who had persuaded his master that estate management was worthy of a gentleman. By degrees he became commissioner of all the ducal estates. Loch's creed was that all men must be brought to work for the greater good. At the

---

* Lord Ronald Gower: *My Reminiscences*

same time his economist's hard eye recognised that 'the demand for the raw material of wool by the English manufacturers enabled the Highland proprietor to let his lands for quadruple the amount they ever produced to him.' The slopes of Sutherland he found 'as much calculated for the maintenance of stock as they were unfit for the habitation of man'. He never doubted the propriety of turning the county into a vast sheep run.

The human wreckage in the glens outraged Loch. It was a savage land where the traveller slept in caves and crossed rivers by swimming them. Although the young men had soldiered valiantly for their country in the Countess's regiment, the Sutherland Highlanders, the elders seemed to Loch to be steeped in drunkenness and torpor. Hovels of crooked timber and bog moss were built on slopes so that the filth flowed away without any exertion by the owner; when the stench grew too great the hut was rebuilt with the same materials a short distance away. Animals used the same entrance as the family and all breathed the same black smoke. Men scorned to do outdoor work, other than to tend illicit stills. Ignorance of cultivation methods was absolute. In hard times the people made nettle broth and a kind of oatmeal pudding with the aid of blood drained from living cattle (defenders of the *status quo* maintained that blood pudding was no more a sign of desperation than the eating of frogs by the French). Although the ocean brought huge supplies of food to their thresholds, the people disdained to harvest it. Wrote Loch: 'They deemed no comfort worth the possessing which was to be purchased at the price of regular industry; no improvement worthy of adoption if it was to be obtained at the cost of sacrificing the customs or leaving the homes of their ancestors.'*

It is possible that Loch would have looked more kindly on the glen dwellers, and even detected latent virtues in them, if his master had not needed their homesteads for sheep. As it was, the prospect of doubling and quadrupling

* James Loch: *An Account of the Improvements on the Estates of the Marquess of Stafford*

the revenues, and his dislike of indolence, clouded his vision. So he urged forward the Sutherland clearances, which had already begun. The people were told briefly why they were to be moved to the coast, and were offered help to build new homes provided they moved 'with alacrity and without delay'. The able-bodied were encouraged to think that the life of a deep-sea fisherman was a nobler and manlier one than lying drunk all day in the Marquess's heather. Those who wished to continue to till the earth would be enabled to do so on sites near the sea. This news was imparted, not by the landlord himself, but by his factors, agents and other creatures, among whom were ministers of the established Church. These last are said to have explained that what was happening was fore-dained of God or alternatively was a punishment for sloth and wickedness.

The first clearances were spread over the years 1800-1820. There are many accounts of what happened, notably by Donald Macleod of Strathnaver, but they have to be treated warily. So do the emollient accounts of the clearances by Loch, by members of the Sutherland family and by that foe of slavery, Harriet Beecher Stowe. It is clear than on occasions harshness was used against those who did not abandon their homes with alacrity, Macleod tells of men with firebrands advancing on villages, people hardly able to snatch their possessions away, the old and sick and pregnant in peril, cattle roaring in fright, great clouds of smoke billowing out to sea. An old woman loses her reason, a man carries his sick children on his back for twenty-five miles, another dumps his three idiot sisters on the lawns at Dunrobin Castle and invites the Marquess's men to look after them. Since the glens were being handed over to moneyed southerners it is not surprising that some of them had a hot reception. On one such occasion the factors 'immediately swore in from sixty to a hundred retainers and the new inhabitants as special constables; and trimmed and charged the cannon at Dunrobin Castle which had reposed in silence since the last defeat of the unfortunate Stuarts.' A message of alarm was dispatched to Fort George and the 21st Foot marched over to see that an English nobleman's plans were not frustrated.* At least Dunrobin did not reactivate the gibbet and quartering-block with which the Earls of Sutherland had once kept discipline. This was far from being the only clash with authority. It looked as though the Marquess's agents were on the run when, in 1816, one of the least popular factors, Patrick Sellar, was charged at Inverness with culpable homicide while clearing Strathnaver. He was acquitted and later won damages from a sheriff-substitute who is supposed to have maligned him; but in the popular belief this was all a miscarriage of justice. A verdict of guilty would have embarrassed not only the Marquess but all the other Scottish landlords busily doing what they liked with their own.

Loch had no wish to pack off surplus people to America, there to fight for living space with Red Indians. He regarded emigration as cowardly. There was work for all in Sutherland, he claimed, so long as there was no irresponsible breeding. In theory he was for early marriage, but when maintenance of a family was left to others it degenerated into 'a selfish gratification of passion in its consequences destroying every right and proper principle of our nature'. The young men of Sutherland were therefore not free to marry until Loch gave them permission; if they disobeyed, there was no land or future for them.

Resettlement did not go smoothly. There was opposition from the tacksmen or middlemen who found themselves being eliminated. In 1812-13 and 1816-17 crop failures drove the inhabitants to the sea shores to scratch for cockles. To those without cattle the Marquess lent money, to those with cattle he sent meal. His agents strove to ensure that nothing went to the undeserving. Sometimes the fishing failed. But by 1820 Loch was able to report that 1,020 persons were engaged in this new industry and that the previous year's catch was 20,060 barrels. The Marquess offered prizes of up to £20 for the most successful boats and there was £20 for anyone who furnished his own boat and manned her entirely with a local crew. An act of 'particular perseverance or praiseworthy

* Donald Macleod: *Gloomy Memories of the Highlands*

intrepidity' could earn £5, a sum equal to the annual wage of an under-housemaid. There was even a tutor in intrepidity, an audacious Dutchman who had been captured in the late wars and had settled on the coast. Besides teaching young men to risk their lives, he showed them how to cure herrings. The Countess made awards to those who built the neatest stone cottages. She also advanced £20 towards a small brewery, in the hope of weaning her people from whisky.*

'A stranger from a distant land he came', wrote the Great Improver's panegyrist. Unfortunately the stranger came all too seldom. His underlings seem to have interpreted humane intentions in a menial spirit. During the clearances the Marquess was building up his reputation as an art patron in London, where Bridgewater House was acclaimed as serving the purpose to students that the Louvre served in Paris. Gillray, never a flatterer, has a drawing captioned 'Maecenas In Pursuit Of The Fine Arts', showing a hook-nosed, stooped, short-sighted, shabby marquess on his way to the auction-room.

As a man of vast possessions he felt the shame of his marquessate keenly. 'You may depend on it, the Marquess wishes to be a duke,' wrote the Hon. H. G. Bennet to Creevey in 1815.† But he still had twenty years to wait. He lived in princely style at Trentham and Lilleshall. At the former it was his custom, as Loch records, to distribute daily

> to every poor object who is travelling along the road, and who applies for the same, a portion of good wholesome bread, in quantity about fourteen ounces to each full-grown man and less in proportion to women and children, with a pint of good table beer. The number of people who received this donation in 1819 amounted to 9,504 men, 2,376 women and 1,789 children, consuming 1,590 leaves and 1,703 gallons of beer. From this charity are excepted all soldiers and sailors receiving the King's pay, all persons residing

* James Loch: *An Account of the Improvements on the Estates of the Marquess of Stafford*
† Sir H. Maxwell (ed.): *The Creevey Papers*

within the parish of Trentham or in its immediate vicinity.

The parish poor benefited, however, on St Thomas's Day, when they received beef, rich soup and milk. Such facts, observed Loch, 'are strongly illustrative of the beneficial effects derived to the poor from the residence of the great families of England on their respective estates; no other country affords an instance of the same kind.'

Not until 1833, after the excitement of the Reform Act, did the Marquess win his ducal coronet. He heard the news at a royal dinner party, when William IV toasted him in his new rank. The elevation was 'for political services to the Liberal Party', but these services had been trivial enough. John Wilson Croker wrote: 'When I told Francis Leveson-Gower six months ago that his father was a Reformer in hopes of being a duke he laughed at me and assured me the poor old man had no such thoughts, but was frightened at the idea of losing his present titles and establishments and supported the Ministers out of mere cowardice and dotage.'* Only six months after achieving his dukedom he died, having been taken ill on a voyage to Dunrobin. There were no unseemly scenes at his funeral, which was characterised by much prayer and a prohibition on whisky.

At once James Loch began to collect subscriptions for gigantic statues by Chantrey of the man who emptied the glens. One of them, thirty feet high on a pedestal of seventy-five feet, caps Ben Bhraggie, overlooking the Dornoch Firth. It had been suggested that Ben Klibreck, 3,200 feet high in the centre of the county, would have been more appropriate, but it was ruled to be inaccessible. The second colossus was reared on the Tittensor Hills overlooking Trentham, and in Shropshire a seventy-foot obelisk was erected on Lilleshall Hill. Had the death of every duke been marked by such indulgences, the country would have worn a strange aspect indeed.

The Duchess-Countess, as she was now known, had also

* Louis J. Jennings (ed.): *The Croker Papers*

spent less time in Sutherland than her responsibilities seemed to require. She who, as a girl, had regretted she could not fight at the head of her regiment, had become a corpulent figure addicted to snuff. 'It was considered a great favour to have a pinch of rappee out of Her Grace the Duchess-Countess of Sutherland's box,' says Lord Ronald Gower. On her visits to Sutherland she left all largesse to her underlings to distribute. Knowing no Gaelic she had to depend on clergymen and others to ascertain whether her people were happy in their new homesteads. After the Duke's death she visited Sutherland yearly and held an old-fashioned court on the lawn at Dunrobin Castle. Her people laid grievances, her factors answered them and her guests looked on. One tenant was refused written assurance that he would not lose his home. 'Weel, my Lady,' he said, 'your hand o' write ye'll no give, and your word is no' worth a damn.'* The Duchess-Countess no doubt learned with distress that the attitude towards the Army recruiters among many of her people was 'Let the sheep fight!' Queen Victoria, who later laid the foundation stone of a memorial to this 'very agreeable, clever old lady', said she was 'adored in Sutherland'.

The faithful Loch, now a Member of Parliament, continued to conduct clearances for the second Duke and was ever ready to defend the family's record. His favourite statistic was that between 1811 and 1833 his master drew not one sixpence in rent from the county, but spent £60,000 improving it. In 1845 he told Parliament that illegal stills had vanished, morals had improved, hundreds of coastal acres had been tilled and Helmsdale was exporting 37,594 barrels of herring a year. 'No portion of this kingdom', he said, 'has advanced in prosperity so much.'† This was in reply to an allegation that a traveller who covered the forty miles from Lairg to Tongue had not seen six houses or six people, only sheep.

Loch's electoral campaign in Wick in 1852 was disrupted by crowds bleating like sheep. Three years later the people

* Joseph Mitchell: *Reminiscences of My Life in the Highlands*
† *Hansard*, 12 June 1845

of Sutherland were asking each other 'the quiet but exultant query, "Did you hear the news? Loch is dead."' * He had received on his death-bed at Englefield Green an honour such as the Great Improver himself might have welcomed, a visit from his Sovereign. 'You know the interest I take in all that concerns the family of Sutherland,' the Queen explained.† In her *Highland Journal* she reproduces the inscription on Loch's memorial near Dunrobin, recording his 'virtuous labour for the land he loved and for the friends he served'.

The rigours of the Sutherland clearances had been well publicised in America. When Harriet Beecher Stowe, author of *Uncle Tom's Cabin*, visited Britain in 1853 she was taken under the wing of the second Duke and Duchess of Sutherland and supplied with facts and figures to rebut all allegations. These she seems to have readily accepted. In her naïve *Sunny Memories of Foreign Lands* she says that in 1845 Sutherland had eight bakers and forty-six grocers' shops 'in nearly all of which shoe blacking was sold to some extent, an unmistakable evidence of advancing civilisation.' Her conclusion was that the Duke's policy was 'an almost sublime instance of the benevolent employment of superior wealth and power in shortening the struggles of advancing civilisation, and elevating in a few years a whole community to a point of education and material prosperity which, unassisted, they might never have obtained.' *Murray's Handbook* for Sutherland in 1867 praises the Duke for removing from the glens those who 'had got an unconquerable habit of starving'.

Although sheep had replaced men, the sheep in turn were ousted when, in certain areas, deer were found to be more profitable. *The Economist* (2 June, 1866) described as 'at once melancholy and discreditable' the sale of a Sutherland sheep farm for conversion to a deer forest. The Norman conqueror, it said, had destroyed thirty-six villages to make a sporting estate in the New Forest; the new feudal lords who used the rights of landed property to 'extemporise wilder- nesses and deserts' were imposing on the community an im-

---

* Joseph Mitchell: *Reminiscences*
† Lord Ronald Gower: *My Reminiscences*

possible strain. John Stuart Mill in his *Principles of Political Economy* had already quarrelled with those Scots dukes who excluded the rest of mankind from the mountains in order to prevent disturbance to wild animals (the Duke of Atholl was a notable offender in Glen Tilt).

As we shall see, the scabs of the Sutherland controversy were picked at by Lloyd George for political purposes in 1913.

THE DUKERIES

20

'The Dukeries' was the name bestowed on that cluster of great estates, with contiguous parks, carved out of Sherwood Forest and belonging at various times to the Dukes of Newcastle, Portland, Kingston, Norfolk and Leeds. Their seats were, respectively, Clumber Park, Welbeck Abbey (formerly a Newcastle seat), Thoresby Hall, Worksop Manor and Kiveton Park. It was an enclave of privilege, a ducal housing estate in the romantic heart of England; a reservation with artificial lakes, long forest rides, vast mansions, temples and follies, all surrounded by stag-headed oaks of great antiquity. Here the ducal landlords enclosed and improved, planted and drained, and for ever built new houses and pulled them down again, sometimes using each other's bricks. Hither they brought the architects and architect-gardeners of the day—now a Talman or a Repton, now a Salvin or a Barry— to ring the changes on fashionable styles, to alter the presentation or context of a building. Sometimes high aspirations faded through lack of resources or for other reasons. Worksop Manor, burned down in 1761, was to have been rebuilt by the Norfolks as the largest and most magnificent house in England, but the death of an heir set a term to this ambition. Between them the lords of the Dukeries held all the forest rangerships and lord lieutenancies. Although the common people were not excluded from these domains, there was no

great welcome for them. The author of a 1797 guide commented that while Clumber Park, with its three-mile Duke's
Drive, provided excellent direction posts, those in Thoresby
Park had strips of wood nailed over the inscriptions, and
in the grounds of Welbeck a visitor looking for a convenient
exit would be sent to the right-about by a broad-faced fellow
saying 'No road this way.' This writer said that in two hours
in Clumber Park, where a sable escutcheon told of a recently
dead duke, 'we saw not a human form', though all round
were 'the sweetest love walks I had ever seen'.* One reason
why visitors were not encouraged was that the Dukeries
formed a large game-preserving area. Because of the depredations of game some farms were let at trifling rents.

If there was a founder of the 'Dukeries' it was Bess of
Hardwick, that compulsive builder who was responsible for
the early versions of Worksop Manor, Welbeck Abbey and
Bolsover. Later landlords had enclosed bigger parks from
the forests, driving the peasants to towns and villages. It may
be that the presence of dukes helped to preserve Sherwood
Forest from plundering, freely though they used its timber
for their roofs and scaffolding. The fourth Duke of Portland,
on whose lands grew legendary oaks with names like the
Duke's Walking Stick and the Green Dale Oak (through
which a carriage could pass), was so apprehensive that Britain
would run out of timber that he planted trees wherever he
could, until his park resembled a plantation. A born improver,
he carried out an imaginative feat of irrigation at Clipstone,
seven miles from Welbeck. At a cost of £8,000, using the
waste of the town of Mansfield, he turned a valley of rabbit
warrens into bright green water meadows, which became
a lure for the inquiring traveller. Not all the Duke's ideas†
were utilitarian. Near Clipstone he built a working folly

---

* John Throsby in Thoroton's *History of Nottinghamshire*
† This public-spirited Duke at his own expense built two vessels,
one a naval brig, to persuade the Admiralty that their warship design
was wrong and that the plans of Captain (later Admiral Sir William)
Symonds were superior. In a test the Duke's vessels outstripped the
Navy's leading frigates. Symonds became Surveyor of the Navy.

called the Duke's Archway, a species of Gothic lodge surmounted by a free school, decorated with effigies of Robin
Hood and other Sherwood heroes. It was meant to mark
the entrance to a broad turf ride through Birkland Forest,
seven miles long. Since the magnates of the Dukeries all
nourished expansive ideas, it is not surprising that they
quarrelled now and then over water-courses and vistas.

By the mid-nineteenth century the dukes were in flight
from the Dukeries. The Dukes of Kingston having died out in
1773, the mansion of Thoresby, former home of the bigamous
Duchess, passed to Earl Manvers. In 1843 the Duke of Norfolk
had pulled out of Worksop Manor. For the sum of £380,000
it was acquired by the fourth Duke of Newcastle, who dis-
mantled most of it. The two survivors of the Dukeries who
now merit notice are the Duke of Newcastle just mentioned
and the fifth Duke of Portland, whose family, the Bentincks,
had taken over Welbeck from the Dukes of Newcastle in
mid-eighteenth century. Between them they offer two remarkable studies in obduracy and eccentricity.

The master of Clumber, Henry Pelham Fiennes Pelham-
Clinton, fourth Duke of Newcastle, was born in 1785 and
inherited the dukedom when eleven. He spent seven years
at Eton. After the Peace of Amiens in 1803 he went to France
where he was taken prisoner and detained for four idle years.
Meanwhile his fortune was accumulating in a gratifying
manner. On his return to Britain he married one of the
richest heiress at large, eighteen-year-old Georgiana Mundy,
of Shipley, in Derbyshire, worth £12,000 a year and possessing
£190,000 besides. To add to his felicity, he controlled six
seats in Parliament.

The Duke had some difficulty in forming views on public
affairs after his captivity ('I find myself a stranger in my native
land'). France had not infected him with liberal ideas. He
deplored the way that 'young and old all flocked to those
tainted shores which had for years been the wonted abode
of vice and revolutionary horrors'. Equally he deplored the
admission to Britain of religious refugees from the Revolu-

tion, 'those lazy inhabitants and worse than useless drones' from monasteries and convents, who were 'unaccountably' allowed to re-establish their communities in Protestant England. It was all part of 'the rising tide of national fatuity'. In 1829 the emancipation of Roman Catholics seemed to him 'a heinous sin, religious as well as political, a suicidal crime', a 'grovelling at the cloven feet of Satan'.*

The Duke's antipathy to Reform exceeded that of the Duke of Wellington. At Newark in 1830 he ejected nearly forty tenants who had voted for a candidate of whom he disapproved, defending his action with the famous cry, 'Shall I not do as I will with mine own?' In the House of Lords he reproached the Attorney-General for joining in the cries of the vulgar and licentious press against one who feared his God and honoured his King. The replies by Earl Grey and the Lord Chancellor were curiously placatory, but despite all the truckling to his rank the Duke was left with the knowledge that his conduct was not admired and that people had a right to resent interference with their electoral freedom.† In the following year the Duke's truculence against the Reform Bill inspired a riot in Nottingham, where a petition for reform had been signed by 12,000. Defying the police and the 15th Hussars, the mob swarmed up to Nottingham Castle, the property of the Duke, and burned it down. It was an uninteresting castle and contained no real valuables. but it was a readily accessible symbol of insolence and privilege. The Duke now feared for the safety of Clumber and set about fortifying the mansion. More than three hundred of his tenants signed a document expressing detestation of the ill-treatment he had received, and pledging themselves to protect his property from plunderers. The Duke was not invited to sit on the Commission which disciplined the rioters and ordered three to be hanged. He was awarded £21,000 compensation against the Hundred of Broxtowe for his sacked castle, which was £10,000 less than he had asked.

* (Fourth) Duke of Newcastle: *Thoughts in Times Past Tested by Subsequent Events*
† *Hansard*, 3 December 1830

It was left gutted as a warning to future generations.

After the Reform Act the Duke valued the loss of his mostly corrupt boroughs at £200,000, a figure of fantasy. He published *An Address To All Classes And Conditions of Englishmen*, regretting the decay of the national finances, agriculture, commerce, public spirit, patriotism and virtue. 'We see unions, associations and other unlawful assemblies usurping the power of the Executive; mob law substituted for the law of the land; and a weak, wicked and mischievous Government fanning the flame of that usurpation for reasons so selfish, culpable and criminal that every honest and well-judging mind must condemn their motives and reprobate their measures.' (Some of it has a very topical ring.) Why, he appealed to the workers, change your benevolent masters for 'the flinty-hearted and despotic Reformer'? They would do better to go back to church; 'religion teaches a man to be contented, to be humble, to be obedient, to be temperate, to be virtuous.' He assailed mechanics' institutes as 'debating societies for radicals, republicans and anarchists of various species, for atheists and for dissenters'.

The Duke's store of political friends gradually dwindled. In 1839, as Lord Lieutenant of Nottinghamshire, he refused to accept two Whigs and Dissenters as magistrates and wrote an insulting letter to the Lord Chancellor. Declining to withdraw it, he was informed that the Queen had no further need of his services as Lord Lieutenant, a post he had held for thirty years. The Duke of Wellington's comment was: 'Oh, there never was such a fool as he is! The Government have done right, they could not do otherwise.' Hoping for sympathy and advice, the sacked Duke called at Apsley House. 'What shall I do?' he asked. 'Do?' echoed his fellow diehard. 'Do nothing.'* Among other disappointments was the defection of his son, Lord Lincoln (later fifth Duke) from true Tory principles to those of Sir Robert Peel. The Duke wrote to the voters of Lord Lincoln's constituency, South Nottinghamshire, explaining that his son had been the victim of bad

---

* Henry Reeve (ed.): *Memoirs of Charles Greville*

counsel and that the doctrine of free trade was vicious and revolutionary. Lord Lincoln was defeated, but found a seat elsewhere.

The harshest critics of the Duke conceded that his views were honestly held and fearlessly expressed. As he himself said, 'they were the result of reflection, not formed hastily, not the adoption of party, not borrowed with an easy indifference from the most fertile stretches of others' wit, but the plain, dispassionate and independent conviction of my own mind.' His forebear, Margaret Cavendish, Duchess of Newcastle, had justified her writings in very similar terms.

The wife who had brought the Duke such riches died at Clumber in 1822, giving birth to twins. Altogether she had thirteen children. He built her a Greek-style mausoleum church at Markham Clinton. His purchase of Worksop Manor from the Duke of Norfolk severely stretched his resources. He was not so proud that he intended to keep up two great seats in the Dukeries; he needed Worksop for the materials. In 1851 the diehard of the Forest died from typhus, and narrowly escaped being buried alive.

Clumber had been a most congenial seat in which to mourn the onrush of ruin and wickedness. His successors began to spend huge sums extending and embellishing the mansion, the architects being Sir Charles Barry and his son. They installed a dining-room for 150 people. They built a Lincoln Terrace a quarter of a mile long, with imported Italian marble, at a cost of £10,000. Then they spent another £7,000 improving the lake and installed on it two vessels, the *Lincoln* and the *Salamanca*. Before the splendours were completed, however, the shadow of disgrace fell over the Dukeries. In 1870 the sixth Duke of Newcastle was ordered to surrender to the Bankruptcy Court and, after much lordly defiance, did so. His creditors accepted 5s in the pound. It turned out that he had encumbered his estates with mortgages and charges amounting to more than £400,000, the interest on which exceeded his income by some thousands a year.

William John Cavendish-Scott-Bentinck, fifth Duke of Portland, born in 1800, at first lived a reasonably normal

life in London society, apart from a tendency to plead ill
health as an excuse for not doing something expected of him.
He held commissions in a profusion of fashionable regiments,
which does not necessarily mean that he did any soldiering.
For a short period he sat in Parliament for King's Lynn. His
mother had been unnaturally shy and in later years it
seemed that the same failing was overtaking the son. Some
wrongly blamed a skin disfigurement which was said to have
turned him into a hideous monster; others were convinced
he suffered from a mental illness; but the sixth Duke of
Portland, a cousin's son who later inherited the estates, had
no time for fancy explanations: the fifth Duke was just shy.
He was not the only noble recluse of his age, for the eighth
Duke of Bedford in later life rarely left his London house
and then only in a shuttered carriage.

The Duke's extraordinary zeal for building, which he
indulged from the day of his succession in 1854, would have
been approved by Bess of Hardwick, who built the first version
of Welbeck Abbey, though she would hardly have relished
his grand design. Right until his death the grounds of
Welbeck resembled a giant constructional camp. The Abbey
had always been criticised as low-lying, but it did not lie low
enough for its new owner, who began to build a second
palace underground. It was as if he anticipated nuclear
warfare. Motives attributed to him include a desire not to
spoil the appearance of the Abbey and an urge to give as
much employment as possible. Those who put it all down to
morbid reclusiveness must explain why the Duke went to
such vast pains to hollow out an underground ballroom
described as the largest private apartment in England (174
feet long, 64 feet wide, 22 feet high), with a hydraulic drop
for delivering up to 2,000 guests, twenty at a time. Of what
use is a giant mechanised ballroom to a hermit? It is all a
tremendous puzzle; and it does appear that even as the
Duke began to transform his seat into one where hospitality
could be dispensed on a princely scale any residual instincts
of hospitality within him shrivelled away until they were
extinguished.

It will be remembered that the sixth Duke of Somerset sent outriders to chase away the inquisitive before his carriage set out from Petworth (his trouble was pride rather than shyness). The Duke of Portland solved the spectator problem by carving out below his park, lake and fields a carriage tunnel more than a mile long, starting from his coach-house, to enable him to come and go unseen. It was lit by sky-lights, which dotted the fields like small greenhouses, and a large number of gas jets. The precautions against being seen seem more than excessive, since the Duke always rode in a coach with drawn blinds. The tunnel was but one of many honey-combing the grounds, just as the ballroom was but one of many subterranean public rooms, among them a long glass-roofed conservatory and a triple suite of library rooms nearly 250 feet long. The kitchens were set up in a converted riding stable, whence food could be lowered into a heated truck which ran on rails for 150 yards to the dining-room. Here it was kept hot in a large steam-heated cupboard.

To maintain the Welbeck tradition of equestrianism, the Duke built a windowless New Riding School out of cast iron, 385 feet long, lit by 4,000 gas jets. It was the second largest riding school in the world (according to the sixth Duke there was one in Moscow where two cavalry regiments could exercise simultaneously). Complementary to the New Riding School the Duke built a Tan Gallop, a glass-and-iron building nearly a quarter of a mile long, for exercising horses in bad weather. Evidently he baulked at the idea of burying a gallop. He was regarded as one of the best judges of a horse in Britain. On big race days his groom could be seen waiting at the telegraph office in Worksop for the results.

The recluse occupied only four or five rooms of the Abbey. In the doors were double letter-boxes, one for incoming notes, one for outgoing, to save the embarrassment of con-frontations. If he required medical attention, questions were put to a valet who felt his master's pulse and reported to the doctor standing outside. Obviously the master of Welbeck could not hope to pass wholly unscrutinised by his hundreds of workmen; in fact, he was able to move among them and even talk to them. There were strict rules: the Duke was to be accorded no sign of recognition or respect whatever. Any man who touched his hat risked dismissal. Tenants were required to pass the Duke 'as they would a tree'. His workmen were paid good wages and each was given an umbrella and a donkey. The domestic staff were also well treated; one maid who left after giving good service had a champagne send-off. The Duke even built a skating rink for his servants and any housemaid who failed to keep out of sight would be ordered there to exercise. For his own recreation he would sometimes walk at night, preceded by a lantern-bearing woman servant who was under orders to keep a forty yards distance and not speak.*

At Welbeck shooting parties were admitted so long as they kept themselves to themselves. Would-be sightseers received permission to call on condition they 'would be good enough not to *see* me' in the event of a chance encounter. To the dilettante Lord Ronald Gower the Duke sent a scarcely legible note saying that the pictures were stored, but that he was welcome to see the grounds. Lord Ronald then drove through a few tunnels and looked at a few oaks. He was told that the ducal follies were worth £1,000 a week in wages to the people of Worksop.†

The Duke had large estates in Scotland. In Ayrshire he inherited the prosperous little port of Troon, on which the fourth Duke spent £100,000. He was known for his good farms, his good schools and churches, his good roads, his superb avenues of apple and pear trees, his kitchen gardens and forcing-houses, his cow-houses with hydraulic screens to protect the occupants from the wind. He was liberal to charities. In his own way, he discharged the duties of a landed magnate to the full. As a London landlord he was almost totally invisible. His town mansion was Harcourt House in Cavendish Square. To reach it he would leave Welbeck by the tunnel and remain inside his coach, with the green silk blinds down, while it was loaded on to a railway truck at

* (Sixth) Duke of Portland: *Men, Women and Things*
† Lord Ronald Gower: *My Reminiscences*

Worksop, travelling thus to London. At Harcourt House, where the gardens were protected by high screens, servants would be ordered out of sight when the carriage drove up. The secrecy inspired wild rumours of oriental orgies in the grounds, with 'singing men', dancing girls and circus riders; neighbours said they could hear horses going round and round on the gravel in the garden.*

The Duke never married. When he died in 1879, in his eightieth year, some 15,000 men were said to be employed on different projects. In his stables nearly a hundred horses led a life of idleness. The new Duke's half-sister, the erratic Lady Ottoline Morrell, wrote an account of the mournful sight that greeted the new owner of Welbeck. His carriage was unable to reach the house without the aid of planks. The big hall was floorless. All rooms were empty except for a convenience in one corner, fully exposed. Furniture was stacked away, pictures lay frameless. Most of the rooms were painted pink and, though sunken, were bright by day. They were heated by warm air. One room occupied by the late Duke was filled with green boxes, all of which contained dark brown wigs. Through a trapdoor from an underground passage Lady Ottoline entered the building which had been the first Duke of Newcastle's riding school. It had been lined with mirrors and hung with crystal chandeliers from the raftered roof, which had been painted in rosy sunset hues. 'The sudden mood of gaiety, that had made him decorate it as a ballroom must have soon faded, leaving the mock sunset to shine on the lonely figure reflected one hundred times in the mirrors around him,' wrote Lady Ottoline.†

The sixth Duke, an outgoing sportsman, was not one to be depressed by this mournful inheritance. Funds were inexhaustible and they were used freely to restore order. In 1881 the Prince of Wales arrived to shoot at Welbeck, escorted through the tunnel by Yeomanry. After winning the Derby in 1888 and 1889 the new Duke gave some of the proceeds to his Duchess, who built a row of cottages for

* *Nottinghamshire Guardian*, 12 December 1879
† Quoted in Duke of Portland's *Men, Women and Things*

elderly estate workers called 'The Winnings'. When the
motor car came Welbeck could field sixteen chauffeurs with
as many travelling footmen, the rule being two on the box
at all times. The skating rink was superseded by a gymnasium
with a head instructor and a Japanese trainer; one of their
functions was to prevent footmen getting fat. There was also
a golf course with a staff of eleven. When the family journeyed
to their Caithness estates they travelled in a special train with
one coach for the Duke and Duchess, one for the children
and governess, one for upper servants, others for lower
servants, and then a string of waggons each carrying a motor
car.* No finer cavalcade ever left the Dukeries. The Duke
was twice Master of the Horse and had the formidable task
of organising the Queen's jubilee processions. Among
monarchs he entertained at Welbeck during his long life
were the Kings of Siam, Portugal, Spain, Belgium and Iraq.

The fifth Duke had left enough material for legends, but
long after his death new nonsensical fancies were being spun
around his grave in Kensal Green. False claimants to titles
were a familiar Victorian scourge, but few had the effrontery
of the rogues who worked up the 'Druce case'. Their con-
tention was that the Duke had lived a double life: not only
was he Duke of Portland, he was also Thomas Charles Druce,
owner of the prosperous Baker Street Bazaar in London.
Tired of his duplicity, they averred, he had decided in 1864
to 'bury' Thomas Druce in a mock funeral, the coffin being
filled with lead, and live out the rest of his life as Duke of
Portland. Had the Duke lived a less eccentric life this con-
coction might have found fewer believers. Enough specu-
lators were found to put up £30,000 in an attempt to win
the Portland estates for the Druce family. At the outset
the leading litigant was the widow of one of Druce's sons,
who complained that she was being cheated of £1,000 a day.
After her removal to a mental home other members of the
family took up the running and 'witnesses' were imported
from America and Australia. The affair reached a climax

* F. J. Gorst: *Of Carriages and Kings*

in 1907 when Herbert Druce, son and heir of the Bazaar proprietor, who had twice sworn that he had seen his father put in the coffin, was the subject of a private prosecution for perjury. To settle the issue, the grave in Highgate Cemetery was opened and found to contain the body of 'an aged and bearded man', identified as Druce. There was nothing more to be said; the conspiracy collapsed.

The sixth Duke of Portland had always treated the Druce claims with contempt. He quotes Lord Rosebery as saying, 'We might as well expect to hear that the late Duke of Westminster was Snelgrove.'*

* Duke of Portland: *Men, Women and Things*

A PRIDE OF SEATS (2)
21

The top league of Victorian dukes was a very grand league indeed. There were many ways of measuring status, other than by assessing length of lineage or admixture of royal blood. One was by enumeration of castles and mansions (taking no account of shooting boxes, London houses, villas and marine residences). Another way was to compare acreage of land or the size of the rent-roll. Other, more whimsical, methods of measuring greatness were to compare the number of miles a duke could march in a straight line without treading on other men's land (Dukes of Sutherland and Dukes of Buccleuch, about 60 miles); or to compare the lengths of frontage of principal seats (Stowe 900 feet, Gordon Castle 570), or lengths of estate walls (Woburn twelve miles, Welbeck eight), or numbers of rooms (Knole, a reputed 365), or numbers of usable guest rooms, or numbers of church livings in gift (Duke of Devonshire, over 40). Not all dukes had State apartments suitable for putting up potentates. The Duke of Atholl had a private army which he turned out at Blair Castle to greet the Sovereign (the Atholl Highlanders, raised in 1839 to support the future sixth Duke at the Eglinton Tournament and kept up to this day).

Each duke had his favourite seat. The lesser mansions might, or might not, be ready to receive him at short notice. One dwelling was often set aside for the heir, another might be used by a dowager duchess. (Dowagers were a real problem; the third wife of the third Duke of Leeds outlived him by sixty-three years and drew nearly £200,000 from the estate.) Unoccupied seats would be left in the care of stewards or bailiffs. Given the slightest opportunity, the servants devised ingenious ways of cheating their masters, mulcting visitors and holding illicit entertainments for their friends. The same profusion of establishments marked all the upper ranks of the aristocracy. Hippolyte Taine tells how in 1848 the Marquess of Hertford said to a homeless French friend: 'I have a place in Wales which I have never seen but they tell me it's very fine. A dinner for twelve is served there every day and the carriage is brought round to the door, in case I should arrive. It's the butler who eats the dinner. Go and settle down there; as you see, it will not cost me a farthing.'*

In mid-Victorian times the Devonshires, who notoriously had no property in Devon, had the following roofs for their heads: Chatsworth and Hardwick Hall, in Derbyshire; Holker Hall, in Lancashire; Bolton Abbey, in the West Riding; Compton Place, near Eastbourne; and Lismore Castle, in Ireland. At the start of the century they also had Londesborough Hall, in the East Riding, but the sixth Duke pulled it down in 1812. By the same marriage which brought Londesborough Hall and Lismore Castle the Devonshires also acquired the Palladian villa called Chiswick House (not really a home, but useful for political breakfasts) and Burlington House, in London.

In Northumberland the dukes of that name owned four castles. Three of them, Alnwick, Warkworth and Kielder, were spectacular baronial fortresses; Prudhoe was built in 1775. In the south they had Syon House in Middlesex and Albury Park in Surrey. The Howards, Dukes of Norfolk, had their main seat at Arundel in Sussex. Until 1843 they owned Worksop Manor, in the Dukeries. Other Howard homes were Scudamore House in Hertfordshire; Greystoke Castle in Cumberland; and Sheffield Manor. As lord of the manor, the

---

* H. Taine: *Notes on England*

Duke of Norfolk was said to hold Sheffield in the hollow of his hand.

Those newcomers to ducal rank, the Sutherlands, had at least five houses in Scotland, the most imposing being the *château*-like Dunrobin Castle, on the North Sea coast. In Shropshire they had Lilleshall; in Staffordshire the great Italianate pile of Trentham; in Buckinghamshire the smaller Italianate pile of Cliveden; and in Lancashire they had Worsley Hall (the Queen visited it in 1851, sailing by festive barge up the Duke of Bridgewater's canal to Manchester). When the uncouth Shah of Persia visited Trentham in 1873 he is reputed to have said to the Prince of Wales that the Duke of Sutherland was much too grand a subject—'You'll have to have his head off when you come to the Throne.'*

The biggest roster of roofs was probably that of the Buccleuchs. In Scotland their principal seat was Dalkeith House, near Edinburgh; it was here that a boy duke entertained the kilted George IV. The Buccleuchs also had Bowhill, a shooting lodge turned palace in Selkirkshire; Branxholme, in Roxburgh; and Drumlanrig and Langholm Castles in Dumfriesshire. In England they owned Boughton House in Northamptonshire and Ditton Park in Buckinghamshire. Their holdings waxed and waned over the years and they could afford to give away houses as wedding presents. From an unpromising start, the Buccleuchs had done uncommonly well, accumulating the spoil of two other ducal families, the Douglases and Montagus.

In 1878 eleven dukes figured in the list of twenty-eight noblemen owning more than 100,000 acres. At the top was the Duke of Sutherland with 1,358,546 acres, of which 1,343,000 were in Scotland. Next came Buccleuch with 458,739 acres, spread over thirteen counties; Richmond with 286,411; Devonshire with 198,665, in fourteen counties; Atholl with 194,640; Northumberland with 186,397; Argyll with 175,114; and Portland with 162,235. These figures take no account of London acreages.

On the holdings listed above the Duke of Buccleuch had

* Sir Philip Magnus: *King Edward VII*

the highest income, £216,026, as against the Duke of Sutherland's £141,679; but the Duke of Norfolk, who owned a mere 44,638 acres, was credited with an income of £269,698, which included big mineral revenues. Although the Dukes of Devonshire and Atholl owned roughly the same acreages, the Devonshire rentals yielded £180,990 as against the Atholl £40,758. The Duke of Northumberland's revenue of £176,048 approached that of the Duke of Devonshire, thanks to big mineral assets. From his 103,760 acres the Duke of Montrose drew only £23,069, chiefly because his lands included such unremunerative masses as Ben Lomond. The Duke of Buckingham and Chandos, thanks to those forced land sales in the 1840s, was down to 10,482 acres, worth £10,080; the Duke of St Albans had only 8,998 acres. The table shows the Duke of Westminster with 19,809 acres outside London, yielding £37,776, but he was easily the richest landowner in London and in the whole country. Other happily endowed London landlords were the Dukes of Bedford and Portland, whose revenues from other parts of the country were £141,557 and £124,925 respectively.*

Queen Victoria, whose private estates totalled 27,447 acres, marvelled at the ample domains of her richest subjects, notably in Scotland. The first kilted duke would meet her at his boundary, escort her to his castle, entertain her and then hand her over to his neighbour. In 1872, standing on a vantage point on the Duke of Sutherland's estates, the Queen noted: 'We got a very extensive view, though not quite clear, of endless hills between this and the West coast—all the Duke's property—where the Westminsters have two, if not three, forests of the Duke's.' Despite bad visibility the Queen could also see some lands of the Duke of Richmond.† Even in England the Queen found herself being passed from duke to duke.

If the Queen could marvel at the amplitude of the ducal life, how much greater an impression might not be created in

* John Bateman: *The Great Landowners* (Compiled from *The New Domesday Book*)
† Queen Victoria: *Our Life in the Highlands*

the mind of a traveller from an unsophisticated land? There is a good account of a visit to Gordon Castle in its heyday (about 1834) by an American journalist, Nathaniel Parker Willis. He reached Speyside by mail coach (taking two seats, one for his gouty leg) and was set down at an immense iron gate surmounted by the Gordon arms. A 'canonically fat porter' admitted him into a rich private world peopled by ladies cantering sidesaddle on blood palfreys, ladies driving nowhere in particular in phaetons, gentlemen with guns, keepers with hounds and terriers at heel, and everywhere a profusion of fallow deer, hares and pheasants. At the castle a dozen 'lounging and powdered menials' were seeing more ladies and gentlemen to their carriages. 'All this little world of enjoyment and luxury lay in the hand of one man and was created by his wealth in these northern wilds of Scotland, a day's journey almost from the possession of another human being,' wrote Willis; 'I never realised so forcibly the splendid results of wealth and primogeniture.' Just before dinner the Duke called at his room, an affable white-haired gentleman of 'noble physiognomy, but singularly cordial address', wearing a broad red ribbon across his breast, and led him through files of servants to a dining-room ablaze with gold plate. He had expected stiffness and reserve among his fellow guests, but found them courteous and genial. Moreover, they had another quality—'I have been struck everywhere in England (*sic*) with the beauty of the higher classes,' he wrote. The nobility and the gentry differed from their peasantry 'as the racer differs from the dray-horse or the greyhound from the cur'. Though he revelled in the company of these self-possessed thoroughbreds, he did not like eating 'with twenty tall fellows standing opposite whose business it is to watch me'. Breakfast, however, offered a rest from supervision. The guests, dressed in fustian, helped themselves in silence, read the newspapers and minded their own business. Until lunch no ladies were visible and the gentlemen rode, shot or played billiards. Visiting the hounds, Willis was told: 'Dinna tak' pains to caress 'em, sir—they'll only be hangit.' He was assured that if a hound formed an attachment to anyone, or showed any sign of superior sagacity, he might be tempted to cut across the scent; and the penalty for that was hanging. The Duchess had with difficulty saved the life of one of the finest in the pack when it began to show appreciation of her presence.

In the afternoons 'there was no class of vehicle which was not at your disposal', Everywhere for miles gates flew open with a touching of hats and keepers saluted in the recesses of the forest. Always there was the 'delightful consciousness that, speed where you would, the horizon scarce limited the possessions of your host.' An 'interesting and affecting' sight was a Gothic school for the estate children. Day by day the beautiful people came and went, bidding adieu to none but their host and hostess. All was informality. A person chose solitude or company as he pleased.*

Willis's host was the fifth Duke of Gordon, known as the 'Cock of the North'. His father had drained the Bog o' Gight to build the castle, which had no grandeur other than that which springs from size. The fishing in the Spey brought the Duke £8,000 a year and was fast increasing in value. Two years after Willis's visit the Duke died and the dukedom became extinct.

Another American visitor, William Hickley Prescott, left an awed account of a visit in 1850 to the Duke of Northumberland's sixteen-towered castle at Alnwick, set in an enchanted deer park with a ten-miles perimeter wall. His bedroom window looked on turrets manned by life-sized stone figures in the act of repelling invaders. After dinner, which was 'a great London dinner over again', the guests heard a concert by musicians brought three hundred miles for the purpose. In the Duke's chapel, the walls of which proclaimed the family's descent from Charlemagne, the whole household of about a hundred assembled for prayers; 'it is an excellent usage and does much for the domestic morals of England', commented Prescott. One day he attended a dinner for a thousand tenant farmers, held in a building of boards and sail-cloth lighted by hundreds of gas jets. There

* N. P. Willis: *Pencillings by the Way*

were galleries filled with ladies of the Castle and the county. 'It was an animating sight, the overflow of soul and sound,' and the cheering made Prescott's head ache. Another day he went to see 1,600 of the Duke's peasants dine. They were dressed in their Sunday best and as they drank to their noble host he thought they would go mad in their enthusiasm. The Duke took it all calmly enough. 'Persons in their condition in England are obliged to be early accustomed to take part in these spectacles, and none do it better than our excellent host and hostess. They are extremely beloved by their large tenantry.' The Duchess had her own school where she helped to teach. When Prescott thanked the Duke for his hospitality the reply was, 'It is no more than you should meet in every house in England.'*

Prescott's host was Duke Algernon, the fourth Duke, a more popular and enlightened Percy than his predecessor. He spent freely improving his estates, built numerous schools and churches, and installed four lifeboats. This did not stop him devoting £350,000 to improving Alnwick Castle, over a span of fifteen years. The first Duke had restored the fortress, employing Robert Adam; but the fourth Duke removed most of the Adam improvements and refashioned the public rooms, with the aid of Anthony Salvin, in Italian cinquecento style. Charged with making a mockery of an ancient English fortress, he replied, 'Would you wish us only to sit on benches upon a floor strewn with rushes?'

When Augustus Hare visited Alnwick in 1887 he found that the sixth Duke and his Duchess had joined the Irvingite cult. The Duchess's father was the last of the apostles in whose lifetime the Lord was due to return. Although a very old man he was still beating up recruits—'and when he dies, what will happen?' The Irvingites gabbled nonsense when seized by the Spirit and this was recorded and treated as prophecy. As calmly as they could, the family waited and watched for the dawn of the millennium, but it was 'terribly anxious work'. When one of the sons fell ill they had him anointed with oil and he recovered. 'It is curious', wrote

* George Ticknor: *Life of W. H. Prescott*

Hare, 'to hear members of the family say casually, "The angel was here on Monday and will be here again on Friday." '
(The Percys were not the only Victorian dukes to be carried away with religious fervour. In 1875 the Duke and Duchess of Sutherland fell victim to the American revivalists, Sankey and Moody. The Duchess would make up parties at Stafford House and transport them to the opera house in the Haymarket for Bible readings; a Lady Barker was nauseated by the mixture of religious fervour and 'the most intense toadyism of the Duchess'.)*

Raby Castle, in Durham, the seat of the Dukes of Cleveland, was another feudal fortress transmogrified—indeed, vandalised—to accord with Victorian taste. In its Barons' Hall the Nevilles had once entertained seven hundred knights and their retainers. The best part of a visit to Raby was the arrival. The guest entering by the Neville Gate was driven into the great hall of the castle and set down at a broad flight of steps; his carriage then passed right through the castle in order to leave. Said a guidebook of 1857: 'When the brilliant gas above combines its glare with that of two enormous fires, and the roof is echoing to the tramp of the horses and the roll of the wheels, the visitor cannot but be struck with this unusual entrance to the magnificent pile.' Under William Henry Vane, first Duke of Cleveland of the second creation, the hospitality of Raby was only for the strong. The Duke was a Whig and a strong advocate of reform, yet with many of the characteristics of a high Tory. It has been said that he acquired six boroughs in order to be given a marquessate and then gave them up during the Reform agitation in order to win a dukedom. A less cynical explanation comes from one who is normally a severe critic of the aristocracy. 'Taunted with being a borough-monger, the Marquess frankly declared that he had purposely at great expense obtained the control of the boroughs because such property was so often used for improper purposes and there was no other mode of counteracting those who used it.' He claimed that his public-spirited

* J. C. Pollock: *Moody Without Sankey*

act had cost him a quarter of a million pounds. It certainly won him his dukedom in 1833.*

From his days as Earl of Darlington, the Duke had been an obsessive fox-hunter. In 1820 he blocked the proposed route of the Stockton–Darlington railway because it threatened his favourite covert. He kept two magnificent packs, one bred large and the other small, and hunted them on alternate days, turning out for thirty-eight seasons without interruption. Both packs were renowned for speed. Tenants were well paid to preserve foxes and high wrath was visited on spoilsports. By night the Duke wrote up the day's events in his journal, praising the brave and lacerating the craven. One day the fox was headed by 'a numerous set of villainous, rascally admirers of Orator Hunt', 'a set of damned, skirting, short-riding, nicking, scut-stinking fellows'.† Drinking with the Duke was as strenuous as hunting, since he had his glasses made so that they would not stand and had to be drained at once. The Duke's unconcealed pride in his descent through his grandmother from Charles II's bastard, the Duke of Southampton and Cleveland, was a 'cause of wonder' to the compilers of the *Complete Peerage*. He was the head of the historic house of Vane of Raby and held a peerage of some antiquity, yet he must needs take his ducal title from 'an infamous adulteress', a title which was 'the actual wages of her prostitution'. This unfastidious, lusty yet not philistine Duke was succeeded by three sons in turn, each of whom scandalously failed to produce a male heir, and the dukedom died out in 1891.

High-perched Belvoir Castle, seat of the Dukes of Rutland, was the gracious 'Beaumanoir' of Disraeli's *Coningsby*. It had been rebuilt over and over again since the Conquest. By the late eighteenth century it was in sad decline. In 1789 that snorting traveller, the Hon. John Byng, found it very dilapidated, under a housekeeper of 'a very drunken, dawdling appearance'. He exclaimed: 'One night's losses at play of the late Duke had furnished this house; at present there

---

* Howard Evans: *Our Old Nobility*
† Sir Timothy Eden: *Durham*

is not a habitable room or a bed fit to sleep in.'* At this
period the building was an uncompromising rectangular
block. The fifth Duke and his Duchess began to remodel it,
with the aid of James Wyatt, as a towered mediaeval castle.
A bad fire in 1816 set back their efforts. Then, Wyatt having
died, the Duchess continued the transformation with the aid
of the Duke's chaplain, the Rev. Sir John Thoroton, the
Duke allowing them to do as they wished. The result has been
derided as a mish-mash of Norman and Gothic, a deformed
phoenix, a triumph of undisciplined zeal. Charles Greville
thought it a 'sad mess' and said the interior had 'enormous
faults which are wholly irretrievable'. The Duchess is commemorated in an astonishing mausoleum, the foundation
stone of which was laid by her admirer, the 'Grand
Old' Duke of York. The work of Benjamin and Matthew
Wyatt, it consists of a neo-Norman shell enclosing a wild
baroque surprise in the form of a white marble Duchess
floating up to Heaven. She is greeted by four welcoming
cherubs—her four dead children—one of whom holds over
her a crown of glory. The scene is theatrically lit by tinted
light from above. The historian of Belvoir, the Rev. Irvin
Eller, considers that the spectacle creates great depth of
feeling, but seems to paralyse the power to express it.†
Perhaps, secretly, he found it vulgar.

Charles Greville attended the Duke of Rutland's birthday
party in 1834. All the villages were feasting on free meat and
ale and the church bells rang in honour of their temporal
lord. Greville's fellow guests, who included the Duke of
Wellington, were 'a rabble of fine people, without beauty
or wit among them'. The host woke this rabble every morning with martial music on the terrace. Every day saw a new
service of plate produced. Touring the castle, Greville found
the cleanliness and order most admirable. The cook produced
400 meals daily. In the servants' hall he was astonished to
find nearly 150 diners listening to an oration by the head
coachman, 'a man of great abdominal dignity', whose 'Cicer-

* John Byng: *The Torrington Diaries*
† Irvin Eller: *History of Belvoir Castle*

onian brows were adorned by an ample flaxed wig'. The Rutland fortunes had clearly revived and the days of baronial hospitality were back.

Greville delivered this assessment of his host:

> The Duke of Rutland is as selfish a man as any of his class—that is, he never does what he does not like, and spends his whole life in a round of such pleasures as suit his taste, but he is neither a foolish nor a bad man, and partly from a sense of duty, partly from inclination, he devotes time and labour to the interest and welfare of the people who live and labour on his estate. He is a Guardian of a very large Union, and he not only attends regularly the meetings of the Poor Law Guardians every week or fortnight, and takes an active part in their proceedings, but he visits those paupers who receive out-of-door relief, sits and converses with them, invites them to complain to him if they have anything to complain of, and tells them that he is not only their friend but their representative at the assembly of Guardians, and it is his duty to see they are nourished and protected.*

The fifth Duke was unhappy about the influence wielded over his son, Lord John Manners, by Disraeli and the 'Young England' Party. This was a romantic Tory movement designed to revive something of the royal prerogative, to counter the doctrines of the big manufacturers and to restore the harmonious interdependence of rich and poor. Lord John wrote a poem, *England's Trust*, which haunted him through his long political life. It contained the lines:

> Each knew his place—king, peasant, peer or priest—
> The greatest owned connection with the least;
> From rank to rank the generous feelings ran
> And linked society as man to man.

It was a sentiment which found easy expression at a ducal

* Henry Reeve (ed.): *The Greville Memoirs*

birthday party. The most anthologised, and most mocked, lines were:

> Let wealth and commerce, laws and learning die,
> But leave us still our old nobility.

Disraeli appreciated 'Beaumanoir' because of its air of habitual residence. The host was not stiff and remote like a Spanish grandee. It was not a gala house to which grand furniture and grand servants were sent express from London, and where the ladies, invisible in the morning, rolled round aimlessly in carriages in the afternoon. At Beaumanoir ladies could be seen all day working gracefully at their embroidery frames.

> How delightful was the morning-room at Beaumanoir; from which gentlemen were not excluded with the assumed suspicion that they can never enter it but for felonious purposes. Such a profusion of flowers! Such a multitude of books! Such a various prodigality of writing materials! So many easy chairs, too, of so many shapes; each in itself a comfortable home; yet nothing crowded. Woman alone can organise a drawing-room; man succeeds sometimes in a library.

This suggests that Belvoir was a marvel of domestic comfort. Other visitors stress its discomforts, notably in winter. Under the seventh Duke (Lord John) the retainers were not only ancient but performed ancient rituals. By night invisible watchmen on padded feet called out the hours with an 'All's well'. By day giant water men with yokeborne buckets of bathwater patrolled the corridors and coalmen 'resembling Bill Sykes' entered the bedrooms of late-rising guests with sacks of coal. Towards dinner-time an old 'gong man' bearded to the waist toured the castle announcing that it was time to dress. No gas was installed until the twentieth century, after the seventh Duke's death.*

* Diana Cooper: *The Rainbow Comes and Goes*

That indiscreet guest Augustus Hare picked up much gossip at Belvoir. He says that a ducal daughter once encountered near the castle a beautiful peasant woman with a missing front tooth. Asked how this misfortune had happened, the woman said that the Duchess Isabella, wife of the fourth Duke, had lost the corresponding tooth and 'forced me to have mine taken out to replace it'. It is true that transplanted teeth were worn (there was a traffic in teeth from the dead of the Napoleonic Wars), but it is hard to credit the notion of a duchess exercising *droit de seigneur* to the point of demanding teeth from the living tenantry.

More than one lord of Chatsworth has felt the strain of having to live like an emperor when his tastes were for quietude. William Spencer Cavendish, sixth Duke of Devonshire, who was a deaf bachelor and the son of Georgiana, was happier eating by himself than with fifty or a hundred; yet he knew that magnificence was his duty and he did not shirk it. In 1811 his coming-of-age celebrations at Hardwick Hall, to judge from an eye-witness account by William Howitt, were wholly scandalous. Howitt, then a youth of seventeen, arrived at the great Elizabethan mansion with 'feelings of wonder and delight', which faded when he found the park littered with the dead-drunk like corpses on a battlefield. Then he reached the seat of hospitality.

I saw barrels standing, spigots running; men catching their hats full and running here and there, while others were snatching at their prize and often spilling the ale on the ground. Sometimes there were two or three trying to drink out of a hat at once; others were stooping down to drink at the spigots; there were fighting, scuffling, clamour and confusion. All round the hall people swarmed like bees. At the doors and gates masses were trying to force their way in; while stout fellows were thumping away at their skulls with huge staves, with an energy that one would have thought enough to kill them by dozens, but which seemed to make little impression.

Inside the hall tenants and yeomanry were stuffing themselves with roast beef and plum pudding, to the loud music of bands. Gate-crashers climbed up the walls to watch and food was thrown up to them. One man fell and was killed, but his body was carried away to an outhouse and the riot rolled on. Another reveller leaped over a wall on the edge of a precipice and was dashed to death. This second fatality cast something of a shadow, but the hard core continued singing, shouting, dancing, tumbling and rolling each other in soot.* Probably only the deaths distinguished this orgy from other coming-of-age celebrations.

In contrast, life at Chatsworth could be excessively staid. Emily Eden wrote, in 1825: 'We have made a rule to accept one invitation out of two. We go there with the best dispositions, wishing to be amused, liking the people we meet there. loyal and well affected to the King of the Peak himself, supported by the knowledge that in the eyes of the neighbourhood we are covering ourselves with glory by frequenting the great house ...'; but, at the end of the second day, 'the depths of *bore* were broken up and carried all before them', and it was necessary to make urgent excuses to leave. 'I have not yet attained the real Derbyshire feeling which would bring tears of admiration into the eyes whenever the Duke observed that it was a fine day.'†

In 1826 the King of the Peak led a dazzling mission to Russia for the Coronation of the Czar, spending £50,000 of his own money. For a visit to Chatsworth by the Queen and Prince Albert in 1843 he fired salutes with eighteen-pounders from the heights, mounted illuminations and fireworks, turned on the high fountains, organised a ball, a concert and a *battue*, and showed his guests a seventy-stone pig. Next year, with bands and an escort of Lancers, he was entertaining the Czar and eight hundred guests to a grand *déjeuner à la fourchette* at Chiswick House, where the Watteau-like scene was enhanced by the presence of an elephant and a llama.

* William Howitt: *Rural Life in England*
† Violet Dickinson (ed.): *Emily Eden's Letters*

Not often was the Duke outshone. There was an occasion at Doncaster Races when he started the day with a coach-and-six and twelve outriders and 'Old Billy Fitzwilliam' (the fourth Earl of Fitzwilliam) fielded a similar equipage; but on the following day 'Old Billy' appeared with two coaches and sixteen outriders and did so for the rest of the meeting. The Duke disdained to compete. Keeping up appearances called for much logistical effort. When the Duke moved from Chatsworth to Devonshire House a waggon was loaded with gold and silver plate, and accompanied by four guards who took with them a stock of Chatsworth-brewed ale. The expedition, headed by four Shire horses, took three weeks, the orders being to proceed very slowly for the sake of the cargo. Police and extra guards attended the resting-places of the waggon and a great deal of treating went on.* Unlike 'Goody Newcastle', the Duke did not divert troops of horse to escort his plate.

The Duke did much to unify the piecemeal palace of Chatsworth. He added the controversial North wing crowned by a self-conscious theatre tower. One of his vistas was spoiled by the remnants of the village of Edensor, which he demolished in 1839 and replaced with a 'model' village about a mile away, still within the ducal park. The Duke's chief labours were eventually devoted to glorifying his gardens. This he did in conjunction with his gardener-architect, Joseph Paxton. The working friendship between bachelor duke and artisan recalls the fruitful association between the Duke of Bridgewater and James Brindley. Young Paxton had not the angularities of Brindley, however: he rapidly acquired enough polish to become the Duke's travelling and shooting companion. His master first met him in the experimental gardens of the Horticultural Society at Chiswick and appointed him head gardener at Chatsworth at £6 a month, with cottage. Paxton was then in his early twenties. A dozen years later he refused an offer to become head gardener at Windsor at a rumoured £1,000 a year. His Great Conservatory at Chatsworth proved an expensive toy.

* Crichton Porteous: *Derbyshire*

It covered an acre, took four years to erect, cost £10,000 and needed £2,000 a year to maintain, including the feed for its two hundred canaries. Fuel was brought to it by an underground tramway half a mile long. Urged on by his ambitious gardener, the Duke began to import rare plants from all over the world. There was great excitement over the arrival of the first *Amherstia Nobilis* from India. One of its staging posts was Devonshire House, where Duke and gardener breakfasted under the leaves. Disappointingly, the *Amherstia* never flowered.* More successful was the giant Amazon water lily, the floral wonder of 1849, with leaves strong enough for Paxton's seven-year-old daughter to walk about on them. The Duke's zeal to import exotics waned after two of his emissaries died on an expedition in North-West America.

So far, the ducal seats noticed have been conspicuous for a blend of hospitality and magnificence. Hamilton Palace in Lanarkshire was a vast treasure-house, but at the time of Alexander Hamilton, tenth Duke of Hamilton and premier peer of Scotland, it was far from being a focus of social and political life. Its greatest day was that on which the Duke received a Pharaoh's funeral.

If the sixth Duke of Somerset was the proud duke of the eighteenth century, the tenth Duke of Hamilton filled that role for the nineteenth century. He was three times a duke (his other dukedoms were those of Brandon in Suffolk and Châtelherault in France), twice a marquess, three times an earl and eight times a baron. A descendant of the two great houses of Hamilton and Douglas, he traced his claim to the Scottish throne by way of the old Regent Arran, first Duke of Châtelherault. In Italy as a young man he developed a keen collector's eye. In 1806 he went as ambassador to St Petersburg and, characteristically, brought home his ambassadorial throne to instal in the throne-room at Hamilton Palace. Pride kept him high above the political battle; so high that in the great world he passed largely unnoticed. His life span coincided almost exactly with that of the Duke

* Violet Markham: *Paxton and the Bachelor Duke*

of Wellington; but whereas no man could have lived a more purposeful life than the Great Duke, no man could have lived a less purposeful one than the proud Duke.

Hamilton Palace was said to resemble Berkeley Square roofed over and set down in the countryside. Its rich art treasures* were open to view, but its historical records were not. In the grounds, as a reminder of the French dukedom, was a mock, four-turreted castle of Châtelherault. The great oaks dating from the Conquest, the herds of milk-white cattle formed a splendid setting. In earlier times the palace had been almost engulfed by the old town of Hamilton, but the houses had been razed and the site enclosed. In the post-Waterloo slump the Duke employed many hundreds of labourers to rebuild the palace in accordance with his royal tastes.

In competition with the British Museum the Duke had bought a superb Egyptian sarcophagus, to which he was very attached. It was supposedly that of a princess whose delicate likeness was incised on its basalt. Whether he intended it from the outset as a receptacle for his own bones is not clear; but as the years advanced he was moved more and more to contemplate its exciting possibilities and even to try it out for size. His own figure was stiff and militarily erect and it was obvious that, when the day came, it would be a tight fit. Some accounts say the interior was enlarged, others that the basalt was too hard to work. A sarcophagus, however royal, was no use without a mausoleum. The Duke therefore resolved to build a death-house which should be the eighth wonder of the world and the first wonder of Scotland. It rose in white stone to 120 feet, towering above the ancient trees, and its dome was visible for miles. An inscription boasted that Alexander, *Dux Hamiltonii Decimus*, had reared *hoc monumentum sibi et suis.* Inside was an octagonal chapel with a floor made of jasper, porphyry and marble. Its doors were replicas of those fashioned by Ghiberti for the Baptistery in Florence. 'What a grand sight it will be when twelve Dukes of Hamilton rise together at the

* They were sold off for £428,000 by the needy twelfth Duke in 1882

Resurrection!' is the boast attributed to the Duke by Augustus Hare. The mausoleum was still not quite completed
when the Duke lay dying, aged eighty-five, in Portman
Square, London. Fearing that he would not fit inside the
princess, he gasped to those round him, 'Double me up,
double me up!' His last earthly journey appears to have
been to buy spices for his embalming.

The body was removed to Scotland and displayed in the
grand entrance hall of Hamilton Palace. Some 3,400 persons,
'decently attired', mounted a black marble staircase flanked
by busts of emperors, and were pointed on their way by
twenty-four mutes until they reached the satinwood coffin
covered with crimson silk, under a pall of Genoa velvet.
Statues of Apollo, Hercules and Mercury were already keeping vigil. After the lying-in-state the coffin was placed in the
black-draped chapel of the mausoleum, now resembling a
sepulchral marquee, and all left except the embalmer and
a party of workmen. According to Hare, who dined out on
such stories, no amount of 'doubling up' would get the body
inside the sarcophagus and they had to cut off the feet. A
lid weighing fifteen hundredweight was finally lowered
over the remains of *'Alexander, Hamiltonii, Brandonii et
Castellerotti Dux'*.

The mausoleum had a six-second echo, described in guide-
books as long-drawn and beautiful. To Hare it seemed that
voices were whispering and clamouring together in the dome.
When the door banged it was 'as if all the demons in the
Inferno were let loose, and the shriekings and screamings
around you are perfectly terrific.'* Underneath was a vault
for the rest of the illustrious Hamilton dead, transferred
from the old Hamilton Church. They included the decapitated first Duke and the mangled fourth Duke, victim
of the notorious four-man duel. The eleventh Duke doubtless
noted the place reserved for him. He too suffered from the
sin of pride, which he indulged at the Court of Louis
Napoleon. Once he was in trouble for breaking the law
which forbade all but the Emperor to drive down the Champs

* Augustus Hare: *The Story of my Life*

Elysées in a carriage drawn by more than eight horses. The Duke exceeded the limit by four.

The twelve Dukes of Hamilton were robbed of the chance to rise together from their exclusive tomb, for the Palace which had once repulsed a town was unable to save itself from mining subsidence and was razed in 1927. The dead dukes were reinterred in a hitherto common field which was annexed to Hamilton cemetery. By then the landscape had been well ravaged by industry.

Most of the great ducal houses were open to the Victorian public. Chatsworth received 60,000 visitors a year. In 1854 Paxton, by then Sir Joseph, told a committee on public houses that as many as a thousand excursionists went round the house at a time. Only one or two men were needed to look after them; they behaved 'exceedingly well'.* A generation later the eighth Duke of Devonshire, surveying his trippers, said, 'I daresay they will bring down the floors some day, but I don't see how we can keep them out.' Lady Diana Cooper, who lived at Belvoir as a child, testifies that trippers poured through all day, leaving an 'asphyxiating' smell, and picnicked everywhere in sight. Her grandfather, the seventh Duke, 'loved his tourists', and allowed them in free.†

By general consent, the finest London residence in Victorian times was Stafford House in the Mall, belonging to the Dukes of Sutherland. It was originally started for the Grand (but penniless) Old Duke of York, with the aid of a £60,000 loan from the Marquess of Stafford, later first Duke of Sutherland. The plans were submitted to that amateur architect, the Duchess of Rutland, for whom the Duke of York cherished a *grand amour*, and she laid the foundation stone (as he laid the foundation stone of her mausoleum). Since the Duke was hopelessly in debt the house had to be sold during construction to the Staffords, who completed it at enormous expense. The young Queen Victoria visiting Stafford House said to the second Duchess, 'I come from my

* J. L. and B. Hammond: *The Bleak Age*
† Diana Cooper: *The Rainbow Comes and Goes*

house to your palace.' Its chief feature was the grand sweeping staircase essential to fashionable receptions. In these august surroundings innumerable distinguished visitors received the aristocratic embrace. Here in 1853 was drawn up the protest of the English ladies against slavery. Harriet Beecher Stowe appeared out of her element when put on parade by the Duchess. 'The magnificent figure of the hostess looked like some splendid bird of paradise mothering under her arms a little black chick,' wrote the eighth Duke of Argyll. The American visitor was much impressed by the stately Highlanders in full costume who greeted her on arrival; but her luncheon was slightly spoiled by the proffered plover's nest, 'precisely as the plover made it', with five speckled eggs, none of which she could bring herself to touch.*

In 1864 Stafford House was *en fête* for Garibaldi, the Italian liberator, flamboyant in red. The Duke's four-horse carriage which bore him there 'literally fell to pieces in the stable, strained to breaking-point by the weight of thousands of strong arms that had snatched at it, clinging to its sides as it passed through a London gone mad with joy.'† The Queen was affronted at the way her favourite Duchess, along with the Duchess of Argyll, fell on Garibaldi and worshipped him. For ten days he held levees at Stafford House; but the Queen was wrong in thinking they had put out a red carpet for him—it was just the ordinary red carpet. The Duchess of Sutherland may have had her radical moments, but all three of her daughters married dukes.

That Piccadilly mansion with a past, Devonshire House, was a building of modest, if not dreary, mien, but the sixth Duke refashioned the State rooms and challenged the Stafford House staircase with one which rose so gently and graciously that going up it was said to be like descending another. The Duke kept untouched the room in which his mother, Georgiana, died. Devonshire House offended generations of Londoners because it was hidden behind a high

* H. B. Stowe: *Sunny Memories*
† (Fifth) Duke of Sutherland: *The Story of Stafford House*

wall. Their complaints were ignored until the 1890s, when the eighth Duke broke the wall with a pair of fine gates from Chiswick House.

Northumberland House, where Oliver Goldsmith addressed a gorgeous manservant in mistake for the Duke, vanished in 1874 to make room for Northumberland Avenue. It was the last of the old noble mansions in the Strand. The Duke received nearly £500,000 compensation, which caused not a few to wonder whether this was the easiest and cheapest way of linking Charing Cross with the new Embankment. In the presence of a crowd the famous stiff-tailed lion, which had dominated the building for over 125 years, was removed for installing at Syon House, where it irresistibly suggests a child's whimsical addition to a toy castle. By the levelling of Northumberland House the Percys lost a useful starting-point for funerals, which used to jam the streets solid all the way to Westminster Abbey.

TO HIM THAT HATH

22

The nineteenth century yielded only half a dozen new dukedoms. Of these, only Wellington's was a reward for high services to the State; the rest were a recognition of wealth or political alignment.

As we have seen, George IV created the unhappy dukedom of Buckingham and Chandos. His successor, William IV, was responsible for two dukedoms, those of Cleveland and Sutherland. Queen Victoria created three new dukes and revived an extinct dukedom.

Her first creation was an Irish one conferred in 1868 on James Hamilton, Marquess of Abercorn, a one-time Groom of the Stole to Prince Albert. The new Duke had his full share of Hamilton pride and as Lord Lieutenant of Ireland was not one to let standards slip. His footmen washed their hands in rosewater before serving at meals and his housemaids wore kid gloves when making the beds. He had ample acres in Ireland to support the highest rank. His seven daughters also did credit to their station: two married dukes, one a marquess and the other four married earls.

The Queen's next dukedom went in 1874 to Hugh Lupus Grosvenor, the prodigiously rich third Marquess of Westminster. Nominally, he was honoured for services to the Liberals, but this was something of a fiction. In 1866 he had seceded into the 'Cave of Adullam' from which renegade

Liberals sallied out to attack the Gladstone Government on the franchise issue. He also split with Gladstone on Irish Home Rule. At one stage his feelings were such that he cast out a Millais portrait of Gladstone from his house. When he returned to heel he declined office and gave silent support only. It is impossible to disagree with his biographer, Gervas Huxley, who says: 'As in the case of the dukedom of Sutherland ... wealth and high standing rather than any outstanding services were the criteria.'* Quite simply, he was made a duke for being a great landlord. His mother, who despised Gladstone, disapproved of the dukedom, rating it as ostentatious; her own husband had never aspired to higher rank.

Most of the Westminster wealth stemmed from a marriage in 1677 at St Clement Dane's, London, between a twenty-one-year-old Grosvenor and the eleven-year-old heiress, Mary Davies, whose scrivener father died in the Great Plague. She was the great-grand-niece of a money-lender, Hugh Audley, whose wealth descended to her. At one period she had to be hidden away in France against kidnappers. In all she brought her husband a hundred acres or so of Mayfair and the whole manor of Ebury, once the property of the Abbots of Westminster, stretching between Oxford Street and the Thames. The land was agricultural but even then its potentialities were seen to be enormous. In later life Mary was headstrong and erratic, and died insane. Her husband, Sir Thomas Grosvenor, was a Cheshire baronet who already owned a valuable estate brought into the family by an earlier heiress; and on it he built the first and most seemly version of Eaton Hall. It was his son, Sir Richard Grosvenor, who laid out and built a large area of Mayfair, where squares and streets bear family names like Grosvenor, Audley and Davies. As a developer he was in as high a class as the Dukes of Bedford who were simultaneously creating Bloomsbury. The building up of the manor of Ebury, much of it the work of Thomas Cubitt, was accelerated when George IV's choice of Buckingham House for a palace rendered the area fashionable. Here,

* Gervas Huxley: *Victorian Duke*

too, in Belgravia and Pimlico, the streets bear family names. Eaton Square and Grosvenor Square alike were enclaves built by aristocracy for aristocracy; and, as on the Bedford estates, privacy and quiet were assured by a system of ducal beadles and barriers.

The Grosvenors' methods of development did not escape criticism on social grounds. Sir John MacDonell, a barrister, published in 1873 a much-quoted book, *The Land Question*, describing how London's dukes exacted 'hundreds of thousands of pounds annually from those who enrich their property'.

> Were they imbeciles instead of good men of business, they must earn more than thousands of toiling artisans; were they Solons or Solomons it would not make much difference. Their position of affluence is independent of virtue or vice, prudence or folly. They exist; that is their service. It was the sole service of most of their ancestors.

Sir John referred to the many private Acts of George III and George IV 'which were studded with acts of favouritism to landlords'. Owners and builders were obliged to level, pave and gravel the streets, but the Grosvenors and Russells as ground landlords were excluded from any responsibility to do so; at the same time they were empowered to erect barriers at will on streets maintained by others, thus enabling higher rents to be charged for exclusiveness. Describing the system as 'shabby and incredible', Sir John asked: 'Which is the more marvellous, the patience of those who tolerate it, or the effrontery of those who flaunt their tyrannical placards before passers-by?'

Frank Banfield, author of a series of exposures in the *Sunday Times* in the late 1880s, said that a dialogue with an intelligent child of the future, would go like this:

> Who caused these houses to be built?
> *The Duke of Westminster.*
> Who paid for the building of these houses?

The Duke of Westminster.
Then they belong to the Duke of Westminster's tenants' children?
No, to the Duke of Westminster's children.
Was the Duke of Westminster very kind to his tenants?
He made them beautify his building land out of their own pockets and took credit for that; charged them a heavy ground rent and at the end of ninety years they were to submit to reversion of the property to his descendants.

In short, said Banfield, the ducal family simply provided the land and drew up the building specifications, happy in the knowledge that so long as London expanded their sons and grandsons would become millionaires. Agricultural crops could fail; rentals never.*

The Grosvenors' family seat of Eaton Hall was rebuilt in 1802 by the first Marquess of Westminster. William Polden designed a vast farrago of Cathedral Gothic, with high stained-glass windows, cast-iron pinnacles and octagonal turrets. Mrs Arbuthnot, who visited it with her Duke, thought it the most 'gaudy concern' she had ever seen, resembling the 'new-built place of a rich manufacturer'; but the young Princess Victoria was captivated by its indiscriminate riches. It certainly provided much-needed employment for hundreds, which was the excuse for many building excesses of the period. It is odd that a family which built elegant homes for other people could tolerate such a fussy folly for their own dwelling. The second Marquess decided to remodel the building in the 1850s, employing England's most accomplished designer of town halls, Alfred Waterhouse. The style of Gothic was modified and further extravagances were added, among them a clock tower not unlike that of Big Ben; and, since the Hall was too vast for normal habitation, a new wing was built for family living. Perhaps the most engaging feature of the revised establishment was the carillon which played 'Home, Sweet Home' when the owner arrived. Less endearing was a giant equestrian statue of Hugh Lupus,

* Frank Banfield: *The Great Landlords of London*

nephew of William the Conqueror. Lupus's nephew, Gilbert le Gros Veneur ('the Great Hunter' or perhaps 'the Fat Hunter') was thought by the family to have founded the line. Genealogists dispute this claim.

The first Duke of Westminster was God-fearing and high-principled, but willing to live with a great deal of outward show, as befitted a Croesus among landlords. His family had the closest of links with the ducal Sutherlands. The Duke's mother was a daughter of the first Duke of Sutherland and he married a daughter of the second Duke. His second wife was a Cavendish. Had there been a monopolies commission to consider ducal marriages, such mergers of land and wealth would surely have qualified for its attention. Westminsters and Sutherlands lived in each other's mansions and hunted each other's game. Both built private railways on their estates, to link up with the trunk networks. Both had London homes which were renowned not only as high temples of hospitality but as forcing-houses for philanthropy. When the second Duke of Sutherland tired of his new Palladian mansion at Cliveden, the Duke of Westminster took it over from him; but in 1893 he disposed of it to the Astors, which infuriated Queen Victoria.

The third Duke of Grafton, in his pious years, had won the Derby three times. The pious Duke of Westminster won it four times, in 1880, 1882, 1886 and 1899. Twice he carried off the Triple Crown—2,000 Guineas, St Leger and Derby. The pride of his stud was Donovan, the Derby winner of 1873, which he bought for 14,000 guineas; the colt's descendants included such punters' delights as Bend Or, Ormonde and Flying Fox. In the Queen's Jubilee year of 1887 there was a suggestion that the Duke should ride Ormonde in the royal procession; instead, Ormonde was brought up to London for the festivities and nibbled orchids at the Duke's garden party at Grosvenor House.* The Duke showed a good sense of values when he paid Fred Archer £500 for riding Bend Or to victory in the Derby but gave the trainer Robert Peck £1,000. Over a period of twenty-five

* Theodore A. Cook: *A History of the English Turf*

years the Duke is estimated to have pocketed £350,000 from
racing, which was roughly the sum he spent on building
farmhouses, cottages, schools, churches and institutions on
his Cheshire estates. According to *The Times*, the Noncon-
formist conscience which was outraged by Lord Rosebery's
racing successes did not resent those of the Duke of Westminster; the Duke 'could pass from a racecourse to take the
chair at a missionary meeting without incurring the censure
of the strictest'.* His benefactions were on a suitably princely
scale. It was said that the city of Chester would at least
hesitate before opposing his wishes. The Duke was not too
exalted to take the presidency of the Metropolitan Drinking
Fountain and Cattle Trough Association, or of the United
Committee for the Prevention of Demoralisation of Native
Races by the Liquor Traffic (his forebears had done much to
demoralise the natives of Cheshire at elections with wine
and ale). The Duke's last Parliamentary appearance was in
advocacy of 'a step in the direction of prevention of cruelty
to women', namely, a Bill to compel shops to provide seats
for assistants. Shop girls, he said, were called upon to undergo
'long periods of enforced sentry duty which would provoke
a mutiny if imposed on soldiers of the Line'. He commended,
in particular, a seat which turned under the counter, as introduced by a Mr Ely, a draper of Peckham.† It cannot be
gainsaid that the Duke, though raised to his dukedom by
wealth, wore the rank well. He at least did not yearn to
enter the Kingdom of Heaven in a rich sarcophagus. He
had been an ardent advocate of cremation and on his death
in 1899 his body was burned at Woking.

About a year after conferring the Westminster dukedom
Queen Victoria asked the sixth Duke of Richmond how it
was that he, who had succeeded to a splendid property in
Scotland, to which he was devoted, had never been made
Duke of Gordon. It was a curious question, coming from
the Fount of Honour. The Duke replied that he had often

* *The Times*, 23 December 1899
† *Hansard*, 11 July 1899

wished to be Duke of Gordon and was much gratified by the Queen's mention of the matter. The Queen took the view that, as the Duke was descended from the last Duke of Gordon on the female side, 'and as his possessions are very large', it would be right and proper for him to have this noble old title; she felt that when such estates passed into English hands they should not be treated as a subsidiary possession. Scotland, she believed, would welcome the revival of the dukedom.* The reference to large possessions gives the game away; it was the only real reason for awarding a fourth dukedom to one who already had three—Richmond, Lennox and Aubigny. The Duke, a Tory stalwart who was Lord President of the Council, received his supererogatory honour in 1876.

Ten years later the Queen offered a dukedom to the third Marquess of Salisbury, after his first term as Prime Minister. The Marquess, expressing deep gratitude, regretted that 'his fortune would not be equal to such a dignity' and begged to decline. 'The kind words in which your Majesty has expressed approval of his conduct are very far more precious to him than any sort of title,' he wrote.† The Marquess was exceedingly rich and it is hard to think that the reason he gave for declining the step was the real one. He went on to serve two more terms of office as Prime Minister. Had he then accepted a dukedom it would have been more worthily earned than most.

In 1889 the Queen raised William George Duff, sixth Earl of Fife, to a dukedom when he married the eldest daughter of the Prince and Princess of Wales. Although he undoubtedly had great possessions—250,000 Scots acres, none of them in Fife—the Queen was reluctant to give him this advancement, thinking it unnecessary and even silly; but the Prince wanted a duke for a son-in-law and made a personal issue of it.‡ Writing to the Empress Frederick the Queen described the match as 'a very brilliant one, in a

* G. E. Buckle (ed.): *Letters of Queen Victoria (2nd Series)*
† Buckle: *Letters to Queen Victoria (3rd Series)*
‡ Sir Philip Magnus: *King Edward VII*

worldly point of view'. The Princess Royal, as the Duke of
Fife's wife became, spent a withdrawn life salmon-fishing.
The Duke had no male issue. In 1900 he was made Duke
of Fife all over again with a special remainder in favour of
his daughters and their sons.

Gladstone twice refused an earldom, but Disraeli allowed
himself to be made Earl of Beaconsfield. In his youth he had
been fascinated by dukes and wrote about them with such
confidence that his father, hearing the title of one of his
novels, exclaimed 'The Young Duke! What does Ben know
of dukes?' In 1848, thanks to the generosity of the ducal
family of Portland, Disraeli was lent £35,000 to buy and
stock with timber the estate of Hughenden, so that he could
live in a style suited to the leader of the Conservative Party.
Unfortunately the eccentric fifth Duke of Portland, on his
succession, called in the loan and Disraeli was forced to go
to the moneylenders in order to continue to play 'the high
game in public life'. Possibly he had dreams of a dukedom,
but one thousand acres were inadequate to support it. He
derived no little satisfaction, however, from having dukes
to serve under him and to entertain him.

If the new dukes of the nineteenth century, Wellington excepted, played little part in public life, the balance was
redressed by a hereditary duke who is unfairly held up as
the embodiment of inertia. Enthusiasm was a quality to
which the heavy-eyed Spencer Compton-Cavendish, eighth
Duke of Devonshire, laid no claim, and it may well be true
that he yawned during his own speeches; yet as Lord Hartington he sat for thirty-four years in the Commons and by
the century's end had held more Cabinet offices than anyone.
Three times he declined the office of Prime Minister, not
out of idleness but for reasons of tact or tactics. The last of
the great Whigs, he broke with Gladstone in 1885 over
Home Rule for Ireland and formed the Liberal Unionist
Party, later becoming Lord President of the Council in
Tory ministries. His record of State offices includes two
spells as Secretary for War. He dispatched General Gordon

to the Sudan and had to threaten resignation in order to stimulate the Government into sending a relief expedition. As Postmaster-General he nationalised the telegraph service. As Secretary for India he had the thankless task of settling Afghan wars. 'His work', says Bernard Holland, 'was done with a weary, or bored, thoroughness, the resultant apparently of a conflict between a strong sense of duty on the one side and on the other a hatred of writing and speaking, and inborn indolence.'* Sidney and Beatrice Webb were predictably scathing about the Duke's failure to understand any complicated measure half an hour after listening to the clearest exposition of it; they complained that he was preoccupied with Newmarket and lay in bed until twelve o'clock. But if a problem had to be mastered, the Duke would worry at it until he saw sense. He grumbled that all his life he was surrounded by people who thought three times faster than he did. Taciturn by inheritance, he despised rhetoric. Gladstone thought his speeches were not elliptical enough; the Duke would 'travel out into the open' with his arguments. However, the eighth Duke of Argyll found it a comfort 'to have a leader who means what he says, and means you to understand what he says'. Often quoted is the advice tendered by the Duke, perhaps unnecessarily, to the young Winston Churchill at a Free Trade meeting in Manchester: 'Do you feel nervous, Winston? I used to, but now, whenever I get up on a public platform, I take a good look round, and as I sit down, I say, "I never saw such a lot of damned fools in my life." ' The damned fools admired his forthrightness and backed his opinions, preferring commonsense to brains and thinking the more highly of him for his philistinism. They would have been delighted at Holland's story of how the Duke was unable to free Lord Salisbury from the library at Chatsworth because neither of them knew which array of false books hid the exit door, which meant sending for a member of the staff. As far as possible Cabinet meetings were arranged so as not to clash with the Duke's 'holy days', or racing days. He drove his own phaeton to the

* Bernard Holland: *Life of the Eighth Duke of Devonshire*

House of Lords, smoking a large cigar and with a collie at his side. If he remembered, he carried with him one of the revolvers he bought after his brother, Lord Frederick Cavendish, was assassinated in Dublin.

The Duke's resources, already vast, had been expanded by industrial revenues from Barrow-in-Furness, built up (with Buccleuch aid) into a booming iron town by the seventh Duke, who also hit on the lucrative idea of turning three old hamlets into the fashionable resort of Eastbourne (Buxton, raised from a hamlet by the fifth Duke, was already a Cavendish town). Yet the inheritor of this empire seemed to lack a philoprogenitive urge. If heirs to the dukedom were needed, his brothers were capable of providing them. He did not marry until 1892, the year after he succeeded to the dukedom, when his bride was a fellow sexagenarian, the widow of the seventh Duke of Manchester, née Louise von Alten of Hanover. As romances go, this was not the most virginal. The Duke, when a young man, had entered the Duchess's orbit just before he became infatuated with Catherine Walters, otherwise 'Skittles', doyenne of the dashing 'horse-breakers' of Hyde Park, in 1862. This hard-swearing courtesan obtained from her protector a house in Mayfair, a fine equipage and, best of all, a pension of £2,000 a year which is said to have been paid until her death in the 1920s. The Duchess of Manchester waited for the association to end and then tightened her grip on 'Harty-Tarty'. Her circle at Kimbolton Castle and Manchester House was a fast one, deeply disapproved of by Queen Victoria. The Queen was incensed to find that the Duchess had coerced the young Earl of Derby into a promise that, if he became Prime Minister, he would give her the post of Mistress of the Robes; a promise which he fulfilled. As a punishment the Duchess was not invited to the Prince of Wales's wedding. She has often been described as the best-looking woman of her day; but she suffered from 'Duchess's disease', meaning that she was haughty, scheming, extravagant and rude. She resented the fact that her husband was unable to keep her in the style to which she aspired. Like everybody else, he knew

of her association with 'Harty-Tarty', but as the outward formalities were preserved he raised no objection. He died in 1890. Two years later the new Duchess of Devonshire embraced the splendours of Chatsworth and Devonshire House, which had long lacked a duchess, with greedy zeal; but if she thought to propel her husband into Downing Street she was disappointed. Sometimes she was called the 'Double Duchess' (though she was not the first to marry two dukes) and sometimes the 'Wicked Duchess'. As hostess she showed a Teutonic insistence that guests should sit upright. Four times during a meal, when Lord Balfour kept sagging, the Duchess ordered, 'Sit up, Arthur! Sit up immediately!' Her grandson, the ninth Duke of Manchester, who tells this story, says she was 'a great snubber'.* Her own stiff figure was achieved with the aid of a corset resembling a medieval instrument of torture. Sir Shane Leslie as a boy was promised a sovereign by the Duchess, apparently because his great-uncle had once courted her. 'She was very fat and closely dressed,' he says, 'and I spent ten minutes searching her multitudinous pockets before I could rescue her purse.'†
The Duke and Duchess gave the most famous of the Devonshire House balls in 1897, to mark the Queen's Jubilee. 'Harty-Tarty' appeared as the Emperor Charles V—a much-admired choice, in view of his Hapsburg features—and the Duchess was Zenobia, Queen of Palmyra, all diamonds and peacock plumes. *The Times* gave more than four full columns to an account of the dresses. Having missed the wedding of the Prince of Wales, the Duchess was determined to be noticed at his coronation as Edward VII. She tried to follow him down the aisle, was prevented by a Guards officer, whom she abused, then fell down some steps, 'to the delight of all'. Mrs Asquith helped her to put her coronet on again and she proceeded as if nothing had happened.‡
The new King had a liking for self-made men, but he remained loyal to the Devonshires, perennial hosts to royalty,

* (Ninth) Duke of Manchester: *My Candid Recollections*
† Sir Shane Leslie: *The Film of Memory*
‡ Henry Blyth: *Skittles*

who could be relied upon to welcome him at Chatsworth with
hundreds of torchmen. It has been said that the Duke was the
only subject capable of forgetting a lunch appointment with
his sovereign. The King had invited himself to Devonshire
House on a certain day and when he arrived the appalled
servants had to retrieve their master from the Turf Club.
After fifty years of public service the Duke died at Cannes
in 1908, the year before Lloyd George began to bait the
nation's dukes for not earning their money.

DUCHESSES FROM AMERICA

23

America was the new land of gold, yet it took the British nobility a long time to tap this fount of heiresses. The New World oligarchy were a familiar sight at receptions, at spas and racecourses, in ocean liners, on the Riviera. Their rich daughters were ravishing enough, their rich widows were eager enough, but the question was: would you really want one in the family? Were they as yet too rude in their ideas of social intercourse?

Three ducal houses which counted the risks and decided to brave them were those of Marlborough, Manchester and Roxburghe. It is arguable that some of the misfortunes which weighed so heavily on Blenheim in the nineteenth century were to be blamed not so much on ducal self-indulgence or agricultural depression as on a culpable failure to marry money. As a result the treasures gathered by one generation had to be sold off by the next, sometimes with no noticeable pang. The seventh Duke, Sir Winston Churchill's grandfather, a church reformer famous for his ingenious and unrelenting opposition to the Deceased Wife's Sister Bill, sought to keep up some ducal state, but his resources were under constant strain. In 1874 he was much exercised over the impetuous decision of his son, Lord Randolph Churchill, to marry Jennie Jerome, daughter of Leonard Jerome, of New York. His misgivings were caused by his knowledge of

Randolph's erratic nature rather than by distrust of an American match, though Leonard Jerome suspected that his daughter was being looked upon as unfit for a duke's son. Certainly the Duke's notions of American society were very odd. In a debate on the Deceased Wife's Sister Bill he related how four husbands had gone to a dance in America and seen their four ex-wives, all remarried, at the same function. He told also of an American father and son whose interlocked marriages resulted in the father becoming the son's son-in-law and the son eventually becoming his own grandfather, at which point he committed suicide.* After much squabbling over financial settlements—for Americans were not used to paying men to marry their daughters—Lord Randolph married his American bride. Meanwhile the Duke's elder son, the Marquess of Blandford, had been living a life abhorrent to a pious father. It was his affair with the Countess of Aylesford, an old flame of the Prince of Wales, which in 1876 provoked a family crisis, and nearly a national crisis. Lord Randolph, with a foolish notion of saving the family honour, had threatened to make public letters written by the Prince to the Countess. The Prince's riposte was to let it be known that he would visit no house where Lord Randolph was received. Disraeli suggested to the Duke that the effects of this ostracism could be avoided if he made 'a dignified withdrawal of the family from metropolitan and English life' and became Lord Lieutenant of Ireland. For reasons of expense, the Duke had no wish to move to Dublin Castle, but he had little option but to agree and to take his tiresome sons with him; the post cost him a reputed £20,000 a year, which meant selling off more and more Blenheim treasures. Sir Winston Churchill's earliest memories are of his grandfather unveiling statues in Dublin.

The philandering Marquess of Blandford, who was the cause of this costly upset, was already married to a silly, practical-joking daughter of the Duke of Abercorn. Her pranks would have been too much even for the second Duke of Montagu. In 1883 the marriage was dissolved and

* E. S. Turner: *Roads to Ruin*

shortly afterwards he became the eighth Duke of Marlborough. As such he entered on a depleted heritage, but could hardly wait to deplete it further. In 1886 the sales of Blenheim pictures and other treasures realised some £350,000, much of which was spent on estate improvements. Leonard Jerome, with whom the new Duke was on good terms, seems to have sown in his mind the idea of marrying a wealthy American. Among those available was the widowed Lilian Hammersley, who was not only enormously rich but very amiable. In 1888 the Duke set off to America to look over this prospect and married her inside a month. Lilian Hammersley's dollars were soon put to good use to install central heating and electric light in Blenheim Palace. These were not the only improvements. The Duke had developed a healthy passion for, and robust faith in, the telephone, which was then an instrument of gross inefficiency. In 1891 he told readers of *The Times* that 'the whole business' of Christiania (Oslo) and Stockholm was done on the telephone and it was intolerable that the British system should be in such a wretched state—'nine times out of ten one abandons the instrument in despair'. For six years, he said, he had had more than sixty French telephones at Blenheim, the exchange being run by a small boy. The Duke was convinced that the future of the telephone lay with private enterprise—he was a director of the Telephone Company—not with the Post Office.*

The Duke did not live long to enjoy his new amenities. In 1892 his valet found him dead in bed and, such was his reputation, rumours instantly spread that he had died unnaturally. Lord Randolph rushed out a statement that the cause of death was almost certainly syncope and the Duke's estate agent revealed that his employer had spent his last evening innocently writing a magazine article on 'Modern Railway Cars'. The inquest attributed the cause of death to heart disease.

The Duke's widow Lilian was so proud of her rank that, in accordance with unhappy precedents, she retained it even when she married Lord William Beresford, with whom she

* *The Times,* 29 August and 5 September 1891

lived as Lilian, Duchess of Marlborough. To a second husband 'it must be galling, one would imagine, to find that his wife still elects to be known by the title bestowed on her by her first husband', wrote the ninth Duke of Manchester, who pointed to the confusion that could be caused if several duchesses of the same name met in a hotel on the Riviera.* In fact, a mild confusion was sometimes caused by a multiplicity of dowager duchesses.

The ninth Duke of Marlborough had no wish to model himself on his father, with whom he had got on badly; nevertheless, he improved on his father's performance to the extent that he took to himself not one rich American bride, but two. He was lugubrious and withdrawn, his nickname 'Sunny' being inspired not by his disposition but by his early title of Lord Sunderland. There was an urgent need, as he saw it, to restore the splendours of Blenheim. Fortunately his temperament did not impair his eligibility in the marriage market. In New York he was marked down by Mrs William Kissam Vanderbilt, daughter-in-law of the Commodore, a social dragon fighting for parity with, if not supremacy over, the Astors. In her daughter Consuelo she saw the key to open the gates to high European society. In 1896 when Consuelo was sixteen her mother was in negotiation with Blenheim. At eighteen she was brought over for the Duke's inspection and saw the lonely feudal state in which he lived. For her entertainment a well-known musician had been brought over from Birmingham to play the Blenheim organ. In turn the Duke was invited to New England, but in the meantime Consuelo lost her heart to an American. By her own account, her furious mother held her *incommunicado*, with the aid of a governess, in the Marble House, that new-built Trianon at Newport; she was told that any disobedience would give her mother a fatal heart attack.† In Cornelius Vanderbilt's account, the mother was ready to shoot any lover of Consuelo's and go to the scaffold, leaving her daughter to live with the blame. The Duke arrived, proposed in the Gothic Room

* Duke of Manchester: *My Candid Recollections*
† Consuelo Balsan: *The Glitter and the Gold*

('whose atmosphere was so propitious to sacrifice') and was reluctantly accepted. On her wedding day Consuelo wept copiously. Years later in a Vatican court Mrs Vanderbilt testified: 'I have always had absolute power over my children ... When I issued an order nobody discussed it. I therefore did not beg her but ordered her to marry the Duke.'*

At Blenheim loyal tenants pulled the newly-weds' coach to the Palace, where the Duke's grandmother 'bestowed a welcoming kiss in the manner of a deposed sovereign greeting her successor'. At this time Winston Churchill stood second in line for the dukedom, but his bumptiousness distressed the family. The Dowager Duchess set the facts before Consuelo: 'Your first duty is to have a child and it must be a son, because it would be intolerable to have a little upstart like Winston become Duke. Are you in the family way?' Consuelo did her duty and the intolerable was averted. The nation has reason to be grateful to her. In 1940 there would have been no enthusiasm for a ducal Prime Minister; promises of blood, toil, tears and sweat come better from a commoner. The reluctant Duchess has told, in her memorable account of life in Vanbrugh's palace, how she slept in a room with a mantel inscribed, on the orders of the previous Duke, with 'Dust, Ashes, Nothing' in black letters. Had the famous Echo been functioning, she could have revenged herself by intoning these words every sunrise and sunset. The Duchess was expected to distribute to the poor the dinner left-overs; she initiated a modest reform by ordering the servants not to mix meat, fish and pudding all together like pig swill. English society took the bemused Consuelo to its heart, which was more than the Duke did. They separated in 1906 and the marriage was terminated in 1921. The Duke then married a second wealthy American, Gladys Deacon, of Boston, who had once inspired a youthful passion in the German Crown Prince, 'Little Willie'. The Duke was by now a Roman Catholic; and it is no small irony that the palace on which he lavished his money was awarded to the first Duke for

* Cornelius Vanderbilt Jr.: *The Vanderbilt Feud*

services against Roman Catholicism. Yet Blenheim owes him a great debt. He restored a noble formality to the setting and, with the aid of Achille Duchêne, installed the superb water terraces leading down to Capability Brown's lake.

The eighth Duke of Manchester, George Drogo Montagu, also married a Consuelo, who in fact was godmother to Consuelo Vanderbilt. She was the daughter of Antonio Yznaga de Vaille, described as of Louisiana, New York and Cuba. This marriage, contracted when the Duke was still Lord Mandeville, helped to restore the collapsed fortunes of the Manchesters, whose revenues from rents, like those of the Marlboroughs, had slumped. The ninth Duke, William Angus Drogo Montagu, son of the eighth, also went to America for a bride. In 1900 he married Helena Zimmerman, of Cincinnati, daughter of a rich rail contractor. The union took place without parental knowledge, but the bride's father magnanimously bought his daughter as a gift the excessively picturesque Castle of Kylemore, on Kylemore Lough, in Ireland. It was a nineteenth century extravagance originally built by a wealthy Member of Parliament, Mitchell Henry, for his wife. Edward VII had considered buying it as an Irish residence, but decided it was too big. The Manchesters already had Kimbolton Castle, in Huntingdonshire, and Tanderagee Castle, in County Armagh. The ninth Duke has left an account of his impecunious youth. Before the agricultural depression, he says, the Kimbolton and Tanderagee estates yielded £70,000 and £25,000 a year respectively, which in days of low taxation made a man 'passing rich'. But when he succeeded to the title he faced a debit balance of £2,000. In 1899, the year before he married his heiress, he was working for William Randolph Hearst, though he does not say in what capacity. He was one of those dukes who, when World War One began, presented their yachts to the Admiralty.*

According to Cornelius Vanderbilt Jr the Duke of Manchester ('an unprepossessing little fellow') had been a suitor of May Goelet, another American heiress, before he married

* (Ninth) Duke of Manchester: *My Candid Recollections*

Helena Zimmerman. In Europe the vivacious 'Baby May' was pursued by all the leading lady-killers and fortune-hunters. 'How I should hate to be May Goelet,' wrote Daisy, Princess of Pless in 1903, 'with all those odious little Frenchmen and dozens of others crowding round her millions!'* After rejecting many proposals, May Goelet accepted the dark and handsome eighth Duke of Roxburghe, who carried her off to Vanbrugh's castle of Floors, near Kelso, with a vast park surrounded by a high interminable wall.

It is a popular belief that the inter-bred British aristocracy derived much benefit, eugenically, from the infusion of American blood. As a proposition it is easier to state than to prove; and the same applies to the tendency of young heirs, at this period, to seek out healthy young actresses and Gaiety Girls. Two actress-duchesses, Lavinia Fenton and Harriot Mellon, have already been encountered. In 1894 May Yohe, an actress, married Lord Francis Hope, who succeeded as eighth Duke of Newcastle; in 1913 May Etheridge married Lord Edward Fitzgerald, who became seventh Duke of Leinster; and in 1933 Marianne de Malkhazouny married the eleventh Duke of Leeds. All three marriages ended in divorce.

* D. Chapman-Houston (ed.): *The Private Diaries of Daisy, Princess of Pless*

DUKES ON THE DEFENSIVE
24

In 1906 a petty comedy within the walls of Alnwick Castle, home of the Percys, symbolised the mounting antagonisms between the Old Order and the New. Supremely unimportant in itself, it expressed in microcosm the distrust between Feudalism and Socialism, between Peers and People, between taciturn privilege and 'articulate' radicalism.

Sidney and Beatrice Webb had gone to Alnwick to carry out research in the ducal records and were living 'in dirt' at the inn. By courtesy of Lady Frances Balfour they were invited to lunch with the seventh Duke of Northumberland and his family. Sidney was wary of dukes. Two years earlier he had ruled that he and Beatrice ought not to be seen in the houses of great people. It was permissible to know them privately, but not to attend their 'miscellaneous gatherings'; upon which Beatrice, who had wanted to attend a party given by the fourth Duchess of Sutherland, author and social worker, sadly put her new dress away.

The Webbs' antennae had told them that all was not well in Alnwick town. There was a heavy atmosphere of snobbishness and everyone seemed fearful of the Castle's displeasure or anxious for the least sign of approval. However, with misgivings, they accepted the Duke's invitation to lunch. It turned out to be no great gastronomic experience. Beatrice claims to have been given nothing to eat but peas and apricot

tart; 'the six men servants, finding I did not take the regulation dishes, denied me the bread sauce, the plain pudding
or another piece of bread.' The Duke was too absorbed in
his dignity to notice this neglect. 'The poor man was in fact
struggling to keep us at a distance, scared by the assumed
attempt of these notable Socialists to get access to the records
of his manor courts.' Beatrice therefore talked to the daughters
while Sidney engaged in pleasant conversation with the
Duchess; but for their efforts, she says, there would have been
heavy silence (these were not the first Northumberlands to
discourage mealtime prattlers). Eventually the Duke realised
that his guests were 'not otherwise than well-bred people',
and relaxed enough to discuss county council business with
Sidney. Beatrice found it possible to award the Duke marks
for being pious, decorous, moral, dutiful, public-spirited, a
good manager, a competent chairman, an active magistrate
and a good landlord. In a typical phrase, she said he was
'prone to good works'. She then cancelled it all out by
describing him as stupid and commonplace, entombed in
'grandiose self-complacency and dull melancholy'.* (It was
the previous Duke whose family were in the grip of the
Irvingites.)

As will be seen, Sidney Webb's plans for nationalising the
coal mines were to horrify the next Duke of Northumberland.
Meanwhile, in those Edwardian years, the battle lines were
being drawn and a more powerful challenger than Sidney
Webb was about to take on the higher aristocracy. In 1909
the Asquith Government of Radicals and Liberals came to
power and the only stronghold of old-fashioned Toryism was
now to be found among the great landowners in the House of
Lords. As Chancellor of the Exchequer Lloyd George brought
in his provocatively named 'People's Budget', designed to
force the wealthy to pay for social reform. The Tory peers
professed to be reformers all, but took exception to the proposed taxes on land values, on unearned increment resulting
from the sale of land, and on minerals.

As a demagogue the Chancellor sensed that maximum

* Beatrice Webb: *Our Partnership*

impact could be achieved by directing public envy and enmity at dukes (or 'dooks', as they were popularly called). Dukes were great landowners; dukes drew vast incomes by owning rather than doing; dukes sat in luxury behind long high walls, cut off from the common people. Lloyd George's Limehouse speech on 31 July 1909 was a rare feat of rabble-rousing and was deliriously received by his 4,000 listeners. His main attack was against those who sat on land waiting to sell it at a profit when the work of the community had sufficiently raised its value. He told how the Duke of Northumberland had held to ransom a county council which wished to buy a site for a school to educate the children of those who worked on his property. The Duke, he said, asked £900 an acre for land on which he paid only 30s an acre in agricultural rates. 'If it is worth £900, let him pay taxes on £900!' exclaimed the Chancellor. The second Duke of Westminster was next accused of 'blackmailing' the London store of Gorringe when its lease ran out by forcing it to pay an increased ground rent, to hand over a 'fine' of £50,000 and to accept elaborate new building plans—all as a punishment for working up a successful business. The mineral-owning aristocrats did not escape attack. They received £81,000,000 a year in royalties. 'What for? They never deposited the coal there.'

The Limehouse speech aroused intense anger in Tory ranks. It also inflamed the King, who described it as a performance of great vulgarity designed to set class against class. The Duke of Westminster pondered whether to sue the Chancellor for defamation, but decided that 'a person attacked from that quarter should find all that is necessary in the way of defence in the fairness and sense of decency still inherent in the community'. In the great riding school at Welbeck the sixth Duke of Portland reminded his massed tenants that he paid out £1,000 a week in wages and that such liberality could not continue if landowners' taxes were increased. Other noble spokesmen said that measures aimed at squeezing dukes would mean bare cupboards for those who looked for employment from dukes. There would be fewer subscriptions to public causes, fewer cups for sports clubs. The popular press followed the Chancellor in the sport of duke-baiting. There was chortling when the Bishop Auckland Guardians talked of building a marble-lined dukes' wing at the local infirmary, with a French cook and chaplain. Anti-duke pamphlets were rushed out. *The Dooks' Domesday Book* contained mock advertisements with testimonials of this order: A Dook writes: 'I find your pen invaluable for reducing subscriptions to football clubs.' The Liberal *Daily News* conducted a running battle with the Duke of Northumberland, whose land monopoly was said to be strangling the towns of the north-east. It reprinted reports of gross overcrowding in cottages occupied by the Duke's miners and of legal pressures on him to put his houses in order. He was also trounced for an amendment he secured to a Housing Bill to the effect that cottages need not be condemned because of damp walls so long as the damp rooms were not used for sleeping in. For the Webbs' host it was not the happiest of summers. The *Daily News* also published 'Fifty Points Against the Peers', one of which listed aristocratic land-holdings as follows: 'Twenty-eight dukes own 158 separate estates with a total acreage of 3,991,811; 33 marquesses own 121 estates totalling 1,567,227 acres; 194 earls own 634 estates totalling 5,862,118 acres; 270 viscounts and barons own 680 estates totalling 13,780,000 acres. In all, 525 peers own 15,201,156 acres.'

Pleased with the way the flames were catching under the ducal pyre, and eager to fan them, Lloyd George repeated his Limehouse performance at Newcastle-on-Tyne. He said there had been a slump in dukes, for which he had no regrets. 'A fully-equipped duke', he said, 'costs as much to keep up as a couple of dreadnoughts; and they are just as great a terror and last longer.' He poked a few laughs at the aristocrat who had one man to fix his collar and adjust his tie in the morning, a couple of men to carry a boiled egg to him at breakfast, another man to open his carriage door and two more to drive him (establishments like this were kept up by professional men earning a fraction of the income of dukes). Why, asked the Chancellor, should 10,000 persons own the land and the rest of us be trespassers? He then cheered his hearers with the thought that though the peers were forcing revolution it was the people who would direct it—which made sensational headlines for the *Daily News*.*

It was not a one-man battle by the Chancellor. He had the eloquent support of Winston Churchill, then in his radical phase. This grandson of a duke had been stumping the country as President of the Budget League, designed to win favour for the new taxes, and had been 'conducting' from the platform a song to the tune of 'Marching Through Georgia':

> The Land! The Land! 'Twas God that made the Land!
> The Land! The Land! The Land on which we stand.
> Why should we be beggars with the ballot in our hand?
>   God gave the Land to the people.

Churchill notified the House of Lords that he would be 'quite content to see the battle joined' between representative government and a 'miserable minority of titled persons who represent nobody'. If they wanted a speedy dissolution of Parliament they knew how to obtain one. Speeches like that of the Duke of Portland, he said, were worth their weight in gold to the Liberals; Churchill's view was that the Duke could easily avoid cutting wages by cutting his personal expenditure. In ducal circles, this went down very badly. The ninth Duke of Beaufort, who hunted six times a week, said he would like 'to see Winston Churchill and Lloyd George in the middle of twenty couple of dog-hounds'. Churchill's cousin, the ninth Duke of Marlborough, viewed the campaign with mild alarm, but the 'traitor to his class' remained a frequent weekender at his birthplace, Blenheim Palace; a circumstance which invited, and received, mockery. A cartoon by Max Beerbohm showed Churchill reassuring the Duke: 'Come, come! As I said in one of my speeches, "There is nothing in the Budget to make it harder for a poor working man to keep a decent house in comfort."' In September 1909, at Leicester, Churchill affected to regret

* 11 October 1909

that the dukes—'these unfortunate individuals'—had been dragged into the fray. They ought, he said, to be left to lead delicate, sheltered lives. It was poor sport to engage them; it was like teasing goldfish. 'These ornamental creatures blunder on every hook they seek ... it would be barbarous to leave them gasping on the bank of public ridicule upon which they have landed themselves. Let us put them back gently, tenderly, into their fountains—and if a few bright gold scales have been rubbed off they will soon get over it. They have got plenty more.' A heckler cried, 'What about your grandfather?'*

Churchill, it is now known, mistrusted the wilder philippics of Lloyd George. He sought reform, not revolution. Tory landowners were certain that revolution of some sort was contemplated. Without calculating the costs, they prevailed on the Lords to throw out the 'People's Budget' and thereby precipitated the great 'Peers or People' electoral battles culminating in the Parliament Act of 1911, which severely trimmed the powers of the unrepresentative chamber. In the Lords' debates on this reform the much-attacked Duke of Northumberland asked: 'What is a democracy? A democracy is simply that sort of government which prevails in one form or another in the decay of a state.' He noted that noble lords were smiling and raising their brows, but he had expected that. 'The proper thing at the present time is to say that all wisdom lies with the people and that a form of government which you would never adopt in your own household or in any business company must be best for the State. But I do not believe it ...' He reminded his hearers that they represented 'in a peculiar degree the education and the intelligence of the country', and that they owed their position to Providence.†

In 1913 Lloyd George focussed his assault on the Scots dukes, with their power to ordain, and maintain, a wilderness. He chose a platform at Swindon to wax eloquent over the rugged, muscular men once bred in remote Highland

* *The Times,* 6 September 1909
† *Hansard,* 16 May 1911

glens, men who 'very nearly conquered England and put their King on the Throne', men who 'did much to arrest the might of Napoleon, the greatest warrior the world has ever seen'. Their reward had been to have their homes burned down. The Chancellor called for re-population, re-afforestation and re-cultivation, none of which could be achieved until the landlords' power had been broken.

A few days after this speech the fifth Duke of Sutherland wrote to the *Daily Mail* saying he would be happy to give the Chancellor a chance to test whether the Highlands could again be made to support a race of rugged, muscular men. He offered the Government 200,000 acres of deer forest at £2 an acre. Almost before the Chancellor could react the Duke had virtually doubled the size of the acreage offered and reduced the price to nearly half. Lloyd George announced that he would regard the offer as a serious one, in spite of the way in which it was made. His land valuers set to work on the Duke's figures and reported that what he was offering was the 'lean, scraggy end of the joint'. The Duke complained of the Chancellor's language and the Chancellor condemned the Duke's 'gratuitous lectures to public men'. Perhaps, said the Chancellor to the Duke, 'in your opinion the price to be paid you should be based on the value that could be got out of the land if it were developed and settled.' The community, he added, would only benefit if the land were restored to 'the condition in which it was, say, a hundred years ago, before it was devastated by your ancestors.' He accused the Duke of making the redress of Scottish wrongs a practical joke, upon which 'all the obsequious and feather-headed mocking-birds of the Tory Party rend the forest with their laughter'. In Glasgow he told an audience that the lords of Sutherland in the eighteenth century had claimed £10,000 compensation for loss of the right to hang their subjects, but had been awarded only £1,000. 'The chariots of retribution are drawing nigh,' warned Lloyd George.*

* *Annual Register*, 1913; and *The Times*, December 1913, January and February 1914

The chariots of retribution were also drawing nigh for the ducal coal-owners, but the outbreak of World War One gave the nation other things to think about. In 1919 calls for nationalisation of the mines led to the appointment of a coal commission under Mr Justice Sankey. Its members included the miners' leaders Robert Smillie, Frank Hodges and Herbert Smith, and the intellectuals Sidney Webb and Sir Leo Chiozza Money. They showed scant regard for ducal feelings. Much of their questioning was directed at securing agreement with their own political views rather than eliciting facts.

The Duke of Hamilton, being infirm, sent his agent, Timothy Warren, to face the inquisitors. Smillie informed him that 'some of us on this Commission' challenged the Duke's right to possess his mines and wanted to see the charters which purported to grant him ownership. Warren was unable to help. When Smillie asked whether the Duke's average income was £240,000, the agent said he did not know. He agreed that the Duke owned Hamilton Palace, Brodick Castle. Châtelherault, Dungavel and Easton Park; and that when the last Duke died the island of Arran had been left to the Marchioness of Graham, then said to be the richest heiress in Britain. Smillie informed the agent that for fifty years the Duke's workers had been living on the edge of starvation, and landless, in the area of Hamilton Palace; to which the agent conceded that there were many slum dwellings outside the Palace walls. He did not know whether the miners in them lived four to six in one apartment. He agreed that if the miners stopped work the Duke's income would cease.

> Smillie: Do you think it would be unjust, supposing he owned the coal, that he, living in Hamilton Palace and being very often on the Riviera and at race-courses and other things should be getting 1s a ton from every ton produced by a miner who risks his life, and that the miner should be getting less than 1s a ton and cutting the coal? Would that be manifestly unfair?

Warren: No.

When asked whether families living in the slums could not be housed in the Palace, the agent replied: 'I am afraid the Palace will very soon cease to exist.'

The eighth Duke of Northumberland, Alan Ian Percy, who had succeeded to the dukedom in 1918, appeared before the Commission in person. This was the members' chance to bait a man who was not only a duke and a coalowner, but an officer and a gentleman. They had written asking for details of his land and mineral holdings, his output, his royalties, his average income and the 'nature of the root of your titles'. It was not the sort of information a Percy was accustomed to revealing, or discussing. However, the Duke said his average royalty per ton for six years had been 6·77d. In the last year his mineral income of £82,450 had been reduced by income tax, mineral rights duty and super-tax to £23,890. As for the root of his titles, he held lands by grants from the Crown, re-grants from the Crown either with or without Parliament's sanction, purchases, marriage settlements, escheat and exchange.

To Robert Smillie's question as to whether it was possible for anyone to own land under English law, the Duke replied, 'Ask a lawyer.' Pressed on similar questions, he said, 'I am afraid I know as little about law as you do.'

You believe the land of England belongs to the ruling king for the time being?—Yes, I believe so.
And he has a right to grant that land to an individual subject?—I believe so.

Having elicited that the Duke did not himself work his collieries, Smillie suggested he was more concerned to draw royalties than to look after his miners' welfare. The Duke replied that all his leases said that houses must be kept in a proper state and that new cottages must be approved by him. It was impossible, however, for him or his agents to get around to see that everything was in repair. To the suggestion that the Northumberland Fusiliers were entitled to a decent house after defending their country, he replied, 'Certainly.'

Frank Hodges, observing that the duke had lost three-quarters of his income by war taxation, asked whether he was now looking forward to some lifting of taxes. The Duke agreed that he was.

You think you are not having enough of the £82,000?— It seems rather a small proportion, do not you think so?

The Duke made it clear that he would oppose nationalisation by any means open to him. It was a step to revolutionary seizure of all land.

Even if the Commission recommended nationalisation, you would use your influence in the House of Lords to defeat it?—Certainly. What has the Commission to do with me?

Taunted with doing nothing for his money the Duke retorted to Smith: 'I am a hard-working man. I am not a privileged man like you. I cannot afford to waste time upon a Commission like this.' He conceded that he was one of those who had 'got through lightly' into the House of Lords instead of having to be elected; denied that he made his money at the expense of the poor or lived in luxury at the cost of human sacrifice; and replied to a sneer that he would personally go round and check the health of his hunters with 'I do not keep hunters.'

Sir Leo Chiozza Money, an economist who was to attain notoriety in the post-war years, asked the simplest and deadliest question. It received an honest answer.

As a coalowner, what service do you perform to the community?—As the owner of the coal I do not think I perform any service to mankind, not as the owner of the coal.

I ask you again, what particular service is it you perform to the State which enables you to draw this £84,000 gross and £24,000 net from the work of mankind?—The fact that I own the minerals.

If science made it possible tomorrow to mine to 20,000 feet, you would still own what they found?—Certainly. Even if it went down to the centre of the earth?—I understand that is the law.

Do you not think it is a bad thing for a man to own as much as you do?—No, I think it is an excellent thing in every way.

Sir Leo suggested that it was unfair that large sums of public money should be spent boring for more coal, which would yield even larger royalties to the owner. The Duke disagreed strongly, saying that the State would reap more in taxes.

Would it not be unearned increment into the pockets of the landlords?—A very good thing for the landowner. Do you think it perfectly just and right?—Perfectly just.

Sidney Webb, who had been the uneasy guest of the previous Duke at Alnwick, did not question the witness; but the Duke told the Commission that he had decided nationalisation would be a disaster after reading a book by Webb.*

The Duke of Northumberland was bloodied but not bowed. His right wing views later became so passionate as almost to threaten his health. In 1922 he supported Lord Salisbury in a damaging attack on Lloyd George's system of awarding honours. He quoted letters from honours touts, one of them offering a knighthood for £10,000, another a baronetcy for £35,000. Honours, said the Duke, were being distributed on a vast scale and with reckless disregard to the services and character of the recipient.† It was good trenchant stuff, which badly needed saying, though it came oddly from one whose qualification to wear the most prized coronet of all came from an accident of birth.

* Coal Industry Commission, 1919; Minutes of Evidence
† *Hansard*, 18 July 1922

DUKES IN DECLINE
25

Between the world wars the old oaks of aristocracy shivered in the fiscal blast. Great estates were sold, great mansions and castles vanished from the map. Yet one splendiferous duke survived, a comet fuelled by the rents of London, leaving a lonely golden trail. He was Hugh Grosvenor, second Duke of Westminster. To his intimates he was Bend Or, after his grandfather's racehorse which won the Derby in 1879, the year of his birth.

Sir Noel Coward has described the Duke as 'a man of notorious personal charm' who, in an earlier age, 'would undoubtedly have glittered with rhinestones from head to foot'.* The third of his four wives, Duchess Loelia, wrote: 'I found the mixture of schoolboy and Roi Soleil irresistible.'† Sir Henry ('Chips') Channon said of him: 'Magnificent, courteous, a mixture of Henry VIII and Lorenzo il Magnifico, he lived for pleasure—and women—for seventy-four years.' But, says Channon, he was restless, spoilt and his life was an empty failure.‡

The Duke was a 'leviathan of wealth' beyond the imagination of Burke. His *Who's Who* entry said: 'Owns about

* Introduction to Loelia, Duchess of Westminster's *Grace and Favour*
† Loelia, Duchess of Westminster: *Grace and Favour*
‡ Robert Rhodes James (ed.): *'Chips,' the Diary of Sir Henry Channon*

30,000 acres in Chester and Flintshire, besides an estate in Scotland and 600 acres in London.' It was, of course, those Mayfair and Westminster acres—the rents of which were constantly being increased—that yielded the bulk of his revenue, estimated at £1,000 a day before 1914, surpassing many a ruler's civil list.

The Duke grew up in that era of vulgarity known as the Grande Epoque. High society had become incurably peripatetic. 'There are people of the highest rank ... whose existence is as much nomadic as that of Red Indians,' wrote a worried intellectual. 'You cannot ascertain their whereabouts without consulting the most recent newspapers ... Their residences, vast and substantial as they are, serve only as tents and wigwams. The existence of a monk in a cloister, of a prisoner in a fortress is more favourable to the intellect than theirs.'* That was written in the 1870s. When the motor car came it was regarded as the final disintegrator of an orderly, settled society. The second Duke of Westminster was very much the creature of this new age of mobility, a nomad *in excelsis*.

The first of the Duke's wives was a Cornwallis-West from Ruthin Castle, not far from the Grosvenors' Cheshire seat of Eaton Hall; her mother, Mrs Mary Cornwallis-West, with an eye to the Grosvenor wealth, is said to have ensured that the children of the two families met as much as possible. It was a happy accident of propinquity which would have tempted the least designing of mothers. Another Cornwallis-West daughter married the Prince of Pless, who had 9,000 miners working for him in the Silesian coalfields and a 600-room castle at Fürstenstein. In the diaries of Daisy, Princess of Pless, the Duke of Westminster crops up repeatedly on the big house circuit of Europe, the habitués of which continually commuted, often in their cumbrous special trains, between the castles of Middle Europe, the palaces of Berlin, the *châteaux* of France and the mansions of England. It was an exhaustive treadmill, but by the end everybody knew everybody. The Duke, inheriting his title at twenty, found

* P. G. Hamerton: *The Intellectual Life*

no difficulty in entertaining royalty, nor did royalty hesitate to accept the hospitality of one far richer than themselves. In the South African war the Duke served on Lord Roberts's staff along with the Dukes of Marlborough and Norfolk, a concentration of blue-blooded gallopers which was dispersed after it drew derisive comment. To be fair, none of the three shirked danger. Back home, the Duke became the society host again. In 1909, when Lloyd George declared war on dukes, Edward VII was a shooting guest at Eaton Hall, travelling two miles in the Duke's estate train to the coverts. It was the King's custom to give free Christmas coals to the poor at Windsor and that December the Duke of Westminster distributed 150 tons of coal at Chester. Judging from his speeding convictions at this period, the Duke was a 'noble scorcher'. One plea in mitigation said 'his car was a very powerful one'. At Richmond, Surrey, the magistrates, imposing a fine of £1 10s, gave him the alternative of seven days imprisonment and then laughed loudly at their little joke. The Duke drove round Brooklands race track on its opening day. On the Solent he was nearly lost in a hydroplane accident. In 1914 he joined Sir John French's staff, 'in an indeterminate position', arriving in a Rolls-Royce car armed with a Hotchkiss machine-gun, with which he 'succeeded in waging minor war on the enemy'.* He was not easy to fit into the Army pattern. In 1916 he was sent with a squadron of armoured cars to Egypt, where he made a 250-mile dash across the desert to rescue from the Senussi sixty survivors of a ship which had been torpedoed in the Gulf of Sollum. For this exploit, culminating in a grand charge, he is said to have been recommended for a Victoria Cross, but received instead the DSO. Later the Duke helped to develop the tank (a fellow duke, the sixth Duke of Montrose, was busy developing the first naval aircraft-carrier†).

After the war the Duke never doubted that the old order was over. If he sold family lands it was not from necessity but as part of a policy of diversification; he became a big

* *The Times,* 21 July 1953
† (Sixth) Duke of Montrose: *My Ditty Box*

investor and landlord in Australia and Canada. As a man
of business he was shrewd: his lavish living had no noticeable effect on his fortunes, which continued to expand.
Many would doubtless have preferred him to found colleges,
save cathedrals from collapse or subsidise great research
programmes, but he lacked the instincts of his contemporary,
Lord Nuffield. He was essentially a Man of Pleasure. In
Coward's *Private Lives*, set in France, Amanda asks Elyot,
'Whose yacht is that?' and Elyot answers, 'The Duke of
Westminster's, I expect. It always is.' (It *could* have been
the Duke of Sutherland's *Sans Peur*.) Over a period of years
the Duke of Westminster had two yachts in commission. For
Scottish and Scandinavian waters there was the steam-powered
Cutty Sark, which had been laid down as a destroyer and ended
up under the White Ensign in World War Two. For gentler
waters there was the *Flying Cloud*, a four-masted auxiliary
schooner built to the Duke's orders, one of the thirty largest
sailing yachts in the world, with a crew of forty. Among
her bizarre features were a porch leading to the upper cabins
designed to resemble the front door of an old Cotswold house
and, in the Duchess's cabin, a four-poster bed. All the vessel
lacked was an organ. 'For everyday work we used the *Cutty
Sark*,' writes the third Duchess, and a very sick-making vessel
she found it. She has left a captivating account of the Duke's
maritime progresses, notably of a cruise along the north
coast of Spain with the use of a Bentley at every port ('we
generally arranged that cars should follow us along the
coast').* Michael Arlen, the fashionable novelist of those
days, once met the captain of the *Cutty Sark* ashore at Cannes.
Ten days earlier, the captain told him, he had been off
Norway waiting to pick up the Duke and a party for salmon
fishing. Instead he received a signal ordering him to drop
all the rods and tackle at Loch More, in Sutherland and steam
full speed for Cannes in order to convey the Duke's party
to a tennis tournament at Monte Carlo. On the following
day the party arrived in six Rolls-Royces from Biarritz,
boarded the *Cutty Sark* and were safely transported to Monte

* Loelia, Duchess of Westminster: *Grace and Favour*

Carlo about thirty miles away. The vessel then returned to Loch More.*

The Duke seems to have sought to create in himself the character of Le Gros Veneur. Like other dukes he stalked deer and shot pheasant; unlike other dukes he harpooned sharks off Scotland and pursued boar with his own hounds from his own *château* of Saint-Saens in Normandy, staffed by his own servants from England. One sport he did not favour, though many British aristocrats did, was the shooting of live pigeons from traps, and he supported the Prince of Monaco's efforts to extirpate it. Wherever he went, as his third Duchess relates, trains were held up for him and priority gangways were erected. His own couriers and courtiers met him everywhere to discharge his public and private errands. He hired bands, orchestras and entertainers as other men hired plumbers. Whenever he began a new courtship jewellers rejoiced.

High-spending magnificos of old were generally men of wit, and even of learning, but if the Duke of Westminster said anything witty or learned it seems to have gone unrecorded. Sir Winston Churchill, who shot stags with him, says he was not good at explaining things or making speeches. Like many of his age, the Duke encouraged practical jests and Churchill was the angry victim of one of the Duke's conjurors who relieved him of his braces. His ration of four wives was not excessive by ducal standards. On the day after he died in 1953 Sir Henry Channon, recording a bad fire next door to his house, wrote: 'It turned out *not* to be the four bereaved Duchesses of Wesminster committing suttee.'†

For some years the Treasury had been taking an estimated ninety-five per cent of the Duke's income. The winding up of his affairs occupied lawyers for many years. Estate after estate was put on the market. In the end the Treasury took about £20,000,000. The richest man in Britain, the combination of Roi Soleil, Henry VIII and Lorenzo, did not qualify for an entry in the *Dictionary of National Biography*

* 'Peterborough,' *Daily Telegraph,* 21 July 1953
† Robert Rhodes James (ed.): *'Chips'*

and his name is hard to find even in name-dropping memoirs.

In the forced selling of ducal land after World War One the melancholy ninth Duke of Marlborough was anxious that the nation should know what it was losing. He therefore wrote a letter to *The Times* on behalf of all those whose 'wealth is no longer fluid but is fixed in great houses and their surroundings'. It was proposed to raze, in the name of social equality, 'fortresses of territorial influence'. The owners had played a part in the national life; they had conducted local administration at no cost to the state; they had practised lavish and comprehensive hospitality and neighbours had been glad to 'put their legs under the mahogany'. Were these houses to become museums?* The Duke feared so. When he died in 1934 Churchill, who had helped to whip up feeling against ducal landowners, sorrowed over the plight of his 'oldest and dearest friend', so heavily pounded by taxes. In the Duke's lifetime, he wrote, the three or four hundred families who had guided the nation and empire had lost their authority, as well as much of their property. The process had shadowed the Duke's life. He knew he belonged to a society which had passed away; and though he liked to think that to broaden the foundations was to strengthen them, the process 'saddened and chilled him'.† Yet Blenheim, under his care, survived and prospered. In the late summer of 1939 the floodlit palace was the scene of a great ball which had the doom-defying brilliance of the Duchess of Richmond's ball before Waterloo.

One duke who strove with some success to keep the twentieth century at bay was Herbrand Russell, eleventh Duke of Bedford, who held the title from 1893 to 1940. Of his immediate predecessors it was said that they could throw £200,000 a year into the Thames and still keep Woburn. Under his rule, Woburn was not a place where neighbours put their feet under the mahogany. To judge from his grandson's account‡ it was a silent, sterile establishment maintained

---

* *The Times*, 19 May 1919   † *The Times*, 2 July 1934
‡ (Thirteenth) Duke of Bedford: *A Silver-Plated Spoon*

for two people: a duke who had nothing to say and a duchess who was almost stone deaf. Victorian formality was kept up, with fifty indoor servants and two hundred outdoor staff. The Duke could afford to maintain two fully staffed houses in Belgrave Square, hardly ever used. He ran the estates efficiently and had no further interests, except the breeding of such rare animals as bison and Père David deer in his park. His political views could not be taken for granted, for in the 1911 debates on the future of the Lords he said he would welcome an elected second house. Nor did he favour the endless amassing of land. To prove his point, he sold off large family estates in the Fens. In 1913 he got rid of the congested, ill-run Covent Garden property which had caused his predecessors to be pilloried, in a perennial *Punch* campaign, as the Duke of Mudford, Lord of Muck, Lord Cul-de-Sac, the Earl of No Thoroughfare and so on. The £2,000,000 proceeds were largely invested in Czarist Bonds, in which the Duke may have been the biggest single loser. He retained the Bloomsbury Squares which, purged of the beadles who tried to keep London's millions from reaching their railway stations, were becoming noisy thoroughfares; but thanks to the ninth Duke their yield had been greatly increased as the leases fell in. In 1914 the Duke turned Ampthill into a training depot at his own expense and, as Colonel Commandant, sent about 12,000 men to the battle-fields. After the war the public heard little about him. He had a yacht, but it was never seen at smart anchorages. According to his grandson, he never carried money, never visited a shop, never telephoned. But if the public heard little about the Duke they heard a great deal about his wife, the 'Flying Duchess' who vied with the 'Red Duchess' of Atholl for the headlines. She took to flying late in life, partly as a form of therapy, finding that the head noises which were part of her deafness were alleviated by altitude, or possibly eclipsed by engine din; but she clearly had an unsatisfied thirst for adventure. From her hangar at Woburn she took part with Captain C. D. Barnard in record-breaking flights,

A HOLIDAY TASK.

Scene—*Mud-Salad Market.*

Duke of Mudford. "SWEET PRETTY PLACE, AIN'T IT?"

Mr. P. (*Inspector of Nuisances*). "NO, MY LORD DUKE, IT ISN'T PRETTY, AND IT ISN'T SWEET! HERE, TAKE THIS BROOM, AND MAKE A CLEAN SWEEP OF IT!!"

The Duke of Bedford (as Duke of Mudford) is pilloried by Punch
for neglect of Covent Garden

notably to India and the Cape. Then in 1937, in her seventies, she took off to complete her two hundredth hour of solo flying and was lost in the North Sea. The Duke lived on, more withdrawn than ever, and almost blind. On the outbreak of World War Two an intelligence department moved into a wing of Woburn; its requests for more room were indignantly turned down. When the Duke died in 1940 the title passed to his pacifist son Hastings, who at one period was dogged by press photographers anxious to see him arrested under Defence Regulation 18b. He attributed his freedom to Sir Winston Churchill, who thought that the imprisonment of peers would give America a false idea of the strength of anti-war feeling in Britain.*

By the time of the Dictators the industrially ravaged 'Dukeries' had only one duke—that tireless host of royalty, the sixth Duke of Portland, who had held the title since 1879 (he died in 1943). Some attempt was made in the 1930s to trim the lavish establishment at Welbeck, but according to one source the only economy that could be agreed upon was to dispense with sealing wax in the guests' bedrooms. Eventually the Abbey with its subterranean suites passed to the military, who still retain it. The neighbouring great house of Clumber, belonging to the Dukes of Newcastle, was pulled down in 1937, leaving a fine church and a fine park (which became an arms dump and was desolated by huge explosions).

The destruction in 1927 of Hamilton Palace, undermined by the colliers of the Dukes of Hamilton, has already been noted; its loss was probably unmourned by the future fourteenth Duke who, as the Marquess of Clydesdale, led the first flight of aircraft over Mount Everest in 1933. Stowe, seat of the spendthrift Dukes of Buckingham and Chandos, became a public school in 1923. In London there was an outbreak of *lacrimae rerum* when Devonshire House was knocked flat in 1924; it was followed soon afterwards by Grosvenor House. More fortunate was Stafford House, which in later years, as Lancaster House, became a Government reception centre.

* (Twelfth) Duke of Bedford: *The Years of Transition*

The owner of Stafford House, the Duke of Sutherland, whose bargain offer of 200,000 acres of deer forest had been spurned by Lloyd George, disposed of 250,000 acres in 1919; and in succeeding years, still selling, he yielded up Dornoch Castle in Sutherlandshire and Lilleshall in Shropshire, but acquired Sutton Place in Surrey. The great palace of Trentham had been demolished in 1911, leaving only a ballroom and a hall; in a humiliating sale Sir Charles Barry's central tower was withdrawn at £50. The Duke was not left wholly without pleasures, for he had a succession of yachts called *Sans Peur* and was able to shoot game all over the world. Having made his peace with Lloyd George he was admitted to Government posts.

The Crown, which had been more than generous to earlier Dukes of Richmond, took back a large swathe of their northern possessions in 1937. Within a span of ten years the seventh and eighth Dukes had died. To discharge the resulting duties, the ninth Duke handed over to the Crown Commissioners 90,000 acres of Speyside, with 450 farms and crofts, along with the communities of Fochabers, Garmouth, Spey Bay, Tomintoul and Port Gordon, with revenues of £50,000 a year. Gordon Castle, where once an impressionable guest exclaimed that 'the horizon scarce limited the possessions of your host', was pulled down. At Goodwood the Duke still had his popular racecourse, but he was best known as a racing motorist. By coincidence another duke descended from Charles II sought fame as a racing driver. He was the ninth Duke of Grafton, who was killed aged twenty-two at the Limerick Grand Prix in 1934, the third duke of his line to die in eighteen years. It was a bad blow to the Grafton fortunes.

Although the territorial fortresses were falling, the list of survivors was not contemptible: it included Chatsworth, Boughton, Badminton, Arundel, Alnwick, Syon, Belvoir, Stratfieldsaye and Inveraray. Their owners were becoming not so much custodians of privilege as custodians of history; and a nation which had lost its awe of dukes was to be increasingly grateful to them for preserving their great houses and sharing them with the public. In the meantime, for dukes as for lesser aristocrats, the period of transition was an anguished one. In self-defence they turned themselves into estate companies. Nominally, they lived at their ancestral seats, but they tended to occupy small houses in the grounds. The great oaks showed scars of lopping and grouting. The dreadnoughts were rusty and obsolescent. More and more the scales of the goldfish were being rubbed off by the jostling of the world. And the day was coming when dinner with a duke—once the aspiration of a rising man of letters, or a well-conducted clergyman—would be purchasable in an inclusive package tour.

INDEX